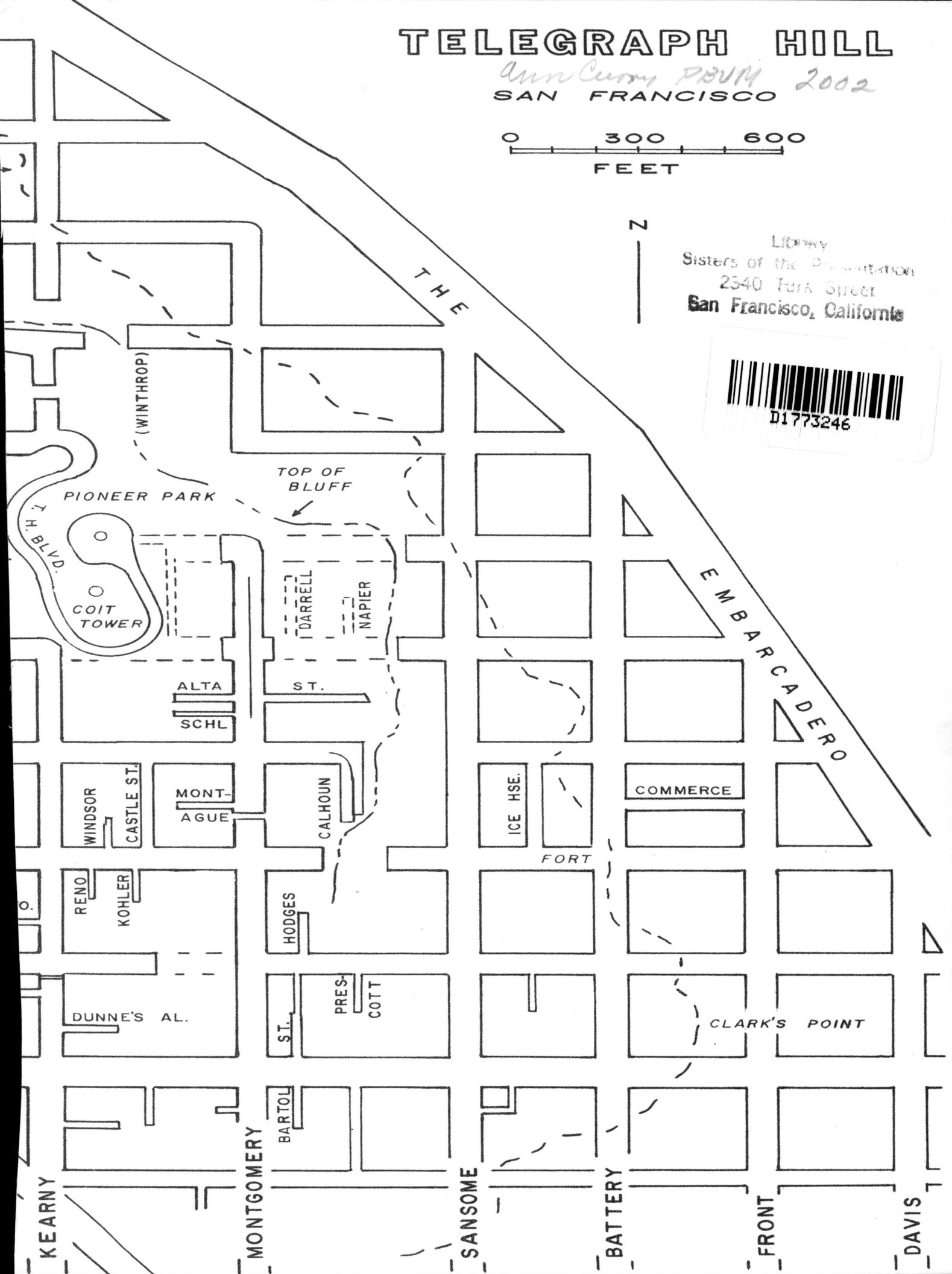

SAN FRANCISCO'S
TELEGRAPH HILL

SAN FRANCISCO'S
TELEGRAPH HILL
DAVID F. MYRICK

TELEGRAPH HILL DWELLERS ◆ San Francisco ◆ CITY LIGHTS FOUNDATION

SAN FRANCISCO'S TELEGRAPH HILL
Copyright ©1972, 2001 by David F. Myrick
First published by Howell-North Books in 1972.
Reprinted by permission of the author
All Rights Reserved
10 9 8 7 6 5 4 3 2 1
Printed through Colorcraft Ltd., Hong Kong

Cover photographs: ©Morton Beebe, 2001. www.photocolony.com
Cover design: Yolanda Montijo

Library of Congress Cataloging-in-Publication Data

Myrick, David F.
  San Francisco's Telegraph Hill / David F. Myrick.--2nd enl. ed.
    p. cm.
Includes bibliographical references (p.) and index.
  ISBN 1-931404-00-3
   1. Telegraph Hill (San Francisco, Calif.)--History.
   2. San Francisco (Calif.)--History.
I.Title

F869.S3 M97 2001
979.4'61--dc21   2001032324

TELEGRAPH HILL DWELLERS is a nonprofit membership organization formed in 1954. It seeks to beautify the hill and protect its basic character, and to perpetuate the hill's historic traditions. P.O. Box 330159, San Francisco, CA 94133. www.thd.org

CITY LIGHTS FOUNDATION is a nonprofit foundation that operates in the public interest, advocating literacy and publishing works of literary merit and community value. P.O. Box 330207, San Francisco CA 94133. www.citylights.com

Table of Contents

Preface to the Second Edition	6
Acknowledgments	
Part 1	
The Place	9
The History	15
The Marine Telegraph	27
The People	35
The German Castle and the Cable Car Line	41
Early Quarries and the Sea Wall	53
The Gray Brothers, Incredible Quarrymen	59
Pioneer Park	69
Coit Tower	75
Telegraph Hill in Print	85
Part 2 North-South Streets	
Sansome and Battery	93
Calhoun	99
Montgomery	105
Kearny	117
Grant	123
Stockton	131
Washington Square	139
Part 3 East-West Streets	
Broadway	147
Vallejo	153
Green	159
Union	165
Alta	177
Filbert	183
Greenwich	193
Lombard	199
Chestnut	205
Francisco and Bay	211
Part 4 Epilogue 1972–2000	217
New Scenes on Old Streets	219
Office Buildings Replace Warehouses	223
The Great Slide on Alta Street	229
Gardens and More Gardens	233
Washington Square and Pioneer Park	241
The Historic District	245
Appendix	251
Bibliography	253
Index	254

Preface to the Second Edition

Because new people on Telegraph Hill often desire more information about the special place where they live, the Telegraph Hill Dwellers has undertaken a reprinting of this book. The additional chapters (Part 4) relate important events since 1972, along with appending some thirty photographs. The earlier index does not cover the new chapters.

After almost thirty years of residence on the Filbert Steps, I returned to my home town but retain valued friendships established while living on The Hill. It is a pleasure to express my appreciation of Larry Habegger of Travelers' Tales, Inc., who lives on Napier Lane, and Nancy J. Peters of City Lights Books for their work in arranging publication as well as of Rhoda Robinson for providing information from her carefully preserved files.

Over the years, the Telegraph Hill Dwellers has commanded increasing recognition. Its recent president, Aaron Peskin, will continue to work for the betterment of San Francisco in his new role as an elected Member of the Board of Supervisors.

David F. Myrick
Santa Barbara
February 2001

Acknowledgments

When I moved to Telegraph Hill in 1952, I became interested in its history and, though much of this intervening period was devoted to other historical projects, I was able to gather considerable information about the Hill and photographs from individual libraries and historical societies. Accelerated efforts in recent years have culminated in this book. It was only because of the interest and kindness of individuals, both off and on the Hill, that this was possible. Some are no longer living but to each and every one of them, including those whose names I never knew or have forgotten, my sincere thanks for their assistance.

Individuals living on the Hill or who have lived here aiding in the development of this story include: Allen and Dorothy Lathrop, Helen McCarthy, Peter Spediacci and his three sisters, Mary Panattoni, Lena Massucco and Ann Marcellino, Helen Oldfield, Mallette Dean, Camilla Hamilton, Mary Martinez, Pearl Rodriguez, Trinity Motroni, Elios Anderlini, Rudolph Friml, Doris Jack, Mary E. Winkler, Grace Marchant, Eda Hoelscher, James C. McCandless and Thomas N. Kearney.

Also Mr. and Mrs. W. Dent Macdonough, Maggie Baylis, Ruth Burton, Armond DeMartini, Mario Cugia, Joseph M. Miller, Manuel Ortega, Mrs. James Wilhite, Janet Livingstone, Marian Francis, Sil Cantella, Robert R. Thompson, Ida Brown and Mrs. Thomas Brown, Victor and Al Merrill, Frances Alfonso, Flora Celli, William Doneri, Peter Zimmerman, Dorothy Erskine, Father Edward DeMartini, Robert and Nancy Katz, Dick and Marge Gray, Sally Tooley and Maurice P. Stergois.

To those people who did not live on the Hill but whose work and associations with the Hill made it possible for them to provide local information, I also express my appreciation. Among them are: Herman Klein, Evelyn Gray, A.L. Horstmeyer, Alice Griffith, Adelaide Cochrane, Mrs. Charles Polk, Chris Heughan, Hon. Richard Sims, Mrs. Charles S. Duncan, Anne Roller Issler, Peter Conmy, Norman Philbrick, Roger Swearingen, Larry Gwynn, Elliot Evans, Karl V. Steinbrugge, Paul Belser, William F. Clewe, Karl Kortum, Jeffrey E. Wetmore, John B. McGloin, S.J., Rev. Robert F. Hayburn, Harold H. Kelley, D.D., Edwin H. Carpenter, Hobart Lovett, Mary B. Connolly and Carl Poch.

The vast resources in libraries and archives throughout the country were tapped for knowledge; the response was gracious and productive. Information came from the National Archives, Library of Congress, The Bancroft Library, California Historical Society, Society of California Pioneers, Special Collections and Newspaper Room of the San Francisco Public Library, California Room of the Oakland Public Library, Sutro Library, California State Library, Library of the California Division of Mines, University of California Medical School

Library, Wells Fargo Bank History Room, California Academy of Sciences, San Francisco Maritime Museum, as well as the libraries of the *San Francisco Examiner* and *San Francisco Chronicle*.

From beyond the California boundaries assistance was provided by the Pennsylvania Historical and Museum Commission, Pennsylvania State Library, Wyoming Historical and Geological Society of Wilkes-Barre, Pennsylvania, New York Historical Society, Maritime Historical Association of Mystic, Connecticut, Peabody Museum, DeGoyler Foundation Library, Hawaii State Archives, Stanford University Archives, Archives of the U.S. Military Academy and the Historical Section Naval Staff, The Hague, Holland.

Also various departments and offices of the City and County of San Francisco: Recreation and Park Department, Department of Public Works, Department of Health, Art Commission, Central Building Permit Bureau, Assessor's Office, Recorder's Office, and County Clerk's Office.

In the various libraries and archives, I would especially like to express my gratitude to individuals who helped to supply answers to my questions. Among them are: Emily McKibben, Irene Moran, James Cantor, Robert Becker, John Barr Tompkins, George P. Hammond and James D. Hart of The Bancroft Library. Maude K. Swingle, Jay Williar, Lee L. Burtis and Peter Evans of the California Historical Society, as well as James T. Abajian and Edna Martin Parratt. John Porter Bloom, Richard S. Maxwell, A.P. Muntz, Jean Sachs, Edwin Flatequal, Elmer O. Parker and Mark G. Eckhoff of the National Archives.

In Sacramento, Allan R. Ottley, William N. Davis and David L. Snyder provided repeated assistance, together with Gladys Hansen, Frances Buxton, Margaret W. Campbell and the ladies of the Wells Fargo Bank History Room, namely, Irene Simpson Neasham, Merrilee Gwerder and Elaine Gilleran.

Others who provided valuable assistance were Albert Shumate, David Lasley, Gordon Chappell, Dion Neutra, Sue Herzog, Elena Bosworth Eaton, Thomas A. Mandas, Charles Mayer, Victor Pangrassi, Dorothy Puccinelli Cravath, Bernard Zakheim, William Hesthal, Teressa Fryworth, Donald O. Roy, Brian Thompson, John Hussey, Larry C. Ames, Jr., Richard Bobier, Robert Levy, John A. Jelenich, Everett M. Hintze, Jean Molleskog, Marguerite Moritas, J.F. van Dulm, Cdr. R. Neth, USN. (ret), Theodore Treutlein, Helen Bretnor, Al Sperisen, and George Woo.

Photographs, both historic and modern, are essential tools in telling the story of Telegraph Hill. Again, people responded to my needs by furnishing contemporary or historic photographs or by assisting me with my own photographic efforts. These people included:

Richard Monaco, Norman Strouse, Frederick A. Reicker, Diane Beeston, Ted Wurm, Don Maskell, Helen Giffen, Matilda Dring, Harlan Soeten, William J. Monihan, S.J., Clare Mashburn and the Lone Mountain College, Roy D. Graves, Gabriel Moulin Studios, George Kraus, E.M. Griffith, Robert Weinstein, Will Whittaker, Walter W. Ristow, Milton Kaplan and Virginia Daiker of the Library of Congress, the Palace of the Legion of Honor, Southern Pacific, the various libraries previously mentioned and especially John Barr Tompkins.

From my parents, Donald and Charlotte Myrick of Santa Barbara, in whose memories this book is dedicated, I have received their constant support and encouragement. To them I am also indebted for their tales of visits to Julius' Castle in the late 1920s; to my Mother for her careful and constructive editorial review of this text and to my Father for his knowledge of botany, which he used to identify some of the flowers hanging from the cliffs by the Filbert Steps.

David F. Myrick
Telegraph Hill, San Francisco
October 1972

Corrections to the 1972 edition:
Page 81 (caption) Later information indicates this was Victor Arnautoff rather than a helper; page 178 (col. 2) Caranzis was an Italian family; page 181 (col. 2) and page 184 (caption) William Wurster was the architect of the apartment building at 261-265 Filbert Street; page 208 (col. 1) Subsequent advice indicates Dr. Grosso had four children and that he was a pharmacist while his son Enrico was both a pharmacist and an optometrist. When needed, the basement kitchen supplemented the upstairs kitchen which was used daily. Dr. Grosso did not make Fernet Branca and he did speak English.

The war with the United States was about over when Mihand Thomas of Mexico City made this print of *Vista de San Francisco de California*, looking north from Rincon Hill. Artistic license was used to depict Telegraph Hill rising majestically from the neat and orderly city against a background in which some of the mountains of Marin County almost became precipices. (—*Wells Fargo Bank History Room*)

More chaotic but more realistic is the scene below, looking at the harbor of San Francisco from the opposite direction. Drawn by Wm. B. McMurtrie in April 1850, it was lithographed by Nathaniel Currier of New York (later Currier and Ives). In the foreground are some goats which were part of the life on Telegraph Hill. The second building from the right is the commission house of Bingham & Reynolds at the corner of Sansome and Broadway. In the harbor are lighters bringing people to the shore while others walk along the Long Wharf, having just stepped off the side-wheel river steamer *Mint*, which brought them down from Sacramento and the gold fields. (—*Library of Congress*)

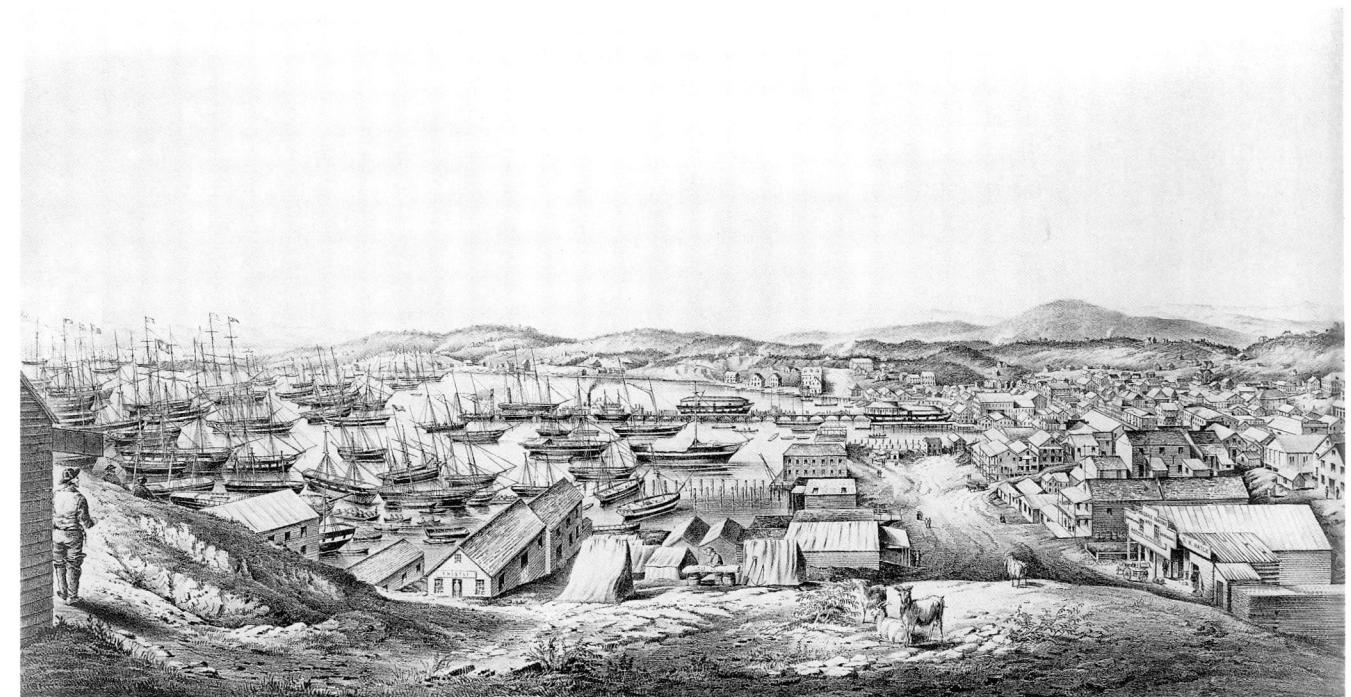

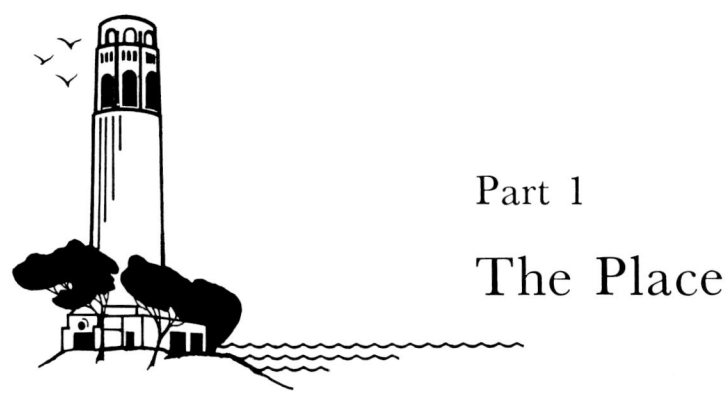

Part 1

The Place

Telegraph Hill is a wonderful place. If you question this statement at all, then wander over to the most northeastern landed part of San Francisco and ask a typical resident of Telegraph Hill, particularly one of the young girls, fresh out of eastern colleges, who have come to San Francisco to enjoy the freedom from academic and parental pressures that comes with distance from home. Pausing in the steps of life before undertaking a home of her own, such a young lady works in the city, has found a "charming apartment with a beautiful view" and knows that she lives in a marvelous world. Her "beautiful view" may not be that of a broad picture window; because of the architecture and location of some dwellings, she might have to peer through a small, awkwardly placed opening to see the outside world. Still, she is participating in the San Francisco heritage, enjoying an outlook from a high place.

But Telegraph Hill is more than a matter of views; it is a way of life. On the streets, climbing the wooden steps or narrow paths, perhaps passing some of the oldest houses in San Francisco, the Hill resident speaks to even the newest neighbor. If time permits, he might help the newcomer move in by carrying a load to the new home. That the new tenant chose Telegraph Hill as his residence gives him a mark of distinction warranting local acceptance and a friendly greeting.

Telegraph Hill is a microcosm of San Francisco. Not only have local events on the Hill been duplicated in other parts of the city, but from a perch on Telegraph Hill a series of residents could have observed most of the major events in San Francisco's history. They would have witnessed the arrival of Captain John B. Montgomery and the hoisting of the flag of the United States, as well as the arrival a few years later of gold seekers from all over the world. Admiral Dewey's return from the Philippines, the great fire of 1906 and the secret ship movements of World War II, Korea and Vietnam would all have passed around them. They would have noted the growth of San Francisco to the south and west to accommodate new arrivals, along with changes and developments in North Beach and the immediate neighborhood.

According to one count, San Francisco has 42 hills. Mount Davidson, south of the center of the city, is the highest, with an elevation of 925 feet above sea level, while Telegraph Hill, at 295 feet, is among the lowest. Actually, Telegraph Hill is two peaks, with the second summit at the southeast corner of Montgomery and Union streets. Although it lacks the glamour of the internationally famous hotels on Nob Hill and does not have tall apartment buildings staring at each other as they do on Russian Hill, Telegraph Hill does share with the Mission District a reputation for the best climate in San Francisco.

The boundaries of Telegraph Hill cannot be defined exactly. Sansome Street may be taken as the eastern boundary, running along the chiseled stone cliffs which time and nature have softened with oxidized sandstone and patches of grass, flowers and tall, graceful eucalyptus trees. A line just above the entertainment zone on Broadway will serve as the southern edge, while Columbus Avenue and Stockton Street form the western limit, although some people residing as far west as Powell or Mason streets think of themselves as living on Telegraph Hill. Francisco Street now

It was a clear winter day around 1935 when this photograph was snapped from a building in the financial district of San Francisco. From the lower left corner, where it crosses California Street, Kearny extends northerly to Telegraph Hill to surmount the Hill on the west side of Coit Tower. Parallel and one block to the east is Montgomery Street. In the center of the photograph are the Hall of Justice and Portsmouth Square, long before it was recast as the cover of an underground garage. To its immediate left are Grant Avenue and Chinatown while in the left background is Russian Hill, then with but a few tall apartments. Between the spires of SS. Peter and Paul's Church can be seen a ferryboat on its way to Sausalito. The completion of many tall buildings would make this scene impossible to duplicate today. On the other hand, the elimination of the large gas tank, just below Alcatraz Island, has served to enhance the view. (*—Gabriel Moulin Studios*)

forms the northern boundary of the Hill. Actually, the topographic features of Telegraph Hill extend beyond these arbitrary limits, and there is no sharp line of personal feelings separating Hill residents from their North Beach neighbors. The North Beach community long ago demonstrated its interest in improving Pioneer Park at the top of the Hill, and Telegraph Hill dwellers shop in the North Beach area, enjoy the cuisine of the many Italian restaurants there and sometimes visit the night clubs along Broadway. A close affinity between the residents and the shipping industry has resulted from the proximity of the Embarcadero and the piers almost at the foot of the eastern slope of the Hill.

Telegraph Hill has had a series of names in years gone by. Allegedly the Spanish called it Loma Alta. Others referred to it as Clark's Point, Prospect Hill, Signal Hill, Windmill Hill, Goat Hill and Tin Can Hill. Those living here today speak of it loyally and proudly as "The Hill," a common practice among the residents of other San Francisco hills, we are told.

From its position at the northern end of the Peninsula, close to the water front and set apart from Nob Hill and Russian Hill by an intervening swale, Telegraph Hill provides spectacular views in all directions. If your windows face the west, you can see Russian Hill, Marin County, the Golden Gate and its fantastic Pacific sunsets. Move to the north side to see Alcatraz with its former penitentiary, Angel Island and San Francisco Bay, its waters changing in color and pattern with tidal currents and variations in the weather. A little further in the direction of the morning sun are the cities along the eastern shore of the Bay — Contra Costa, as one county is so aptly named. Step around to the southern slopes of the Hill and the city with its myriad details opens before you, and once the night takes over this view becomes an intricate electrical display.

San Franciscans are protective of their spectacular views. Whenever a fair outlook is endangered by a skyscraper or some other construction, the residents — almost like an eruption — march on City Hall to vent their wrath upon sometimes forgetful municipal officials. However, Telegraph Hill dwellers do not think of the views as their exclusive possession; on the contrary, they readily share the panorama with visitors from all over the world. Coit Tower and Pioneer Park are accessible to all without restrictions. A road leading to the summit of Telegraph Hill beckons to automobiles with license plates from distant states, although in the summer months wiser tourists approach the summit on the No. 39 bus. On the return trip a stroll down the streets or stairs leads visitors past multicolored houses surrounded by small but well-manicured gardens.

Sometimes the best views on Telegraph Hill are not those of the Bay or the Golden Gate. This is especially true when people forget that a picture window can work both ways. Several years ago a well-known restaurateur lent his Alta Street apartment to a friend one warm summer evening. That same evening a cocktail party in an apartment on neighboring Filbert Street adjourned to the roof to enjoy the view. The Bay was spectacular, as always, but one person was rewarded by a more intimate view and advised his friends to turn around. From the back of the Alta Street apartment a pretty girl ran toward the window, then dashed into the back room. The fact that both she and the man chasing her were stark naked made the view considerably more interesting, but much to the disappointment of the observers the scene was not repeated.

Then there is the story of a man who was considering changing his bachelor status. Living next door, in sight of his apartment window, was a happily married couple whose relationship our friend hoped to emulate; the fact that the wife was properly endowed in both face and figure added more than just a touch of envy to his feelings. One evening as the couple was getting ready to attend a formal banquet, the woman was ironing her gown while her husband, dressed in his dinner jacket, was lost in the evening paper. Apparently she was ready to go; her hair was just right and only the gown remained. Our bachelor was at a loss to understand the husband's indifference while his wife — totally and delectably nude — worked over the ironing board. Concluding that even the best of marriages can be hopelessly dull, our man gave up all thoughts of marriage and, when last heard from, was still a bachelor.

Not everyone on Telegraph Hill wants a view, as the following episode suggests. Along the Fil-

Slashing across this aerial photograph taken in 1969 is Columbus Avenue, separating Russian Hill (lower left) from Telegraph Hill and North Beach. The relandscaped Washington Square, adjoining Columbus Avenue, is flanked by Union and Filbert on the east-west axis. The many white specks in the picture are automobiles; a long line can be seen approaching the parking area in the circle at the top of Telegraph Hill (Coit Tower is just below). Abrupt cliffs line the east and north sides of Telegraph Hill. In the upper left are the old sailing ship *Balclutha* and docks for the train ferries and Fisherman's Wharf. (—*Cartwright Aerial Surveys*)

The view from Telegraph Hill on a clear moonlit night is spectacular. The suspension cables of the Bay Bridge linking San Francisco with the East Bay cities help to frame the lights of downtown Oakland. Down below, along San Francisco's famed Embarcadero are Pier 17 (partly hidden) and, in better view, Pier 15.

bert Street steps on the east side of the Hill are two tall and stately trees. The Lombardy poplar has been there so long that its history is now lost, but not so the near-by redwood. Some time ago, probably in the early 1930s, a man and his wife occupied an apartment on Darrell Place, but their unhappy marriage caused the husband to seek solace in the arms of a girl living in a small house on the Filbert Street steps. The only impediment to this otherwise idyllic tryst was that the wife had a splendid view of the girl's bedroom. Even though the shades were scrupulously drawn, the thought of the angry wife's scowling countenance bearing down on the little red house made the girl uneasy. So as a shelter the husband planted a redwood tree before the window, hoping that the branches and the girl's security would grow together. The tree has done well, but the several human relationships have not. The girl soon tired of the arrangement, moved away and got married, while the man and his wife were divorced and moved off the Hill.

Although when the U. S. Coast Survey made this map only ten years had elapsed since the days of the '49ers, much open space still existed on Telegraph Hill, in spite of the many warehouses and docks constructed along its east side. Meiggs' Wharf, monument to an unrealized land speculation, extends into the Bay from Francisco Street between Powell and Mason streets. Soundings are in feet within the dotted line and fathoms beyond. Contour lines show rises of 20 feet. (—Library of Congress)

The History

According to some versions of San Francisco history, Telegraph Hill was noted by Portolá in 1769 and seven years later de Anza gave it the name Loma Alta. Romantic as the thought of these events is, nowhere will they be found in the diaries of Crespi and Font, who accompanied these expeditions.

Scant attention was given to Telegraph Hill in the early days of Yerba Buena. In the early 1840s settlement was limited to the dairy ranch of Juana Briones on the west side of the Hill near Filbert and Powell streets; Señora Briones also maintained a potato patch in what is now Washington Square. After she moved to a larger ranch down the Peninsula in the 1870s her Telegraph Hill property, referred to as the Spanish Lot, was used for baseball games and even today it is an athletic field.

During the Mexican War, San Francisco Bay rested quietly under Mexican rule until Captain John B. Montgomery sailed the *Portsmouth* into the harbor and raised the U.S. flag at the plaza on July 9, 1846. The plaza has taken the name of the ship, while the captain's name is remembered in the street that today links the financial district with Telegraph Hill.

Two days after his landing, Montgomery ordered a signal pole to be erected "on the hill off the point of Yerba Buena" so that a sentry could furnish timely warning of approaching ships. Next on the agenda was the construction of a fort on this hill, and Lieutenant John Stoney Missroon was assigned to the task. The site he selected overlooked the harbor, whose waters then extended as far inland as Montgomery Street. Building materials came from the mud flats of Mission Creek; the adobe was cut into squares, dried and brought to the base of the Hill by the schooner *Sarmiento*. At that point the hard work began as sailors toiled up the hillside, each with an adobe section on his back, much like a string of ants. It was dull work and the days were hot. Not far away were several "saloons" and the toilers would slip off to purchase a few bottles of *aguardiente* and cache them near the fort. The welcome news was whispered from one man to another and soon small groups disappeared around the Hill to tank up till they could hold no more. At the end of each day a rescue party was dispatched to drag them summarily down the Hill to the boat. A night in the brig for the offenders and a dozen lashes next morning started off the new day, which promised the same monotony as the one before.

Within a few weeks Fort Montgomery was finished and ready for business, with a flagpole, planks for the floor, and cannon captured from the Mexicans. No shots were ever fired from this fort and it soon fell into disuse and became known as Missroon's Folly. Now not even a plaque marks its location, at the northwest corner of Green and Battery streets, since the hill that supported the fort was leveled long ago. Only the name Battery Street recalls its existence.

Clark's Point

William Squire Clark was born on the frontier of Pennsylvania in 1807. Coming across the plains to California, he arrived in Yerba Buena in the fall of 1846. Although he found the country under martial law, he escaped the confinements of military service by volunteering for guard duty when needed and thus was able to engage in business.

When Isaac W. Baker arrived in San Francisco in January 1850, he made this sketch of Prospect Hill, which he later acknowledged as Telegraph Hill. The north side of the Hill was sparsely settled. Men climbed the Hill to watch for incoming ships. (—Bancroft Library)

The Yerba Buena harbor was shallow and lighters were used to land goods on the beach; the most practical landing place was at the rocky point below Telegraph Hill. There Clark built his house using "some adobe, with pieces of lumber . . . and bullock skins on the outside to prevent the winter rains from washing it down."

Yerba Buena was renamed San Francisco early in 1847 and at the same time the alcalde granted Clark a lot near his house on which he began construction of a warehouse and wharf. After spending two months near Corte Madera in Marin County cutting redwood trees, Clark completed his facilities, and before the end of September 1847 he was advertising his warehouse services "at the Stone Pier, foot of Broadway." And so Clark's Point took its name; by today's maps it was at Broadway near Front Street, but in early times the name embraced all of Telegraph Hill.

The stone pier was a good investment, but it was really too small to be practical. Clark sought to lengthen his pier, but he would need pilings and a pile driver; wood there was in plentiful supply, but there were no pile drivers then in California. Learning that a whaling ship ballasted with pig iron was in port at Sausalito, Clark successfully negotiated with the captain for 1200 pounds of the iron, and by lashing the blocks together he made a serviceable hammer. For $100 he purchased the windlass of a wrecked ship and soon the pile driver was erected. Clark's assistants, a carpenter and a blacksmith, had never seen a pile driver in operation, and there were some adjustments to be made before it functioned properly. A crisis arose when the hammer fell in the water and was lost in the mud. However, a newly arrived ship was discovered to have a large piece of scrap iron on its manifest, owned by Dr. Samuel Merritt. Clark bought the iron and work was soon resumed.

Though the wharf had passed from Clark's ownership it was finally completed, and on September 22, 1848, the *Belfast*, 163 days from New York, was the first ship to tie up at this pier. The event was said to have been responsible for a reduction in the prices of many goods and a simultaneous increase in real estate values, since ships were then able to unload directly and avoid the costly lighterage.

Located at the foot of Broadway and measuring 150 feet (later extended to 250 feet), Clark's was the first wharf north of Panama to be built on pilings. Then the construction of the Central or Long Wharf began in July 1849, and within a short time, as the shallow part of the Bay was filled, more piers appeared along the water front. At the eastern base of Telegraph Hill were Buckelew's Wharf on Green Street, Cunningham Wharf between Green and Vallejo, and Law's Wharf near Union Street.

Clark's career was successful but not always smooth-running. While he was on the city council, two other councilmen, William D. M. Howard and William A. Leidesdorff, bitterly disputed his method of handling city funds, which were used for part of the construction of the wharf. Then Jacob P. Leese challenged Clark's title to the land underlying his warehouse; twice the matter went to the California Supreme Court, but the dispute was settled and Clark retained possession. When he died in 1889 Clark was reputed to have been one of California's early millionaires.

Trouble in 1849

By the end of June 1849 some 15,000 immigrants had responded to the magic word—"Gold!" According to the *Alta*, this number included 5000 Americans, 6000 Sonorans, 2000 Chileans and the remainder from other countries. In the East fantastic tales of California's riches made good newspaper copy: golden bullets were used to kill California buffaloes and a railroad was under construction, "the rails of which were fabricated of the purest gold."

While this misinformation was being circulated throughout the land east of the Missouri River, a forest of masts dominated San Francisco harbor as crews abandoned their ships. Grass-covered Telegraph Hill blossomed first with tents and gradually with houses. In September 1847 an advertisement had been placed for a "pleasantly situated Frame House and Lot, North East Corner of Vallejo and Montgomery Streets," which was for sale "cheap." But a year later the boom was on and W. S. Clark was advertising five lots for sale only a few blocks away.

The settlement of Telegraph Hill in 1849 extended from the water-front warehouses up and over the summit to Kearny Street and two blocks further to Stockton Street. The section between Broadway and Union was shared by people from both Chile and Australia; the part east of Kearny was known as Sydney Town, while Little Chile occupied the area west of Kearny. Residing in Sydney Town were some of the less attractive discards from the land down under, the Sydney Ducks, who teamed up with former members of Stevenson's New York Volunteers and vagabonds in general to form the Hounds in February 1849. Initially their chief form of entertainment was parades, but as summer approached they changed their name to The Regulators and their sorties became marauding expeditions; the robbery and extortion of saloonkeepers were their specialty. When one of their men was killed during a quarrel in the tent of a Chilean shopkeeper there was considerable excitement, but nothing untoward took place for about three weeks. Then on Sunday night, July 15, 1849, The Regulators set upon the defenseless South Americans like a whirlwind. While fife and drum played, tents were torn down, their contents stolen or smashed and the human occupants were beaten or shot. The shrieks and cries of women and children were heard mingling with the demoniac laughter of the ruffians. The Regulators made a night of it, fortified with liquor stolen from the tent saloon of Domingo Cruz on Clark's Point.

The public was aroused and a force of 250 citizens was formed to arrest the culprits. Nineteen Regulators were rounded up for trial and, to insure justice for the accused, two attorneys were appointed to defend them. After due deliberation the jury found some of them guilty and imposed maximum sentences of ten years in prison on two men, with lighter penalties for the others.

Renewed trouble two years later was halted by the Committee of Vigilance. At that time 91 were arrested, of whom about half were released, 28 were ordered to leave California and four were hanged. With a third outbreak of violence five years later a second Committee of Vigilance was formed and quickly hanged two murderers.

California Joins the Union

With the growth in population, the City of San Francisco was incorporated in May of 1850; six years later it would be consolidated with the county to become the City and County of San Francisco.* As the city's affairs became more settled, important structures were erected around Telegraph Hill. On the east side was the Fremont Hotel, operated by John Sutch. Above it, at the southeast corner of Sansome and Vallejo,

---

*To be governed by a Mayor and Board of Supervisors.

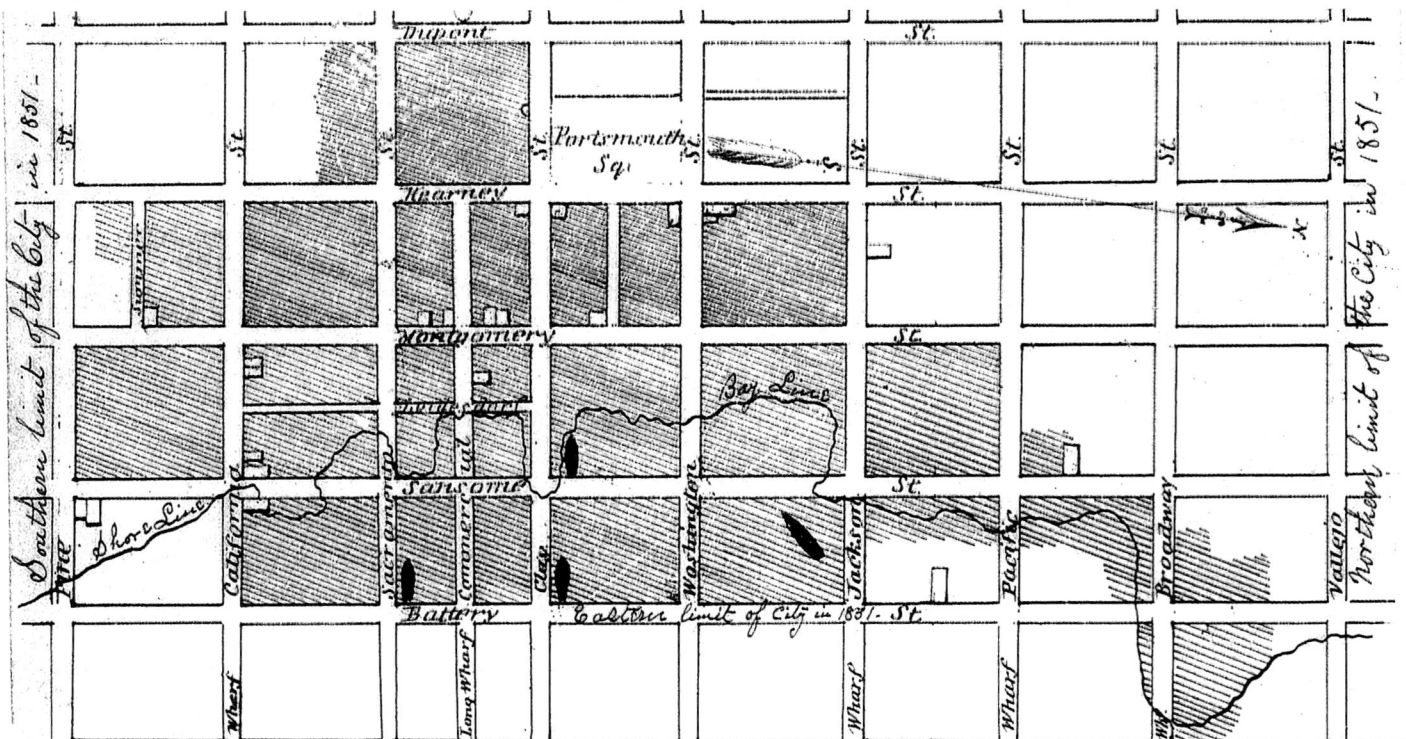

MAP of the BURNT DISTRICT of SAN FRANCISCO, Showing the Extent of the Fire.
Buildings Saved marked thus ▢

Of the early fires in San Francisco, the most calamitous took place in May 1851. In the lithograph by Justh & Co., whose premises luckily were beyond the fire limits, people can be seen running up Telegraph Hill to seek refuge near Hudson's windmill (upper left) while in the foreground weary men carry provisions up Russian Hill. The fire was so extensive (see map) that the loss was reputed to be around $20,000,000. (—Bancroft Library)

was the cemetery with the caskets of the seamen who had died aboard the *Congress* and the *Savannah* in 1846-47. (In 1857, when this part of the Hill was excavated for ship ballast, the coffins were interred in the new Yerba Buena Cemetery near the present Civic Center.) On the west side of the Hill was St. Francis Church, while near-by — and catering to different interests — was a bull ring. At the summit the Marine Telegraph, which gave the Hill its name, was established in 1850.

Although California became part of the Union on September 9, 1850, the news was not known for certain in San Francisco until the *Oregon*, decorated with flags, came steaming into the harbor several weeks later. A celebration was in order and Mayor John W. Geary appointed a committee to make appropriate arrangements. The celebration, a parade followed by patriotic orations, was held on October 29 and went off with "pomp and circumstance"; that night signal rockets were set off from Telegraph Hill.

During the 18 months from the Christmas of 1849 to June of 1851 San Francisco suffered an epidemic of six major fires. The big fire of May 4, 1851, the fifth and worst of the series, was the only one to burn part of Telegraph Hill. Starting in a paint shop on Portsmouth Square, the fire spread rapidly to the north, jumping Broadway and continuing over the high ground to Clark's Point. Everything east of Sansome Street, except for two buildings on the corner of Vallejo, was consumed. Colonel Poore's building, built over the Bay, marked the northern limit of the fire damage. The near-by warehouse of Dewitt & Harrison was saved with 80,000 gallons of vinegar — an expensive substitute for the unobtainable water.

San Francisco took on a different appearance after the fire as new structures replaced the old. Ed Gilbert of the *Alta*, writing about Telegraph Hill in August 1851, mentioned the changes taking place:

> This hill and those around which have stood for so long, like giant sentinels, guarding the slumbers of our broad and beautiful bay, are fast becoming covered with houses, and their original appearance ere long [will] be lost and forgotten.

He then went on to report that streets were being laid out and that houses were "thickly thrown" on both sides of the telegraph. The sound of hammers and saws shaping houses on the Hill clashed with a low-pitched booming below. In June 1852 Battery Street between Green and Union was absorbing the rocky foot of Telegraph Hill as workers blasted out a lower road level. Lots formerly at street level on the west side of Battery suddenly found themselves as much as forty feet above the traffic.

Independence Day, 1861

On the evening before the Fourth of July in 1861 a large crowd of San Franciscans was treated to a pyrotechnic preview of the festivities, held in the business section of Montgomery Street. More spectacular, however, was the blaze that broke out at 9:15 that same evening, starting in a house at the northeast corner of Kearny and Vallejo. "All Telegraph Hill seemed to be on fire," was one description, as the flames spread along the streets to consume about a dozen houses. Gen-

The Ringling Brothers Circus was ready to accommodate readers from other lands, as demonstrated by this poster. (—*Chinese Historical Society of America*)

erated by the fire, great clouds of sparks swarmed over the houses that stood on the eastern declivity of the Hill; everyone expected these shacks to go but they escaped unsinged.

For a while there were serious doubts that the horse-drawn fire engines could negotiate the steep and partly graded streets. Finally Engine No. 6 was dragged up Montgomery and along Vallejo to attack the fire from the rear. Engine No. 14 was employed in the same manner, approaching the fire from Green Street. "It was like scaling Olympus but the giants did it," remarked one spectator. Those engines which could not get close to the fire sent up long hoses and poured streams of water into the inferno. A number of "pretty little cottages" at the north edge of the fire were spared through the combined efforts of man, beast and machine.

The Telegraph Hill landlords, along with their Italian and Mexican tenants, suffered a dead loss, since insurance companies were not interested in such "remote areas" as the Hill. The scattered hydrants and water cisterns — none of the latter were located east of Dupont — were too few in number to comfort insurance underwriters, especially in view of San Francisco's history of fires. Also, cisterns required proper attention and some expense, for filling a 20,000 or 30,000 gallon tank cost $2.50 — a sum of more importance to the city budget then than now.

But the next day was Independence Day, the first of four the divided nation was to witness. Except for the Pony Express and steamer mail, California was isolated from the Atlantic Coast until the telegraph line was completed in October 1861 and the railroad eight years later. Since there was a faction of Southern sympathizers in California, a strong display of military might was scheduled for the holiday to forestall any possible moves against the Union cause. Washington Square was the marshaling area for the big parade that morning. All around the park and on adjoining streets were various military units which gradually took their appointed places in the procession moving along Powell Street.

That night 20,000 people, braving the wind and the cold fog, were drawn back to Washington Square to watch the finest pyrotechnic display ever seen in California. Besides those in the square, the glare of bursting rockets revealed hundreds more observing the spectacle from the windows of homes on Russian and Telegraph hills.

The War Between the States finally ended without leaving any scars on Telegraph Hill, and time moved on through the next decades in a regular pattern with few events of note. At noon on April 23, 1870, Blossom Rock, a navigational hazard in San Francisco Bay, was scheduled for demolition with 43,000 pounds of black powder. The announcement of the blast brought a large gathering to the slopes of Telegraph Hill. The crowd grew restless when the detonation was delayed for two hours, but those who did remain were rewarded with the sight of a great column of water which "rose majestically" some 200 or 300 feet. More lasting developments on the Hill were the purchase of land for Pioneer Park in 1876 and the construction six years later of the turreted German castle followed by the cable car line.

Earthquake and Fire

The most historic of all events in San Francisco's past is the earthquake of Wednesday, April

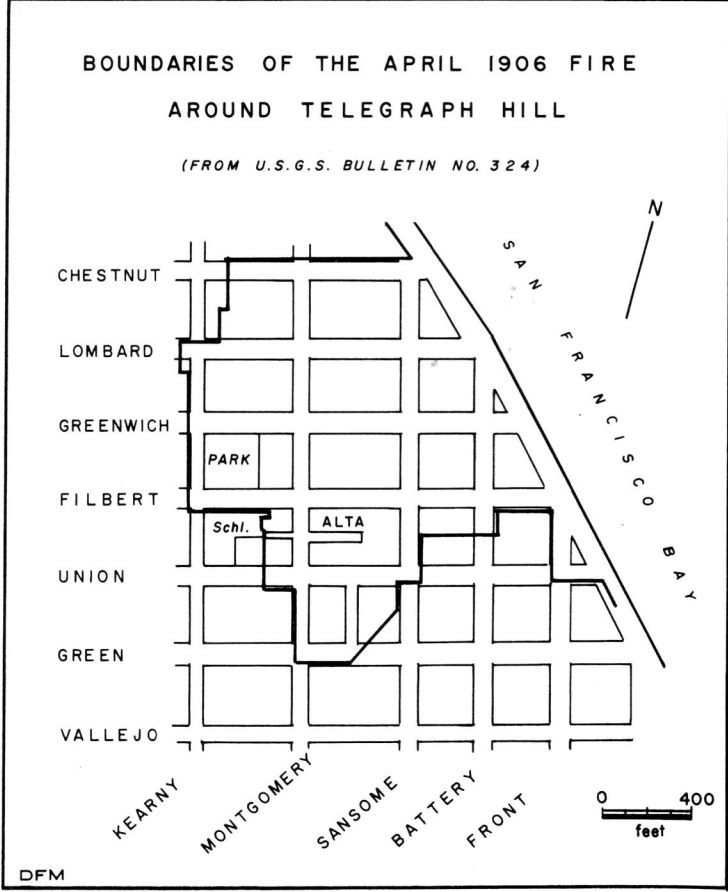

Although the fire had been extinguished, smoke hung over the city for many days. In this photograph, taken from the Ferry Building (which escaped the flames), Telegraph Hill can be observed in the background with the undamaged houses along Union Street. In the lower left is the track of the Clay Street cable car line. (—*Library of Congress*)

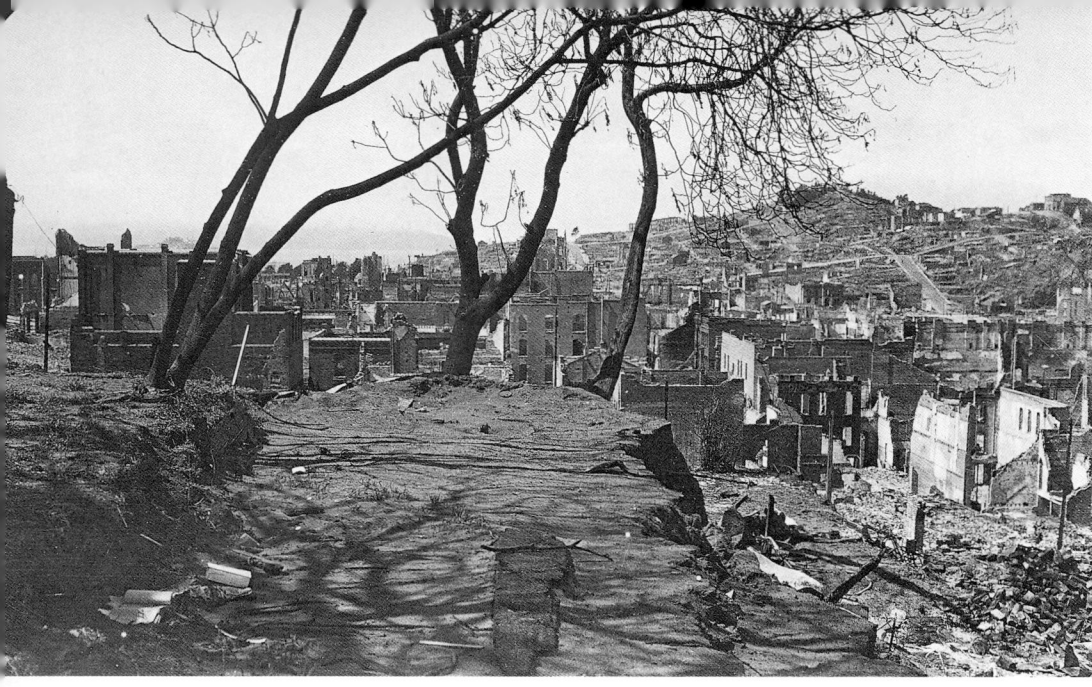

The fire was over and the veil of smoke had lifted from San Francisco when Arnold Genthe recorded this stark and quiet scene with his camera. The only surviving structures were the buildings on Telegraph Hill (upper right). (—*Palace of the Legion of Honor*)

18, 1906, and the disastrous three-day fire that wiped out much of the city. The fire consumed 490 city blocks and another 32 blocks were partially burned; 28,188 buildings were destroyed, according to the count published in the San Francisco Relief Survey. The burned area was generally east of Dolores Street and Van Ness Avenue, and because a part of Telegraph Hill was one of three small enclaves to escape the flames, some of the oldest houses in San Francisco are here today.

The fire — really a multitude of fires — spread rapidly. Within 24 hours the downtown section had been consumed and people were being warned to leave their homes. When the Barbary Coast and Chinatown were threatened, refugees escaped by climbing Telegraph Hill and then descending the Filbert and Greenwich stairs to the water front, where boats took them across the Bay to safety.

On Friday all hope for the Hill was abandoned when the flames crossed Pacific Avenue near Kearny and throughout the night strong winds swept the fire up the slopes of Russian and Telegraph hills. With the flames approaching, it took little more than a suggestion to persuade the frightened people here to evacuate their homes and follow the other refugees. While the people waited on the water front for a boat to take them to Oakland, a freight car full of chickens was broken open by the soldiers, who told the refugees to help themselves. A large caldron was set up and soon the tempting bouquet of chicken broth was in the air. But just before serving time the boat blew its whistle and the people were herded aboard, sadly leaving the caldron of soup behind.

Not unexpectedly, there was confusion everywhere. Giovanni Doneri and his family, heeding the advice of the soldiers, left their flat on Telegraph Hill and proceeded to the Embarcadero. While they waited for the boat, the urge to retrieve some prized possession was so strong that Giovanni and his oldest son climbed back up the stairs to return home. That was the last Mrs. Doneri and her other children saw of them for some time. Cinders were flying about when the two Doneris arrived at the top of the Hill, and the soldiers there gave them wine-soaked burlap bags and ordered them to join the volunteers beating out sparks and small fires.

The volunteers had evolved a plan that envisioned saving most of the buildings along Montgomery Street by supplementing natural barriers with firebreaks and using wine to cool the walls and roofs of remaining buildings. Pioneer Park was one barrier, and the brick walls and adjoining playground of the old Garfield School on Union Street were another. The unprotected gap between Upper Alta and Filbert streets was a problem, but by demolishing some buildings a firebreak was created and, as flames from the west neared Kearny Street, a backfire was started. This effort — plus liberal applications of wine to cool the sides of the buildings destined to stand — did the trick in that quarter.

Sparks from the burning buildings were landing on the shingle roofs of houses along Montgomery and its cross streets, but the ever-watchful volunteers made quick work of them. Covering the walls with burlap soaked in wine saved the three-story structure which contained Doneri's flat, at the southeast corner of Montgomery and Union, but the buildings across the street were consumed by the fire.

While wine was used to great advantage in fighting the blaze at the top of the Hill, broken casks in a winery at the bottom filled another need. No water was available immediately after the earthquake so the people drank wine, the only potable liquid in the city. Horses and dogs, who were equally thirsty, lapped up the wine spilled in the streets; their antics soon proved that four legs are no better than two when the grape takes effect.

North Beach was about the last district to be consumed by the conflagration as backfires along Vallejo Street to the Bay proved to be ineffective. It was not until Saturday morning, April 21, that the last blaze was extinguished.

The Changing Scene

The Italians had scarcely settled on the Hill in large numbers when the Spanish started to arrive, followed later by the Chinese. Around 1920 artists and would-be artists began to occupy the Hill, and Harry Lafler's famous Compound on Montgomery Street was a center for the Bohemian life. But all that was soon to change. The opening of Telegraph Hill Boulevard in 1923 brought more people to the summit to enjoy the view, and a year earlier Julius' Castle had begun serving its famous 65-cent lunches. As roads and trails on Telegraph Hill were graded and paved, the influx of outsiders grew, a trend that accelerated with the completion of Coit Tower in 1933.

Already alarmed by the invasion of their quiet domain, the artists became even more alienated as they watched modern apartment houses rise on the Hill. Gradually they did the only thing they could: they simply moved away to Twin Peaks, Potrero Hill and more distant places. The new tenants on Telegraph Hill found the same Spartan furnishings — unreliable hot water, old-style iceboxes, a dual-burner gas plate for a stove,

---

Already the ashes had been brushed aside and frame buildings began to appear when this photograph was taken. The brick walls of old St. Francis Church (right) still stand but the almost new walls of the three-story kindergarten on Union Street (left) suffered badly and the building was torn down. Further up the Hill on Union are the walls of the old Union Grammar School. Some of the buildings along Montgomery Street remain today. (—*California Historical Society*)

drafty windows — but they loved the views and the charm of the Hill and were willing to pay a little more rent to enjoy them. To designate anything as a "first" risks quibbling over definitions, but possibly the first modern apartment house on the Hill was the building at the corner of Chestnut and Kearny (199 Chestnut), erected in 1931, followed four years later by the building at 1441 Montgomery Street.

The tide was then turning more strongly; even the august *New York Times* gave precious space, in the issue of April 19, 1936, to report the changes. Tom White, in an article subcaptioned "San Francisco's Historic Bohemian Quarter Succumbs to the Forces of Economics and Modernism," compared the past with the then current situation. During World War II apartments were sublet to military personnel when the regular tenants went overseas. After the war artists were even harder to find on Telegraph Hill; young lawyers, bankers, stockbrokers, nurses, teachers, stewardesses and secretaries made up the active scene.

The Fight for Survival

When the Greenwich Street cable car line discontinued its operations in the 1880s, Telegraph Hill was left without public transportation of any kind. True, there were streetcar lines operating around the Hill — Sansome, Broadway, Columbus Avenue and so on — but no matter how skilled or obliging the operator, the streetcar patrons could not ride to the top of the Hill.

Then on July 30, 1939, Municipal Railway bus route No. 11 was established to carry people from the intersection of Union and Powell streets up to Coit Tower. On October 6, 1946, the route was extended to include a segment from Powell to Montgomery via Union Street; revisions on other lines were reflected in the renumbering of this U-shaped route to No. 39 on February 1, 1949. Three buses built in 1939 comprise the fleet, with only one in use at a time while the others run elsewhere or are in the shop. The line is part of the local scene and a friendly rapport exists between the regular drivers and their patrons. Drivers will bend the rules a bit to wait for passengers who might be momentarily delayed or stop in the middle of a block to accommodate someone on a rainy day. Like the corner grocery, the transfer point at Union and Stockton serves as a community meeting place.

The riders of the No. 39 line are a loyal and determined lot, as the Municipal Railway management found in 1954 when it attempted to curtail drastically the hours of bus service. A great hue and cry arose, and people banded together to protest, with the result that plans for reduced bus service were shelved.

However, the concerned citizens, having won the battle of the bus, instead of disbanding decided to become a permanent organization under the name of the Telegraph Hill Dwellers. Their first meeting was held in the Schaeffer School of Design on March 24, 1954; heading the group were Fred Meyer as president and Mrs. Raymond Theill as executive vice-president and "chief instigator." The general purposes of the Dwellers are to beautify and preserve Telegraph Hill, making it a better place to live and visit. Their projects have been varied and numerous, including tree planting along sidewalks, placing utility wires underground, preserving height limits, installing litter containers and directional signs, improving relations with civic officials, issuing *The Semaphore* and holding neighborhood parties and dinner meetings. The group's success has not been automatic but reflects the hard work of subsequent officers and many volunteers among the 600 dues-paying members.

Early in 1956 promoters sought to "redevelop" a large portion of Telegraph Hill at a cost estimated from $7.5 to $25 million. The term "blighted area" was loosely tossed about, even though some of the buildings in the section generally bounded by Vallejo, Grant, Filbert and Montgomery or Calhoun streets were less than two years old. Five hundred unhappy residents at a mass meeting in February 1956 heard the plans explained in English, Italian and Chinese — but all had the same adverse reaction. When Mayor George Christopher gave his support to the Hill residents, after visiting the "blighted area," the redevelopment talk subsided.

A month later a different development group proposed an 11-story apartment building to replace a post-fire apartment house on the west side of Montgomery just south of Union. This threat

Taken from Russian Hill, this classic photograph with the pretty young ladies smiling for the cameraman against a background of billowing smoke tends to minimize the calamity. However, within the next few days there were to be dramatic changes as the fire marched relentlessly in all directions. All of the buildings in the picture were burned, including the Merchants' Exchange (large building with a cupola in the center of the picture) and the Hall of Justice (left), where the heat of the fire wilted the steel-frame tower. (—Arnold Genthe photo, Palace of the Legion of Honor)

of a tall building spurred the campaign to extend the forty-foot height limitation from Union Street southward to a line 120 feet from Broadway. On June 4, 1956, the Board of Supervisors voted approval of this measure. In spite of a farewell party, the old building still stands and any vacancies it has are gobbled up.

The automobile brought new dimensions in living to the Hill, as well as more congestion for city streets. On Telegraph Hill, finding a home for the car is even more difficult than finding housing. Older apartment houses were built without garages as autos were then beyond the reach of most people; newer buildings were often constructed with an inadequate number of stalls until the one-for-one (auto space per housing unit) law became effective in December 1955. Because of the Hill's topography certain streets cannot be graded for vehicles, and in the two and a half blocks of Montgomery between Montague and Greenwich over 100 dwelling units are without access to a graded street, a matter which further aggravates already crowded parking conditions.

Residents of Telegraph Hill demonstrate considerable pride in their community and a tenacious approach to problems. When a tree-planting program was begun in the spring of 1956, what first appeared to be a simple project became quite involved as explanations to hesitant residents and the approval of several city departments were required. The concrete sidewalks had to be cut and the proper trees selected, and of course the individual property owners had to co-operate. Before the trees were in place, Mrs. (Dorothy) Morse Erskine spent many hours guiding the program and then planted some of the trees herself. Other examples of community pride will be found in the individual care given to gardens and homes.

WATCHING FOR THE STEAMER.

News from home was a precious commodity in the days of '49. Letters from loved ones had to take the long tedious voyage to Panama, thence across the isthmus to await the northbound Pacific Mail steamer to San Francisco. Once the mail ship was sighted as it entered the Golden Gate, homesick Argonauts could scarcely contain themselves as the ship rounded Clark's Point to anchor in the harbor. The excitement was contagious; men rushed to the summit of Telegraph Hill to cheer the incoming vessel and fervently pray for some message from home. (—*California Historical Society*)

The Marine Telegraph

Telegraph Hill received its name from the semaphore placed on the summit in 1850 to advise the city of the approach of ships. The first signal pole, erected by the military in 1846, had long since vanished; probably its wood brightened the hearth of some shack on cold winter evenings. With the new Marine Telegraph in operation, as a vessel made its way through the Golden Gate the lookout arranged the two arms of the semaphore to indicate the type of craft. Certain arrangements could stimulate a burst of activity in the town, particularly when the arms indicated the arrival of a Pacific Mail steamer, which meant that long-awaited mail from the East Coast would soon be on hand. In the early years men rushed to the crown of Clark's Point to welcome the ship, while others hurried down to the post office to get a place near the head of the line. With as many as 13,000 letters to be processed from a single ship, several hours of waiting were necessary. For those who wished to avoid standing in the muddy street, a place at the front could be purchased for as little as five or ten dollars.

Almost forgotten is the name of John K. Duer, the man who sparked the idea of a system of ship indicators. Appointed a midshipman in 1836, Duer joined the Pacific Squadron in February 1848, serving first aboard the storeship *Southampton* and later on the frigate *Savannah*. Early in 1849 he walked into the newspaper office of the *Alta California* and told the editor of his idea for a code of signals for California harbors. Impressed, the editor enthusiastically described the plan in the issue of February 1, 1849.

Receiving some support, Lieutenant Duer worked out the details and specifications in a room on the second floor of the Merchants' Exchange Building owned by Dunbar and Gibbs. The day before Christmas in 1849 this building was destroyed in one of San Francisco's early fires, along with Duer's plans. Subsequently a new Merchants' Exchange Building was erected on Montgomery Street, and Duer was able to redraw his plans. With financing arranged, work on the project began in January of 1850 when a Mexican War veteran, known only by the nickname Churubusco, started hauling timbers to the top of the Hill. As to how the site for the signal station was acquired there are two conflicting reports: one states that the land was leased from two pioneers, E. V. Joice and M. L. Callender, while another attributes ownership to settlement on the ground.

Ned Boehme, who had come from Philadelphia the previous August, and William Mercier, who had worked with Duer in the preparation of the plans, soon began constructing the station. A strong mast was set in the ground and around it they built a two-story house measuring 18 x 25 feet; at the peak of the roof was a platform enabling the men to arrange the signal. When the building was finished Boehme and Mercier lived upstairs, spending their time cooking and keeping house, watching for ships through a telescope and arranging the semaphore. Boehme recalled that light refreshments were served in the downstairs room for people who ventured up the Hill.

Official notice of the station's completion was accorded by the *Alta* when the following request appeared in the issue of April 19, 1850:

> To Pilots — Pilots will confer a favor upon the proprietor of the Marine Telegraph by requesting masters of vessels bound in to hoist their colors at the masthead instead of the peak.

On that same day the Marine Telegraph made its first report when with a single wooden arm it indicated "vessel in distress inside." The English bark *Daniel Grant* had struck Blossom Rock but luckily managed to dislodge herself. At sunset another bark appeared, the *Malony* from Trinidad Bay, and she moored without difficulty.

A reference to "Duer's telegraph arms" appeared in the *Alta* of September 17, 1850. Also in that issue was a short article beginning:

> Yesterday morning — Were you on Telegraph Hill yesterday morning? No! Ah! How much you missed of the fresh and beautiful . . .

From there the writer went on to praise the scene, but the article is significant as it is one of the first times the name Telegraph Hill appeared in print. After that the name Clark's Point faded away. "Signal Hill" was one of the few landmarks noted on the U.S. Navy chart of the Bay in 1850, but that soon gave way to the present name.

Boehme had left his job at the station after a few months, and Lieutenant Duer departed for New York on August 23, 1850. It was probably about this time that the Merchants' Exchange and the signal site passed into the hands of G. F. Sweeny and T. E. Baugh; according to one account they paid $6000 for the property. At the same time Mr. Swat of the Merchants' Exchange was peddling copies of a "beautifully lithographed sheet of signals now in use at the telegraph station in this city."

About Sweeny and Baugh there is some confusion, traceable to *The Annals of San Francisco*, an important source of the city's early history. This book introduces these men on page 465 saying, "early in 1849 this enterprising firm had erected a station house on Telegraph Hill. . . ." However, on page 824 the book contradicts itself, advising that George F. Sweeney [*sic*] arrived in California in October 1849.

George Francis Sweeny was born in Tyrconnel, Ireland, in 1815 and came to the United States. Sailing from Philadelphia around Cape Horn, he arrived in California on October 12, 1849, according to his membership certificate in the Society of California Pioneers. His brother, Myles D. Sweeny, was the first president of what is now The Hibernia Bank. George Sweeny's partner, Theodore E. Baugh, was a native of Philadelphia.

The Merchants' Exchange and the Marine Telegraph brought prosperity to Sweeny and Baugh. The telegraph and the meanings of the various positions of its wooden arms were part of the lives of the knowledgeable men of San Francisco. One evening when *The Hunchback* was presented in a local theater, an innocent actor appeared on stage with outstretched arms to ask, "What does this mean, my lord?" Before the other player could respond, a loud voice from the audience brought down the house with "Side-wheel steamer!" But while the Marine Telegraph performed admirably, it still did not meet the demands of those impatient to have even more advanced notice of arriving ships. For this reason, Sweeny and Baugh established an outer station at Point Lobos in 1851. Located beyond the Golden Gate, six miles from Telegraph Hill, the lookout there arranged his signals and the inner station on the Hill repeated them.

This visual system was cumbersome at best and inoperative in adverse weather, so Sweeny and Baugh prepared to replace it with an electromagnetic telegraph line. They filed a petition with the City Council on June 14, 1852, to build a line from Point Lobos, entering the city via Broadway (Larkin Street marked the city limits at that time), down Stockton to Sacramento Street, where the Merchants' Exchange was then located, on the south side just east of Montgomery. There subscribers would be notified of shipping movements as reported by the telegraph. Work began promptly; wires were strung on thirty-foot poles, and men were schooled in the Morse code. When the clipper ship *Crescent* appeared on September 11, 1853, she had the honor of being the first ship reported by the new system, which was one of the first telegraph lines in California.

That very night some malicious person cut down two poles on Broadway for his own use, and a few days later someone cut the wires near the Exchange. This vandalism was too much for the two partners, who appeared at the council meeting of September 27 and got an ordinance passed establishing penalties for disturbing this vital communications link. The poles were a tempting source of firewood.

This primitive oil painting by an unknown artist executed in 1850 has long delighted aficionados of early San Francisco history. White tents of recent arrivals dot the green slopes of Telegraph Hill under Old Glory, proudly waving from the mast of the Marine Telegraph. But the fort, shown here perched on the bluff at Clark's Point, rightfully belongs more to the north (on the right side of the Fremont Hotel), if William Eddy's *Official Map of San Francisco* of 1849 is to be believed. (—*Wells Fargo Bank History Room*)

The electric telegraph was formally opened on September 22, 1853, with a sumptuous midday dinner at the Point Lobos station. More than 300 people attended, including the consuls of England, France and Denmark. When everyone was properly stuffed the speeches and toasts began, led by T. H. Selby, a smelter operator and later mayor of San Francisco. Toasts were drunk for practically everybody, and J. S. Henning, the builder of the telegraph line, was not forgotten. Then messages were sent to town and answered; the party did not break up until five in the afternoon.

The new arrangement certainly expedited ship reporting, but it completely by-passed Telegraph Hill and people on the street soon lost the habit of glancing up at the Hill to see what kind of ship was arriving. However, the name Telegraph Hill was firmly established, although the Hill was used for the Marine Telegraph for only three and a half years.

The downstairs part of the former lookout station was still a taproom, and now a telescope for sight-seeing was installed. On the side of the main building the word TELESCOPE was painted in large letters visible from the center of the city. Perhaps the sign induced some people to undertake the climb, but the hike to the summit was not to be taken lightly, and every pilgrim making the ascent felt that his achievement should be recorded for future generations. Out came the handy pocketknife and soon another name appeared on the clapboards of the building. Eventually the walls were covered with names: someone estimated as many as 40,000 of them. Once his name was carved into the wall, the visitor

Inner Telegraph Station.

Outer Telegraph Station.

The Inner (first) Telegraph Station served its purpose much better when the Outer Station was added at Point Lobos to relay notice of arriving ships beyond the Golden Gate.
(—Annals of San Francisco)

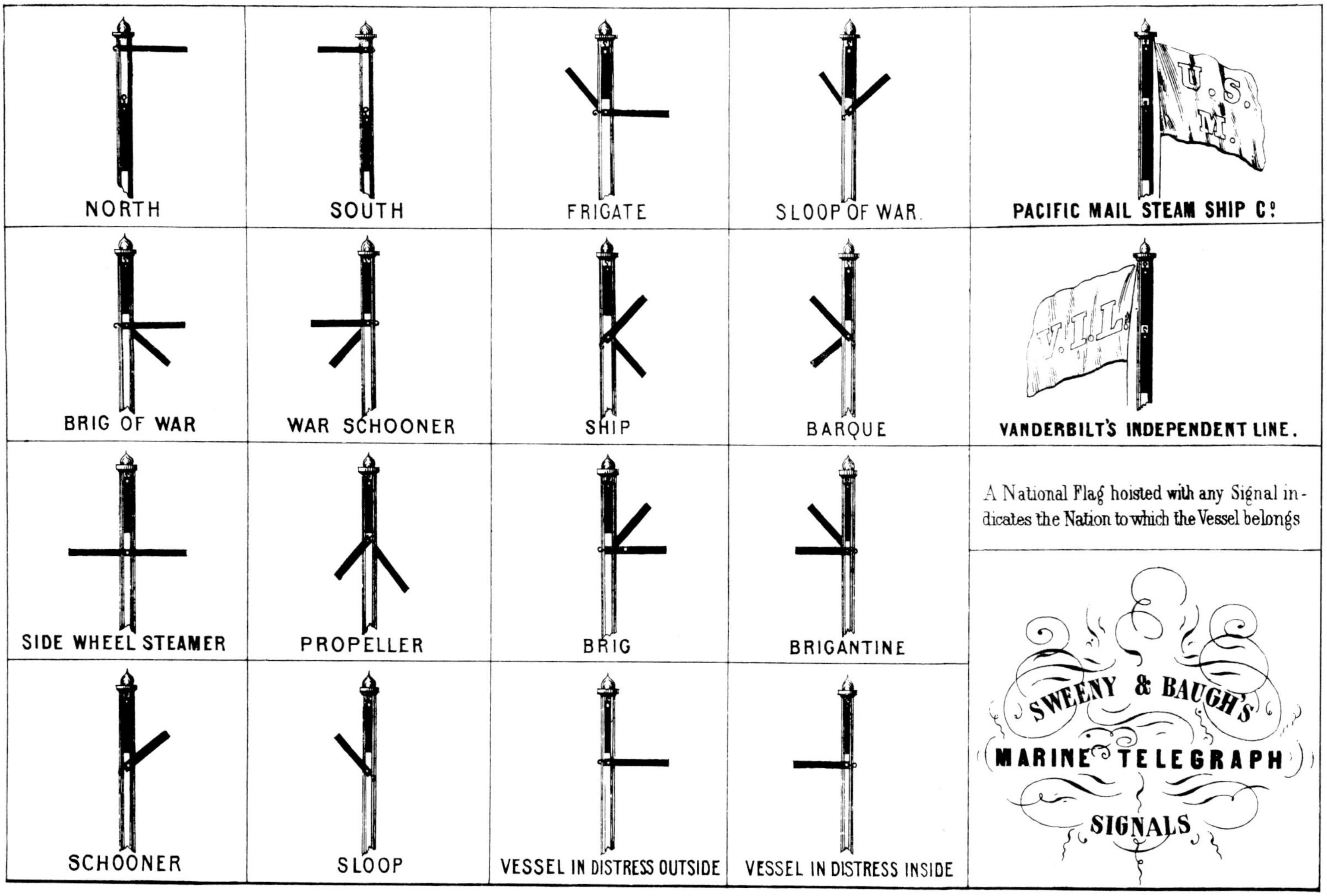

NORTH	SOUTH	FRIGATE	SLOOP OF WAR.	PACIFIC MAIL STEAM SHIP Cº
BRIG OF WAR	WAR SCHOONER	SHIP	BARQUE	VANDERBILT'S INDEPENDENT LINE.
SIDE WHEEL STEAMER	PROPELLER	BRIG	BRIGANTINE	A National Flag hoisted with any Signal indicates the Nation to which the Vessel belongs
SCHOONER	SLOOP	VESSEL IN DISTRESS OUTSIDE	VESSEL IN DISTRESS INSIDE	SWEENY & BAUGH'S MARINE TELEGRAPH SIGNALS

Precise information concerning the initial telegraph signals is lacking, as samples of the "lithographed sheet of signals" peddled by Mr. Swat in the summer of 1850 are yet to be found. Similarly, the engraving filed February 17, 1852, by Sweeny and Baugh with their copyright application has been lost. Only because R. P. Bridgens filled the wide border of his 1854 map of San Francisco with pictorial and other information do we have a record of the signals.
(—Library of Congress)

stepped into the taproom for refreshment and, if his pockets jingled with silver and the day was clear, he produced the necessary two bits for a look through the telescope at the wonders of the East Bay and Marin County.

This place of pleasant diversion met a dramatic end at three in the morning on December 7, 1870, when a strong southeaster passed over the city and destroyed the station. When dawn came, all that was left was kindling wood, and even that was gone by nightfall as a steady stream of neighbors carried away armloads of it for firewood. Except for a few goat fences, the summit of Telegraph Hill was once more untouched by the works of man.

George Sweeny died in 1859, but the Merchants' Exchange continued to be managed by Baugh and his brothers until 1865, when a group of dissatisfied businessmen established a new Merchants' Exchange. For a time there were two buildings of that name in San Francisco, then about 1870 Baugh renamed his the U. S. Court Building. With his other real estate investments, including his share of the Sweeny and Baugh tract on Cliff House Road, Baugh was able to live comfortably in San Francisco until his death in 1881.

Incoming ships continued to be reported from Point Lobos until 1961, and the last lookout station there was erected in 1926. The Marine Exchange lookout station on Pier 45 D is still in operation today.*

The Time Ball

In a number of cities in the United States during the last century, the exact moment of noon was designated each day by the dropping of a time ball. The ball, a hollow metal sphere two to six feet in diameter, was hoisted to the top of a twenty or thirty-foot shaft and allowed to fall precisely at noon. In a port like San Francisco, the time ball played an important part in checking the accuracy of ship chronometers.

Ship captains determine their longitude by comparing local time, as derived from celestial

---

*Lookout stations using semaphores to indicate impending ship arrivals were used in other parts of the world. One example is the system in use in the 1880s at Willemstad, Curacao, in the Netherlands Antilles.

An explanation of the intricacies and merits of Barrett & Sherwood's time ball was the subject of an advertisement in the *Alta* of September 15, 1852. (*—San Francisco Public Library*)

---

observations, with Greenwich time, as shown on their chronometers. The accuracy of the chronometer is of paramount importance, and on arriving at each port the captain took his instrument to one of the local watchmakers for testing which involved several days in the shop. With the record of fires sweeping downtown San Francisco in the early days, captains were reluctant to leave their chronometers ashore for the required time. Samuel Barrett and Robert Sherwood, watch and chronometer makers, offered a method of checking the

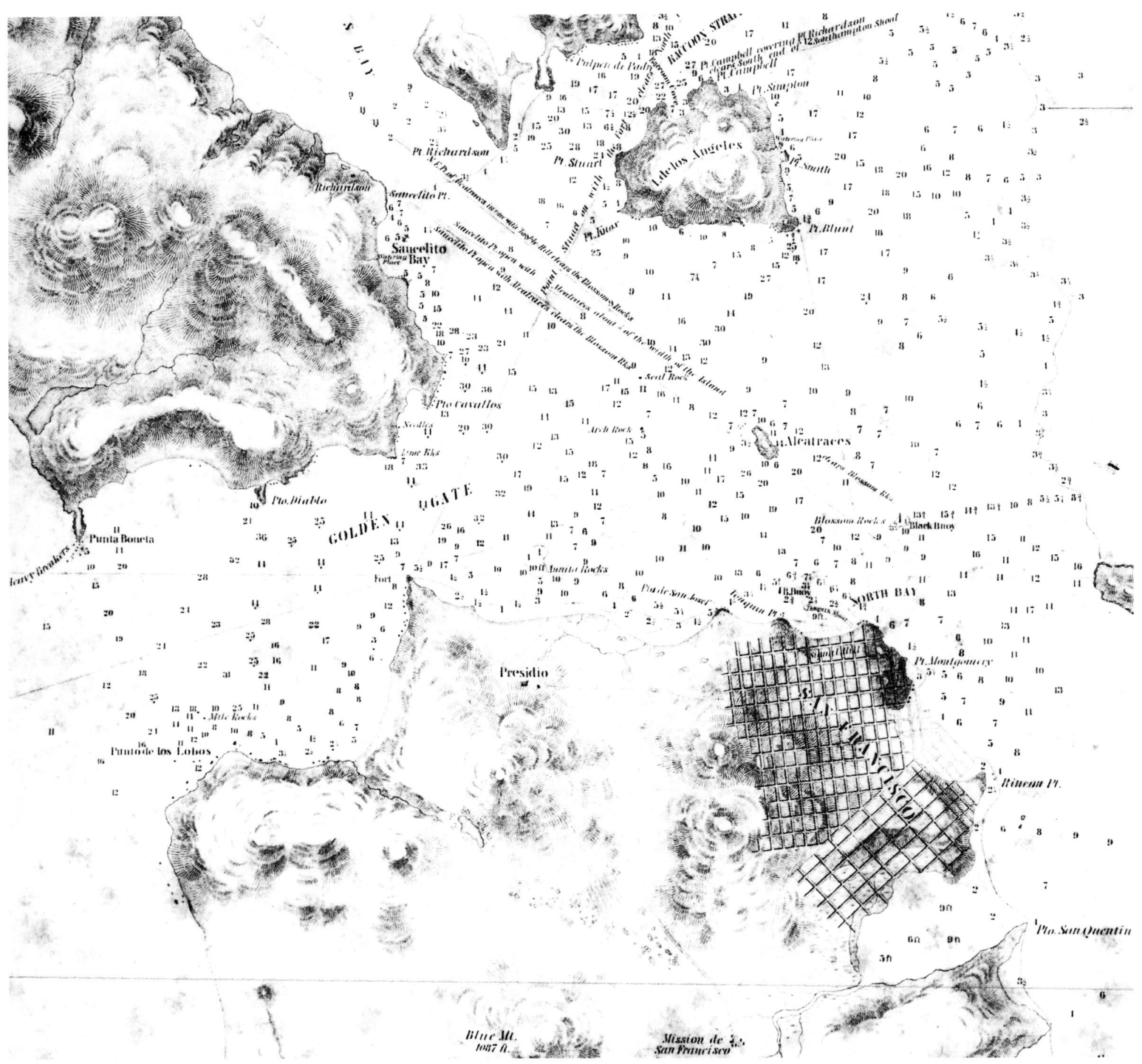

This 1850 chart of the Bay of San Francisco by Cadwalader Ringgold, Commander, U. S. Navy, offers topographical names which do not exist today. Some have been changed and others have vanished. Signal Hill is Telegraph Hill, of course, and Blue Mountain is part of Twin Peaks at the western end of Market Street. Blossom Rock, a menace to navigation, was removed, while Point Montgomery and Point San Quentin, now separated from the Bay by filled land, have fallen into oblivion.

The outer signal on Point Lobos was in a commanding position to relay early notice of incoming ships; later when the electric telegraph line was installed there was no need for the inner station on Telegraph Hill. In those times it was a long journey to Mission Dolores. (—*National Archives*)

precious instruments without removing them from the ships. Prevailing upon Sweeny and Baugh, they used the signal pole on Telegraph Hill for a time ball; beginning on May 20, 1852, it was dropped at noon every day except Sunday. The key to the financial success of this venture was that the exact time of the ball's release was kept secret. For several days a captain would record his observations of the time ball according to his chronometer, then he compared his record with Barrett and Sherwood's tabulation at their City Observatory, paying a small fee for this service.

It was only a matter of weeks before a rival service appeared, and again it was on Telegraph Hill. Joseph McGregor (1814-67) of Perth, Scotland, had settled in Valparaiso, Chile, but came to California in October 1848 on hearing of the gold discovery. Dealing in chronometers, charts and other navigational paraphernalia, McGregor and his partner, David Anderson, established the San Francisco Observatory at 215 Green Street, on the east slope of the Hill. Following the British tradition, they dropped their time ball at one o'clock rather than at noon.

These two services seem to have lasted only a few years. However, in 1885, shortly after the German castle was completed on the crest of the Hill, the time ball resumed its daily appearances, although the operators are unknown. As the fortunes of the castle waned the time ball was moved in 1898 to the new Ferry Building and then to the Fairmont Hotel in 1909, where with Frederick Shaefle as one of the operators it functioned until June 30, 1937. This time ball is now on display aboard the *Balclutha*, the old sailing ship maintained by the San Francisco Maritime Museum.

The New Flagpole

In 1961 the P.&O.-Orient Lines wished to commemorate the arrival of its newest and largest ship, the *Canberra*, as she entered San Francisco harbor on her maiden voyage from Southampton. Taking a leaf from the past, the steamship company offered to underwrite the cost of a sixty-foot flagpole, semaphore equipment and an appropriate plaque, all to be erected on Telegraph Hill. Obtaining the approval of the Art Commission, it raised the pole at the northwest edge of the circle at the summit.

As a prelude to the arrival of the *Canberra* on July 20, 1961, the California Historical Society sponsored a program consisting of speakers, the unveiling of the plaque and music from the Sixth Army Band. At midmorning, when the bow of the ocean liner poked through the fog, a 13-gun salute was fired from the Hill using borrowed cannon. The band then played "God Save the Queen," the Union Jack was hoisted on the new flagpole and the crowd departed to welcome the ship as she docked at Pier 32, some distance from Telegraph Hill.

Telegraph Hill appears on a number of lithographs of early San Francisco. This lithograph, the work of a London firm, shows the busy harbor as seen from Telegraph Hill in 1851. The windmill on the Hill belonged to Mr. Hudson, who used it to grind spices. (*—Library of Congress*)

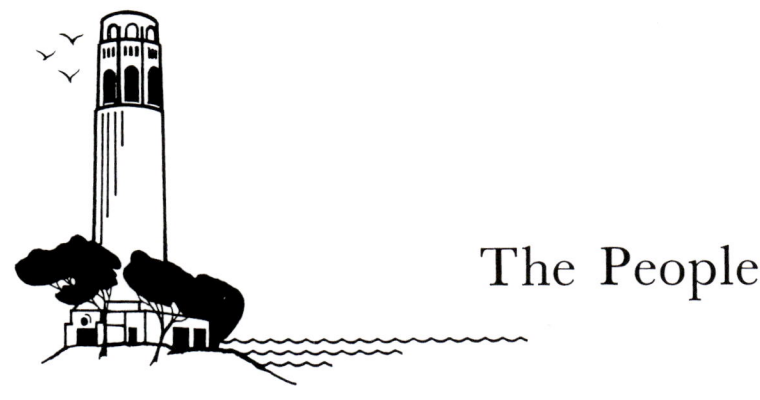

The People

Short of unpredictable natural phenomena, it is the people in their particular ways, individually and collectively, who make up the history of a community.

Telegraph Hill today is occupied by people from many different nations. But back in 1880 the census revealed that about three-quarters of the residents came from Ireland; of the remainder, Germany provided the largest share and the number of Italians about equaled the Portuguese. A few gave Massachusetts or New York as their birthplace, and there was a scattering of men from Norway, Sweden and Denmark, most of them working as stevedores or seamen. Living among the Germans in the 300 block of Green Street at that time were seven Chinese laundrymen named Ah Sang, Ah Loy and so forth.

The Italians now constitute the largest national group on Telegraph Hill, a situation which arose with the heavy immigration around 1900. They generally settled on the west side of the Hill (Sunny Side), while the Irish preferred the top of the Hill and maintained their last stronghold on the east side (Twilight Side). They did not always live in harmony; one Irish gang — appropriately known as the Rock Rollers — in any conflict quickly positioned themselves above the enemy, for then gravity was on their side. After the 1906 fire many of the Irish moved from Telegraph Hill to Rincon Hill, and after the 1915 Panama-Pacific International Exposition closed, the Italians built new homes in the Marina District. However, Italian is still an important language in North Beach (the Latin Quarter) and on Telegraph Hill. Sitting on a park bench in Washington Square, one hears Italian phrases punctuated by English — or more accurately, American — words.

Another segment of the Hill population was from Spain, and even today the Spanish and the Italians both are very conscious of their separate national origins. Most of the Spanish people who arrived here around 1900 came from Hawaii. One young girl, Francisca Seone, left Galicia in northwestern Spain in May of 1899, traveling with her brother and niece. After the seemingly interminable thirty-day voyage aboard a packed vessel, Francisca arrived in Hawaii, where she met and married Antonio Bergantino, the head jailer of Hawaii, who had previously emigrated from a neighboring district in Spain. The new couple came to Telegraph Hill in 1901 and subsequently built the flats at 103 and 105 Alta Street.

One day in 1914 the people living on Alta Street were startled to see a long parade of men, women and children laboriously climbing the Filbert Street steps, each lugging an armload of possessions. Natives of Andalucia, they had left Spain to work as contract labor on the Hawaiian sugar plantations. When they had received favorable letters from fellow countrymen living on Telegraph Hill, these families had carefully hoarded their meager earnings for passage to San Francisco. The Spanish people brought with them customs which at first set them apart from their neighbors, and resentment developed when some charities favored them over equally destitute Irish families. The constant twanging of Spanish guitars was another disturbance; one Celtic resident to this day finds the sound unbearable.

During the summer months the Spanish people packed asparagus in the canneries at Fairfield or Rio Vista and enjoyed a vacation during the winter. Others set themselves up in business. Roque (Rocca) Martinez, for example, operated a small cigar factory behind his house, first at 1423 Montgomery and later at 310 Union Street.

Among the different groups on Telegraph Hill there are those who sparked the community's development or contributed to the folklore of the neighborhood. Some of the more illustrious residents and visitors warrant individual attention, but they constitute only the smallest fraction of the thousands who have lived on the Hill at some time.

Some Illustrious Individuals

Perhaps the pioneer of the better-known Telegraph Hill characters was the scalawag Henry Meiggs, often referred to as "Honest Harry." Meiggs came to California from New York in 1849 with a shipload of lumber, which he disposed of at fancy prices, then he went into lumbering in California's redwood country.

Watching the rapid growth of the inner harbor, Meiggs reasoned that the congestion would soon require expansion of the water front at North Beach. He built a wharf extending from Francisco Street, between Powell and Mason, and confident of the glowing future of North Beach he invested heavily in its real estate. The only trouble was that the city expanded in the opposite direction and Harry, in spite of his winning smile and glib tongue, was soon strapped for cash. He solved this problem handily by obtaining illegal possession of San Francisco city warrants — in effect, promissory notes — which he used for collateral for personal loans.

The bubble burst in October 1854, but by that time Harry Meiggs and his family had quietly left their home at Broadway and Sansome and were already on the high seas bound for South America, where Meiggs would remain for the rest of his life. The exit had been carefully planned to avoid arousing any suspicion; to maintain the impression that the house was still occupied, Mrs. Meiggs' canary birds were left behind, chirping away in their cages.

People were lured to California for reasons other than gold, and some came to provide theatrical entertainment. In July of 1851 Junius Brutus Booth, Jr., arrived in San Francisco with his mistress, actress Harriet Mace. They soon settled on Telegraph Hill and stayed there until they went back east the following spring. When they returned to San Francisco in July 1852 they brought with them not only the younger brother Edwin but also Booth's father, whose arrival aroused great excitement in California. Junius Brutus Booth, Sr., returned east in September and died a few months later; Edwin Booth toured the gold country and then left for the Atlantic Coast. But Junius Booth, Harriet and their daughter continued to live in the Calhoun Street house, the attic of which was filled with theatrical props of all kinds. Appearing often at Maguire's Opera House, Booth stayed on in San Francisco until 1864.

Many years later, a movement arose to give the little cottage at 5 Calhoun Street some permanent recognition as the former home of the great actor, and a suitable plaque was cast. The dedicating group converged on Calhoun Street but they could not find the house; even worse, quarrying operations had undermined the lot so badly that it was about to join the rubble at the foot of the Hill. There was nothing for the party to do but trudge downhill, thwarted in its endeavor.

Other theatrical people occupied the Hill in the 1860s. Mrs. Sarah Thayer lived in the 400

Henry Meiggs (opposite) and Edwin Booth (above) were two famous personalities who resided on Telegraph Hill in the early days of San Francisco. (—*Wells Fargo Bank History Room*)

block of Green Street, just west of Kearny, while across the street was the home of John L. Stackhouse, a scenic artist with the Metropolitan Theater. Mrs. Stackhouse's neighbors raised their eyebrows when she graciously invited Adah Isaacs Menken and other colorful ladies of the stage to stay with her family. In the last century such California stage personalities as Samuel and James Murdock, Catherine Hayes, Lewis Barker, Elisa Biscaccianti, Laura Keane and Lola Montez were reported to have found temporary shelter on Telegraph Hill.

The legal profession was also well represented. William Sherman Fitch lived a few doors west of the Thayer house. George C. and R. H. Waller maintained their law offices in the Montgomery Block, but they resided on Montgomery Street between Green and Union. Around the corner on Green was the home of Colonel George W. Grannis, an expert rifleman and a partner in the venerable law firm of Halleck, Peachy & Billings.

When James Ross moved to his Marin County ranch in 1862 he sold his property near the crest of the Hill at 311 Green to his neighbor, William B. Agard the importer. Agard moved into the house and lived there for many decades. Ross' move to Marin and his subsequent developments in that county are remembered in the town bearing his name. Another Green Street resident active in Marin County was Samuel P. Taylor, whose Pioneer Paper Mill there was the first on the Pacific Coast, dating back to October 1856.

Montgomery Street, climbing sharply from Broadway, provided "Montgomery Hill" as an alternate name for Telegraph Hill. Levi Mastick, engaged in the lumber packet business, lived on the west side of the street just below Green. Another member of the family, attorney E. B. Mastick, resided at the southwest corner of Union and Calhoun but later moved to Alameda. His house was well known because it was constructed largely of mahogany. Then at 8 Calhoun was the residence of John A. T. Overend, proprietor of the steam printing press that turned out the *Evening Bulletin*.

Translated, these Chinese characters say, "Telegraph Hill." In Cantonese, reading down, they would sound, "Teen-Po-Sun." (—*Ton Gee of Toy Sun Cleaners*)

From Hunters Point to Rincon Hill, around to Telegraph Hill (right center) and westward to the Golden Gate, this 1877 Currier and Ives print illustrates the close affinity of Telegraph Hill people and the maritime world. At their doorstep, in the harbor and at the docks, were ships from all over the world disgorging cargoes into the warehouses of commission merchants and providing employment for sailors, stevedores, warehouse laborers and craftsmen, many of whom lived on Telegraph Hill.

On the north (right) side of the Hill was the dry dock, and on the southwest side St. Francis Church looms prominently. Behind the busy part of the city were acres of sand dunes, now covered with row houses. (—*Library of Congress*)

Charles Warren Stoddard, posed on a footbridge in a rural setting, spent part of his early boyhood on Telegraph Hill. His writings of the South Seas, coupled with his personal enthusiasm, led Robert Louis Stevenson to his first cruise to Tahiti in 1888. (—*Silverado Museum*)

Stoddard and Stevenson

Born in Rochester, New York, Charles Warren Stoddard (1843-1909) came to California at the age of 12. The family moved into a brick house on Union Street, directly opposite the Union Grammar School — "a pretentious building for that period," Stoddard later wrote. The long stairway down to the docks, the corner grocery and the small but carefully tended gardens were among the things that fascinated this sensitive young man. "Above and beyond the school-house Telegraph Hill rose a hundred feet or more. Our street marked the snow-line, as it were, beyond it the Hill was not inhabited save by flocks of goats that browsed there all year round, and the herds of boys that gave them chase, especially of a holiday," wrote Stoddard in his book, *In the Footprints of the Padres*. After school, when not chasing goats, Stoddard and his friends gathered discarded tin cans for recovering the soft solder, which they sold to merchants for pin money. After two years this happy boyhood life in San Francisco was interrupted by a trip to New York, and it was not until 1859 that Charles returned.

Stoddard's literary career progressed from poetry to essays to books, and after a trip to Hawaii he became a journalist for the *San Francisco Chronicle*. He also became part of the erroneous legend wherein Stoddard was living on Telegraph Hill at the time he met Robert Louis Stevenson, the British novelist. This tale is well preserved in books and articles and has even been set in poetry. Old-timers occasionally point to the small apartment at 287 Union as Stoddard's home some ninety years ago.

Contesting a romantic legend is not a popular task, but all evidence leads to the conclusion that in his adult life Stoddard lived on Rincon Hill, then a more significant residential area, and that he first met Stevenson elsewhere. However, the two men did become close friends for the few months in 1880 that Stevenson stayed in San Francisco. Telegraph Hill was not unknown to Stevenson; indeed, after describing Stoddard's house on Rincon Hill in chapter eight of *The Wreckers*, Stevenson mentions Telegraph Hill, which some readers may have commingled with the previous paragraph to place Stoddard's home on Telegraph Hill.

In more recent times, noted visitors have been entertained in Telegraph Hill homes. After Helen Forbes died, her apartment at 60 Alta Street passed into the hands of Mayris Chaney Martin, a recognized professional dancer, whose friends included Mrs. Franklin D. Roosevelt. Often a guest in this apartment, Eleanor Roosevelt was a gracious visitor, admiring the Afghan dog of one lady and pleasantly acknowledging friendly recognition by other neighbors.

A few blocks away, at the crest of Filbert, is the home of Whitney Warren, an expatriate of New York who divides his time between San Francisco and his ranch in the Sacramento Valley. His quiet dinner parties, with guest lists of distinguished statesmen or movie and stage personalities, are famous but only occasionally get into the local society pages. When Princess Margaret of Great Britain and her husband, Lord Snowdon, were in San Francisco in November 1965, a small dinner party at this home was one of their scheduled activities. Some neighbors, apprised of the event, were on hand to give the royal couple a neighborly welcome.

Probably the greatest party of all time was held on the deck of The Compound on Calhoun Terraces to honor the Shah of Iran when he visited the city in June 1958. Elaborate preparations were made by the hosts, Tom Kearney and Jake and Bob McNear; the U.S. State Department inspected the premises and, though somewhat appalled by the primitive environment, approved the prepared guest list (which inadvertently omitted the hosts' names). At the appointed hour, with several hundred neighbors gawking, three black Cadillacs arrived to disgorge the bowing Iranian officials. The party was a great success, but while some people to this day are convinced that the Shah was there, the truth is that he never appeared, presumably because of the advance newspaper publicity.

HARPER'S WEEKLY.
JOURNAL OF CIVILIZATION.

Vol. XXX.—No. 1535.
Copyright, 1886, by Harper & Brothers.

NEW YORK, SATURDAY, MAY 22, 1886.

TEN CENTS A COPY.
WITH A SUPPLEMENT.

A mounted sword contest at San Francisco. (—*Drawn by T. de Thulstrup from Photographs*)

The German Castle and the Cable Car Line

It was a cold and foggy summer morning in 1873 when the Clay Street cable car line began operating on Nob Hill in San Francisco. This was the city's first cable car operation and its builder, Andrew S. Hallidie, nervously watched its fledgling movements. Soon it was apparent that Hallidie, already a successful wire rope manufacturer, had scored again and within a few years other cable lines stretched along San Francisco's streets. Not all of them were destined to be prosperous.

Frederick O. Layman, a capitalist and real estate man, envisioned a cable car line running up Telegraph Hill. Realizing that local residents could not provide sufficient traffic, he planned to establish a resort near Pioneer Park similar to the Cliff House on the ocean side of the city.

In applying for a city franchise on March 13, 1882, Layman outlined his route along Kearny Street, from Pacific Avenue to the sea wall. The proposed route was broken into three segments: the first part spanned eight blocks from Pacific to Chestnut Street, on the north side of the Hill; there people would descend by a 130-foot vertical elevator, and then continue by the third link for the remaining few blocks to the Bay.

While most visitors to the resort were expected to use the cable cars, Layman told the Streets Committee of the Board of Supervisors that he wanted to encourage the patronage of those who preferred their own conveyances. Kearny Street, he explained, would be the most appropriate route for carriages from the downtown area, but to make Kearny a practical street the part running along the west side of Pioneer Park would have to be graded. As the park was city property, Layman allowed that the gracious thing for the city to do would be to pick up the $4000 tab for this work. That Layman's real objective was to obtain a good base for his cable road did not escape official notice, and some doubts were expressed as to the propriety of the city's going to this expense to aid a private venture. While some committee members objected to Layman's proposal, Supervisor John McKew of the Second Ward adopted a politically more practical attitude. Not only would the construction payroll spread munificence in two wards — Kearny Street was the dividing line between the First and Second Wards — but the proximity of the cable line would certainly offer no detriment to McKew's own business, a wood and coal yard on Union just west of Kearny.

The committee sanctioned Layman's request, subject to the proviso that city improvements for Kearny Street would be withheld until construction of the cable road was well under way. Layman's proposal was then presented at a full meeting of the Board of Supervisors, and they went along with the committee but added a few restrictions. These included the usual five-cent fare limit, a maximum speed of eight miles an hour and the requirement that cars were "to be provided with sufficient brakes and other means of stopping when required." When the ordinance came before the mayor, that august gentleman demonstrated his legal training by raising a number of well-founded objections; the terms of the franchise were revised accordingly and approval was granted on May 1, 1882.

Next on the agenda was a corporate home, so on May 9 the Telegraph Hill Railroad Company was organized, with an authorized capital stock of $100,000. Among the incorporators were a Swiss banker, a real estate man, and Matthias Gray, a music publisher and wholesaler of band instruments. Since Mr. Gray's large home was on the southwest corner of Kearny and Lombard, perhaps he thought the cable line projected past his front door would provide convenient transportation to his downtown store. Gustav Sutro was another incorporator; a cousin of Adolph Sutro, of the Comstock tunnel fame, Gustav and his brother Charles were partners in the investment house of Sutro & Company.

In the spring of 1882 one part of Mr. Layman's plans began to take form as the sound of hammers and saws provided musical evidence that work was under way on his observatory at the summit of Telegraph Hill. Having in mind the occasional strong winds that 12 years earlier had destroyed the old semaphore station, the promoters took pains to make the structure solid. In appearance the two-story, octagonal wooden building suggested a German baronial castle.

Layman contemplated that the operation of the castle's public facilities would be managed by others. To that end he placed advertisements in the *Chronicle* and the *Alta,* as well as the German-language *Demokrat,* as follows:

> TO LET: The Telegraph Hill Observatory, Restaurant and Concert Hall, now in the course of construction. . . . Desirable parties can get favorable terms . . .

Messrs. Wertheim and Vogelsang leased the castle and chose July 4, 1882, for the opening. Several hundred people struggled up the grade that day to satisfy their curiosity about the new ornament on Telegraph Hill. Once there they could quench their thirsts and perhaps squint through a telescope at the myriad sights around the Bay.

While the German castle had become a tangible reality, the other part of Layman's project remained ethereal. Shortly after incorporating the Telegraph Hill Railroad, he advertised that the stock subscription books were open and assured the local moneymen that the cable road "promises

Frederick O. Layman built his castle in two stages. This single-story observatory, completed two years before the cable car line, was the forerunner of the grander structure. (—*Society of California Pioneers*)

HO! FOR TELEGRAPH HILL.

After construction of the Kearny Street line had been suspended, *The Wasp*, in one of its traditionally satirical cartoons, taunted Layman by suggesting various means of ascending the Hill. Undismayed, Layman pasted the sketch in his scrapbook and built on Greenwich Street. (—*California State Library*)

to be one of the best paying investments." However, after he had spent two months in unsuccessful promotion, the *Examiner* declared that the cable line "promises to be a first class bubble." Though Layman made some further progress, he had actually begun his long walk down the path of trouble, and failure would haunt him in this venture. Some minor work had been performed on the grade when the contracts were cancelled on July 25, 1882, following which the company filed a petition to disincorporate.

The trouble was that the part of Kearny Street traversing Telegraph Hill was too narrow for both a cable car line and normal traffic. When residents found surveyors' stakes only two feet from the sidewalk, they objected. On Sunday, August 6, Layman invited everyone to a meeting at the observatory to explain the project and hopefully to convince them that the personal inconvenience would be minor compared to the advantages of the cable car. The neighbors failed to be persuaded at that or at subsequent meetings.

Some of the details of the project were revealed at these gatherings. Andrew Hallidie estimated the cost of the new cable line to be $66,629.75, the largest items being the engines and machinery to power the cables ($14,000) and the six cars with grips ($10,000). W. H. Milliken, an engineer retained by Layman, made a second estimate, starting with Hallidie's figure and adding 25 per cent for contingencies plus another $20,000 to buy the castle and $10,000 to enlarge it, bringing the total to around $110,000. These estimates reflected a change from double-track operation to a single-track line with three turnouts. The Chestnut Street elevator was discarded in favor of a 440-foot sloping trestle down to Bay Street so that cars could move over the 3700-foot line in a matter of ten minutes.

In the steep part of Greenwich Street, No. 1 negotiates the grade. Not enough patronage came from these houses to support the Telegraph Hill Railroad Co. (—*Roy D. Graves collection*)

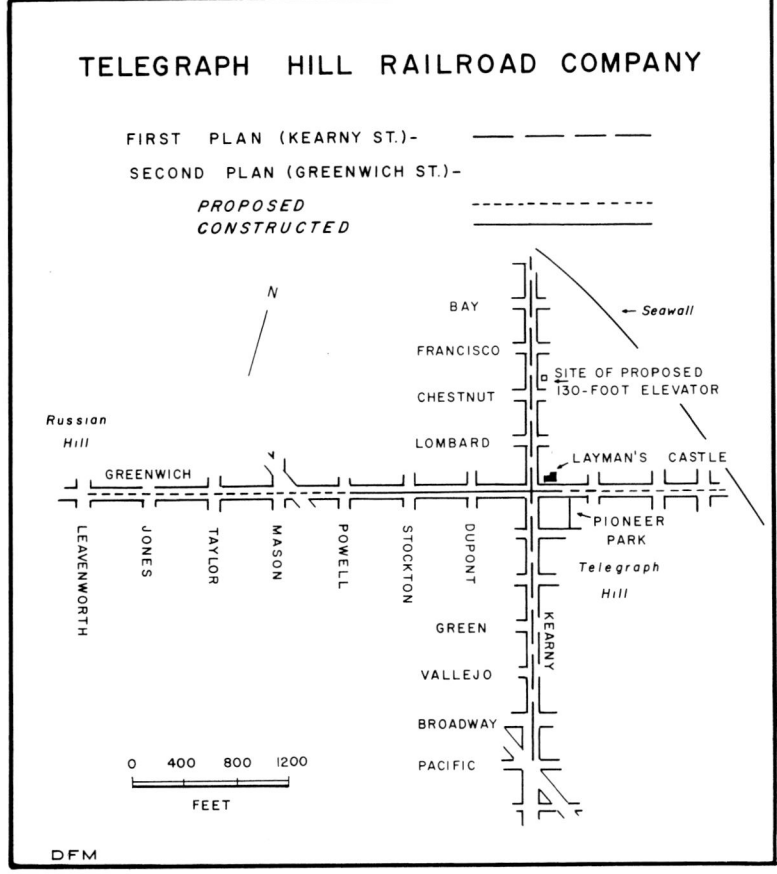

A Change in Location

Layman was trapped. Only a small number of people were willing to labor up the Hill to patronize the refreshment stand in the castle. The managers had tired of the empty premises, terminated their lease and departed. Without public conveyance there could never be adequate patronage at the observatory, yet the Kearny Street residents made things so difficult that Layman's cable line was an impractical dream.

Kearny Street provided the only direct route from the business center of San Francisco, but Layman was not ready to acknowledge defeat. There were other less desirable routes, involving transfer to a connecting line to reach the downtown area, and Layman took this course as the only way to salvage his investment in the castle.

So in October 1882 he appeared before the Board of Supervisors to seek a franchise for another line, this one running along Greenwich Street from Leavenworth to the summit of Telegraph Hill and then down to the sea wall. Again his efforts to secure a franchise encountered delays. Mayor Maurice C. Blake had a penchant for exercising his veto power, particularly in the matter of cable cars; in fact, Supervisor William Bodfish of the First Ward became so annoyed that he publicly declared he had "just about enough of these veto messages." Fortunately for Layman, an election was approaching and the voters put Blake out to pasture. The new franchise received favorable consideration by the supervisors and was approved on November 14, 1882.

Though the authorized route was 4700 feet long, Layman considered it financially expedient to build only the 1400 feet between Powell Street and the top of the Hill. Money was still a problem, and for a year he kept the presses busy turning out one prospectus after another. By the time the fourth had been circulated, Layman managed to find 22 subscribers with the necessary funds; perhaps the offer of a one-year free pass with the purchase of ten shares of stock — $100 — helped to sway the hesitant. Besides major commitments from Gustav Sutro, the law firm of Chickering and Thomas, the Fredericksburg Brewing Company of San Jose and several trustees, there were smaller pledges of $500 or less. One piano tuner promised all of fifty dollars.

When the treasurer, Sutro & Company, reported that ten per cent of the subscriptions had been paid in, Layman was able to file incorporation papers for the new Telegraph Hill Railroad Company, early in December 1883. Layman was named president, with Gustav Sutro vice-president and Andrew Baird secretary. William H. Milliken continued as chief engineer, a job for which his long record as a mechanical engineer qualified him. He had invented a hydraulic-ram elevator and more recently had been engaged in the construction of the Presidio and Ferries Railroad, also in San Francisco.

Construction Begins

On January 9, 1884, the construction contract was awarded to Joseph Fazackerley, the contractor who had supervised the building of the Presidio and Ferries Railroad. Under the contract Fazackerley was to build the line from Powell Street along Greenwich to the observatory, as delineated in Milliken's drawings; he was also to

Altogether the T.H.R.R. had three cars, but only two were in use at one time. Here No. 2 pulls into the passing track just below Dupont (Grant Avenue) to allow No. 3 to continue its journey down to Powell Street. For car No. 2 the steepest part of the climb lies ahead. The long flights of stairs leading up to the substantial homes indicate the amount of street grading accomplished in prior years. (—*Roy D. Graves collection*)

The same view, some eighty years apart. In the top photograph is the enlarged castle overlooking some of the more pretentious homes on Telegraph Hill. Just above the sea wall, Dupont terminates in the center of the picture; Stockton is to the right.

In the scene below, taken in 1971, apartments cluster on the Hill, which is crowned by Coit Tower. The masts of the *Balclutha* are silhouetted against the autumn sky. (—*Top, Society of California Pioneers; bottom, Diane Beeston photo*)

furnish the cable and two cars, pledging to complete the job by April 1, 1884. For all this he would receive $17,350 in cash and $3000 in fully paid stock of the company.

When the contract was signed, Fazackerley was busy finishing some work on the Omnibus Railroad and Cable Company, and he took no steps to initiate work on the Telegraph Hill Railroad, except for asking Milliken to order rails from the Pacific Rolling Mills. As one week of inactivity followed another, Milliken in desperation enlisted the aid of Sutro, who was also heavily involved with the Omnibus Railroad. Fazackerley soon got the message, and as February began his graders started excavating the roadbed along Greenwich. Others in his crew began blasting an engine room 32 feet square and 15 feet deep out of the solid rock at the top of the Hill.

Milliken arranged for Alfred F. Knorp, a San Francisco furniture maker and millman, to build the three cars according to Milliken's plans at an agreed price of $1125 each. The cars were generally similar to those used on the Presidio Railroad, except that the rear of the cars was 12 inches higher than the front. As they would run on a fixed route with grades up to thirty per cent, this feature made it possible to keep the longitudinal seats nearer to a level position while the cars moved along the grade.

Milliken and Layman visited Knorp's shop several times as the cars were being made. Milliken usually did most of the talking, and Layman's remarks were confined to his desire that the work be done well. This quest for quality workmanship extended to the roadbed, where the tracks were stabilized by iron cross braces, similar to the Market Street cable line. Quality became almost a fetish. For example, after the ties and stringers had been tamped to Mr. Milliken's satisfaction, Mr. Sutro came along and ordered the job done all over again. Iron rails had been part of the initial plans but Layman and Sutro decided that steel rails would be installed, even though the cost was somewhat greater. Also, the chimney of the powerhouse was built taller, and the walls around the machinery thicker than called for in the original plans.

In April the cars were ready, and the rails and power plant were in place by May. The cables, from the Hazard Manufacturing Company of Wilkes-Barre, Pennsylvania, were the last major item to arrive. Finally on May 23, 1884, the cars were set on the track and a few hesitant trial runs were made.

Meanwhile, at the crest of the Hill workmen were feverishly toiling to complete the enlargement of the crenelated castle. Telegraph Hill was soon graced with a truly imposing edifice, now a four-story building 140 feet long, 40 and 50 feet wide and 62½ feet high. When Gustav F. Walter and Rudolph Hopf took over the management of the new castle the stature of the enterprise grew, as these men for some time had operated the Vienna Garden at Sutter and Stockton with considerable success.

The Telegraph Hill Railroad, unlike most of the cable lines in the city, was a funicular railway. Typically, San Francisco cable cars are powered by a moving cable, which the operator of the car mechanically grips as needed. On the Telegraph Hill Railroad, both cars were permanently attached to the moving cable, with the ascending and descending loads balancing each other. By means of an electric signal in each car the operator's instructions were transmitted along the specially constructed cable to ring bells in the powerhouse at the top of the Hill; acting on these signals, the engineer set the cars in motion or brought them to a stop. For emergencies there was a braking system on each car which could be actuated by the operator, but the usual procedure was for the two cars to move or stop at the same time.

The scheduled public opening for the cable car line, first set for June 1, 1884, was postponed until June 13 — a Friday, for the superstitious — and that day did bring bad luck, as the line was not in working order. No further date was suggested for the opening, and while the bugs were being worked out, local residents enjoyed free rides — until June 22, when a nickel fare was charged. Five days later the completion of the Telegraph Hill Railroad was formally celebrated, and invited dignitaries toured the system. The climax of that day was a fine collation spread for their enjoyment at the observatory. Speeches were made and A. H. Wands, boss of the connecting Omnibus Railroad, toasted the success of the new venture.

Newspapers spread the word that the line would be opened on Sunday, June 29. Telegraph Hill's summit, long reserved "for adventurous boys and reckless goats," was now accessible even to the most timid soul. Estimates of patronage that day ranged from 2000 to 3000. Those who entered the observatory found not only a dazzling display of comestibles and potables but also enjoyed musical entertainment galore, with the program headed by the Vienna Garden orchestra.

But Layman's ill fortune continued to pursue him and not all went well that day; the crowds were there but the facilities failed. In spite of several weeks of trial operations, the essential tail rope slackened during the afternoon, bringing the system to a halt. A quick thrust of the knife was intended to cure this, but someone miscalculated and the rope was left just one inch too short! However, the crisis was resolved when a block and tackle was brought and the rope was stretched. Later in the day Layman was due for another unwelcome surprise when leaking gas in the pavilion forced an early closing.

Notwithstanding the glowing forecasts in Layman's several prospectuses, the Telegraph Hill Railroad failed to pay its stockholders any dividends. Not only was traffic light but revenues were even lower than initially contemplated. The transfer system with the Omnibus Railroad meant that the connecting line got the cash fares of the homeward-bound passengers while the Telegraph Hill Railroad received nothing for its work except paper transfers. Another difficulty was that two cars had to operate at the same time, thus precluding the economies of tailoring the service to varying traffic levels.

Layman relinquished the reins in December 1884, and Gustav Sutro became president. In the following month everyone in the company was embarrassed by a lawsuit growing out of a misunderstanding over the authority of the chief engineer to order materials while the responsibility of payment rested with the contractor.

Just when the Telegraph Hill cable line gave up the ghost has not been determined, but several educated guesses place the date at "about 1886." Some reports say that runaway cars with serious consequences helped to clinch the demise. One man, an Episcopal minister who had lived on Lombard Street as a boy, recalled seeing the tracks in place up to the time of the 1906 fire; it was not a happy sight: a partly washed out grade and rusty tracks choked with weeds. For many years the cars were stored in the Howard Street carbarn. Layman went back to Hamburg, Germany, where he died on September 2, 1889, at the age of 44; Gustav Sutro continued in the investment business until his death at the age of 69 in 1897.

Duncan Ross and His Broadsword Contests

Even though the almost empty cable cars continued to serve the castle for a time, there was nothing spectacular to draw people to the summit of the Hill until Duncan C. Ross began staging his exhibition broadsword contests. With a Herculean frame and weighing a trim 217 pounds, Ross had gained a public following through his professional wrestling matches and other athletic achievements. During an enlistment in the Royal Scots Greys, one of the British heavy cavalry regiments, he had been an instructor of swordsmanship.

Ross was the victor in a mounted broadsword contest in Kentucky around 1879, but the first contest on the Pacific Coast took place in San Francisco on February 25, 1885. In Central Park (at Eighth and Market) he met Sargeant Owen Davis of the Presidio and scored a narrow victory. Though the match failed to evoke favorable press notice, it did attract 1800 people, mostly drawn by some good publicity before the event. The announcement of this "assault at arms" advised one and all that this contest should be recognized as a rare sight usually available only to a privileged few. As the two horsemen galloped towards one another, each endeavored to strike his opponent's armor, thus scoring one point, and a match generally totaled 21 points. A blow on the helmet did not score and hitting a man below the armor or striking his horse evoked a one-point penalty. The swords used were regulation cavalry sabers with the points dulled but

"TELEGRAPH HILL OBSERVATORY," SAN FRANCISCO, CAL.

Large influxes of visitors around the observatory were the exception; patronage of both the cable car and the castle were disappointing. Perhaps because the lithographers, Joseph Britton and Jacques J. Rey, were personal friends of the proprietor they suggested its popular acceptance.

the edges honed to razor sharpness. Protected only by ordinary helmets, iron masks and cuirasses (padded jackets), the contestants sometimes suffered spectacular and painful injuries.

Ross was encouraged by the size of the group witnessing that first contest and decided to offer repeat performances. Taking over the Telegraph Hill observatory, he had one corner of the ground below the castle leveled, and an area about forty by fifty feet was fenced in to form an arena. In that somewhat medieval setting the crowds were treated to the sight of two men, mounted on horses and dressed in modified armor, hacking away at each other to the clang and clash of steel. Presumably some of the onlookers also stepped into the observatory for an occasional glass of spirits.

"There are always several thousand spectators, who no longer climb up the steep slope of the hill, but are drawn up by a cable road, one section of which has a grade as steep as the roof of a house . . ." read the cover story of *Harper's Weekly* for May 22, 1886. The article's graphic descriptions of the sometimes bloody contests probably caused proper Bostonians to question the veracity of the magazine's subtitle, *A Journal of Civilization*.

Ross took on all kinds of challengers, including an Australian police inspector and an Italian tamale peddler, and he emerged victorious in all contests but one. Sergeant Charles Walsh, who had been with General Sherman in the Atlanta campaign and who held a record of 11 successful sword contests in Mexico, had the distinction of being the only man in a year of weekly contests to beat Ross. But in the return match the following Sunday, Ross defeated Walsh in the nineteenth round. However, after a year of performances the public's interest dwindled. Even an overzealous attempt at authenticity — a heavy blow split Ross' helmet and nearly finished him — failed to hold the spectators, and the Sunday afternoon demonstrations soon became just a memory.

Still, Ross' connections with the sporting world attracted to the observatory such regular patrons as Charlie Mitchell, Paddy Ryan and Pony Moore, all big names on the boxing scene. Even John L. Sullivan stepped up to the bar for a drink and a convivial chat with Duncan Ross. Newspapermen frequented the establishment, and once when two men of that profession had a dispute, arrangements were made for them to settle things at the observatory. The encounter was scheduled for two in the morning and word drifted around the newspaper crowd that there would be a big fight at Duncan Ross' place. The police also caught the word; they slipped up the Hill to arrest not only the participants but all of the spectators as well, marching them down to the jail for the night. After that, Ross departed from the scene and was not heard from until 1898, when he lost his title as broadsword champion at a matched staged in Ohio.

In 1887 Otto Liebman tried his hand at running the observatory, but one year was enough for him. Next came Emile Marsky, who managed to last for two years, although it was necessary for him to find supplementary employment as a bookbinder.

By this time the castle had a reputation as a "hoodlum resort." But although forlorn and forgotten, "Layman's Folly" had become a landmark in the city, inviting questions from travelers who approached San Francisco by ferry. After a decade several legends circulated about its origins: one was that Adolph Sutro had built the castle, and another had it that both the observatory and the cable car line were constructed by Duncan Ross, using $50,000 his father had given him. Then there was the delightful story that Santa Claus used the abandoned structure as a toy warehouse each December.

In later years the castle came into the possession of Charles Sutro, Gustav's son. And then in January 1895 the *Call* reported that the "castellated ruins" had been sold to a party in Chicago and that the building was to be restored as an attractive resort with promenades, including the repair of the old cement wall around the periphery of the Hill. However, the Chicago investors vanished before making any improvements.

The building remained just as it was for another five years until Sutro sold the castle and the underlying lots to The Gray Bros. Crushed Rock Company. It was hoped that the quarry operators had at last reformed and would now join in the preservation of Telegraph Hill. At first the Gray brothers had planned to dismantle the observatory for its lumber, but seeing that the structure was well preserved they decided to convert it into living quarters for their quarry employees. Whether or not this plan ever materialized is not known.

The final chapter in the history of the observatory was written on the morning of July 25, 1903, when two neighborhood teen-agers, Walter Bush and Willie Main, discovered crackling flames at the base of the wooden tower. They also noted a number of small boys suspiciously scampering away from the scene. Rather than chase the youngsters, Willie turned in the alarm while Walter went into the building to rouse the Emile Vincent family, which occupied the second story. Seizing a pair of fire extinguishers, Walter exhausted their contents with little effect. Meanwhile Vincent, whose job as a night watchman for the Emporium department store required him to sleep in the daytime, slipped into his clothes. Mrs. Vincent took their two children, Emile and Otelio, out of the building while her husband began throwing personal belongings out the window. Only when Mrs. Vincent screamed to her husband to run for his life did he dash out of the building, running through the front entry which was by then wreathed in flames.

The time was about 1890; the German castle sat forlorn at the summit of the Hill, the public had lost interest and the cable car was stilled. To the right of the castle, at the top of Filbert Street, is the Lafayette Primary School. Below at Grant Avenue is SS. Peter and Paul's Church; next down is St. Peter's (Episcopal) Church and below that is the dome of the Russian Church. (—*Southern Pacific*)

By the time the fire department arrived, smoke and flames were billowing from the windows of the wooden structure. Considerable difficulty was encountered in pulling Engine No. 5 up Filbert Street, even with six of the largest horses in the department, but hundreds of excited boys appeared on the scene and provided eager and helpful hands to pull hoses up the Hill. In spite of the great volumes of water being poured into the building, the fire was fanned by the wind and continued to make headway until the tower at the east end of the castle fell with a loud crash, scattering embers in the dried grass and on the roofs of a dozen homes. Numerous small fires quickly blossomed but were snuffed by the alert firemen.

After an hour the last of the flames flickered out, leaving only the flimsy shell of the west end of the building. Not only was the fire costly for the Gray brothers — insurance companies refused to cover it — but it was a double loss to the Vincent family, as it destroyed a source of income as well as their personal possessions. About three months before the blaze Emile Vincent had reopened the old castle as a resort, with a bar and weekly concerts, charging a ten-cent admission fee. They had been doing a "first class business," lamented Mrs. Vincent in the wake of the fire.

The ruins were sold to a scavenger named Louis Bacigalupi, who put a force of men to work dismantling the structure. Even with a guard on duty people came in droves the next day to gather firewood. Huge loads of wood toddled off seemingly without assistance but actually supported by pairs of small legs. Timbers holding up the shell were also taken, which increased the danger of collapse. At about eleven on the morning of August 1, 1903, five men were working on the roof when the remainder of the building fell with a loud crash, but they escaped injury. The noise signaled the time for more wood gathering, and many Telegraph Hill stoves that summer and autumn were fired with the remains of Layman's Folly. A famous landmark of some twenty years was gone, and once again the summit of the Hill was empty.

Telegraph Hill was quarried for many purposes; much of the rock after only a short journey ended in the Bay to form the sea wall. Initial construction of Section 5 of the sea wall is indicated by the temporary trestle in the 1885 picture above. Just beyond the pile driver a wharf is undergoing readjustment as Front Street, the former bulkhead line, will soon be landlocked by the new sea wall. In the background, morning sunlight sparkles in the wake of the ferry steamers bound for Oakland and Alameda. (—*San Francisco Maritime Museum*)

Carrying away a few rocks at a time, these horse-drawn wagons carved out the Hill. (—*Muybridge photo, Bancroft Library*)

Early Quarries and the Sea Wall

A hundred and twenty years ago Telegraph Hill was considerably larger than it is today, and several processes account for the deterioration. In early times ships were ballasted with rock from the Hill. Later, as the city grew, peripheral streets were lowered to provide suitable grades for horse-drawn vehicles and to transform hillside lots into commercial property. But the greatest damage was done by those who quarried the rock for street paving and bulkhead work.

At the time of the Gold Rush, sailing ships bringing supplies to San Francisco often could not find return cargoes and had to sail away empty. To avoid having their ships bob over the seas like corks, captains filled their holds with rock. Telegraph Hill was conveniently located at the water's edge, and upon application of a few charges of black powder its slopes yielded enough ballast to stabilize the homeward voyage. In Liverpool, Sydney, Valparaíso and New York the rock became street pavement or fill as needed; Telegraph Hill became the most widely disseminated hill on earth.

Originally the southern flank of Telegraph Hill extended across Broadway before dipping down to the lagoon at Jackson Street near Montgomery (sometimes derisively called Montgomery Lake or Lake Como). Broadway, at first a narrow passageway cut through the Hill in the summer of 1850, was doubled in width that autumn — no easy job as some of the cuts were 25 feet deep — and then widened again in 1863-64. Today multiple-story buildings hide most of the cliffs along the southern edge of the Hill.

Elsewhere, street work was almost continuous. In November 1855 a fine level road was opened around the water side of Telegraph Hill, from Meiggs Wharf near Powell Street to Broadway. Tolls were collected at an office on Stockton Street. The crest of Stockton was also being lowered, a slow process since the work was carried on through solid rock.

The First Sea Wall

From 1863 until February 7, 1969, the San Francisco harbor was administered by the Board of State Harbor Commissioners. Many improvements were made under the direction of this board, including two separate sea walls that required thousands of tons of rock. In the summer of 1867 bids were requested for constructing three sections of the first sea wall. There would be one short section extending 650 feet along Front Street, between Union and Vallejo, while the others would be south of Pacific Avenue. Alexander H. Houston, a prominent railroad and street contractor, was awarded the contract.

For his rock, Houston arranged to quarry a part of Telegraph Hill along the west side of Battery Street near Vallejo. Planning an unusually large blast, he secured authority from the Board of Supervisors and soon had a large force of men piercing the Hill with a sixty-foot tunnel and two small lateral tunnels. Thirty-nine 25-pound kegs of black powder were strategically placed in the tunnel and the opening was closed with sand and gravel. The "Great Blow Out" was scheduled for nine in the morning on November 4, 1867.

Long before the appointed hour the hillside was covered with spectators. Actual firing was delayed for twenty minutes while the workmen warned neighbors away from the site and advised

Martin Vice, boat builder, established himself along the road around North Point. Stone (at right) was also unloaded from river scows. Below, about ten years later on July 4, 1875, with flags billowing in the breeze, the tug *Monarch* is about to be launched from the Merchants (Cousins) Dry Dock. Capt. Millen Griffith stands on the pilothouse; the *Rescue* (at left) was built for him at the same place. After the launching, good cheer was dispensed in the Dry Dock Exchange (left). (—*Top, Wells Fargo Bank; bottom, San Francisco Maritime Museum*)

the closest residents to remove personal belongings from their homes. Tension mounted as horses were drawn away and all business was generally suspended.

The blast was fired, but there was no great upheaval of the hillside. The spectators had to be content with a huge cloud of dust and the noise of stones clattering against windowpanes and wooden clapboards. Three or four houses at the top of the Hill were "pretty well peppered from attic to ground floor," but the owner, Judge John McHenry, was not concerned since his home at 212 Broadway was not endangered. Besides, he was anxious to have those lots lowered so that they could be used commercially.

Rocks were hurled from the mouth of the tunnel with great violence. One twenty-pound rock followed a course through a number of obstacles. It crashed through the window of one house, passed under the staircase and out through the opposite wall; across the alley its progress ended when the rock embedded itself in the side of another house.

Near the base of the Hill the rear of the stable belonging to Thomas De Vries and James B. Chase was demolished by a huge mass of rock, while another pile of stones, deposited on Battery Street, blocked the entrance to their stevedoring and ship-ballasting firm.

Even though the audience was disappointed by the show, the big blast was considered news by the press as far away as Napa. Mr. Houston was satisfied with the results, estimating that 6000 tons of earth and rock were brought down and three times that amount was loosened.

The Next Attack on the Hill

When these sections of the sea wall were completed no further work was done; Telegraph Hill and the "zigzag" or "sawtoothed" pattern of the water front around it remained relatively undisturbed. However, the docks and streets angling into the Bay, picturesque as they were, caused shoaling which required expensive dredging. To remedy this difficulty T. J. Arnold, engineer of the sea wall, proposed a new bulkhead line that would curve gracefully around Telegraph Hill. Adopted in 1877, the plan was implemented by building a new sea wall, section by section. The first five parts, from Powell around to Filbert, were constructed between 1878 and 1881, while the next two, from Filbert to Vallejo and down to Pacific, were built in 1884-85. The balance was completed in succeeding years, all forming the base for the Embarcadero of today.

Andrew Onderdonk, best known as one of the contractors of the Canadian Pacific Railway, took some of the early sea wall contracts. However, when he tried to quarry rock from Telegraph Hill he was hauled into court. The litigation lasted from 1880 through 1881 but delayed the blasting only temporarily.

W. D. English & Company, contractors for the fifth section (from near Filbert to Vallejo), found the proximity of Telegraph Hill an irresistible temptation. The owners of high-level lots who wished their property lowered co-operated with Mr. English, while others sold their lots to him. A petition was filed with the supervisors in May 1884 to authorize the lowering of Sansome Street, but during an investigation of the matter, after the damage had been done, a number of the property owners who had refused to sign the petition appeared to testify, while those who had favored it could not be located — which threw some doubt on the petition's validity.

However, City Hall sanctioned the quarrying and the wreckers began tearing away at the east side of the Hill, just at about the time Layman was putting the finishing touches to his cable line on the other side. With each blast the top of the Hill shrank westward, threatening the "old Rookeries," which dated back to the days of '49. A particularly heavy blast on the morning of June 1, 1884, brought down a large quantity of rock and a long series of landslides followed. Within the next year ten houses on Union, Calhoun, Alta and Green streets became uninhabitable; some slid off the cliff to become kindling wood. Tenants on those streets were harder to find because of broken windows caused by the blasting, reported Mrs. Barber, the widow of chronometer maker Joseph McGregor (she had owned the property at 215 Green since 1852).

Mrs. Bernice Houston, a widow with five children, saved her home only by moving it off the lot at 4 Calhoun, where she had lived for twenty

Presumably these men at the end of Meiggs' Wharf are resting from arduous toil. The camera has momentarily diverted their attention from the construction work on the sea wall. The year is 1880. (—San Francisco Maritime Museum)

years. Also on that street, Elizabeth Overend was driven from her home after living there over thirty years. Eliza Kelleher, dependent on rents from her two houses on Union Street, was approached by Mr. Schuyler of the contracting firm after her first house had been undermined and had gone down. He offered to buy the lot, but at a distressed sale price. Then he asked, "Is that other house out there rented?"

"No," she answered, "Why?"

"Because it would not be safe for anybody to live in it. Go up and live in it yourself, and you will get killed, and you won't have any damages."

Shortly after midnight on July 24, 1884, a fire began in a house on the bluff at Sansome and Union. Firemen encountered great difficulty in dragging hoses up the steep incline, but the blaze spread slowly, consuming only six houses in the course of an hour. Only three were occupied and the residents had time to remove their belongings. The vacant dwellings owned by the contractors were already doomed.

The cliff receded westward and became higher as it approached the crest of the Hill, one estimate being 120 feet high. Along with the tumbling houses, the flight of stairs at the foot of Union Street became a casualty. Down below, Sansome Street was cut through early in 1885, though it remained "in miserable condition, not passable" for many months.

Residents at the top of the Hill repeatedly sought legal recourse to preserve their homes, but court injunctions and petitions filed with the Board of Supervisors were to no avail. One member of the board, John T. Sullivan, a bootmaker living near the blasting, was able to hold off the grading of Green Street. Threatened with defeat at the next election by parties associated with the contractor, he told them he could "stand defeat as good as any other candidate." Sullivan was replaced by a Turkish bath operator.

Providing sea walls and low-level commercial lots were not the only needs Telegraph Hill served. The continued growth of the city created an insatiable demand for crushed rock to be used in paving, concrete manufacture and fill. In 1893 there were six major quarries and several smaller ones in San Francisco, but a dozen years later the operators numbered 14.

Not every hill makes a successful quarry; a low incidence of shale is essential. The best locations were around Twin Peaks, where the Gray brothers operated the Blue Rock Quarry ("blue rock," a form of basalt, is actually gray in color). On Telegraph Hill, at Green and Sansome streets, they employed thirty to forty men and produced 35,000 cubic yards annually in the early 1890s, the largest output in the city. That was also a "blue rock" quarry, but mixed with the rock was a lot of unstable shale which was susceptible of slippage, especially after a rain, a factor causing many problems on the Hill.

For about three-quarters of a mile the east and north faces of Telegraph Hill were marked with quarries. In addition to Gray Bros., there were the smaller operations of Wetmore Bros. and John Kelso, but those firms lived in the shadow of the former. For twenty years the Gray brothers made life miserable and sometimes hazardous for residents on the Twilight Side of Telegraph Hill.

Everyone posed for the cameraman when he recorded the spindly walkways and the Union Street steps before they, along with many of these houses, became victims of the quarrymen in 1884. (—*Bancroft Library*)

GRAY BROTHERS' QUARRY, SANSOME & GREEN STS

The rock crusher of the Gray Bros., as it appeared at the top of their billhead. (—California Historical Society)

Long after the quarrying was over, an inspection party visited the scene of a rock slide in 1924 at the corner of Sansome and Filbert streets. Houses along Alta Street peer over the precipice, while the Filbert Steps are at the right. The wires above and the tracks in Sansome Street are for the street car line.

This site has long since been occupied by a single-story building which was rented to a ship stevedoring firm and more recently to a wholesale antiques importer. (—Dept. of Public Works)

The Gray Brothers, Incredible Quarrymen

Of all the scoundrels in San Francisco who persistently flouted the law, the Gray brothers were perhaps the worst. Their aggressive tactics caused much suffering to innocent parties, and it was only after two murders that their free-wheeling operation was closed down. They were the incredible quarrymen.

Although the brothers grew up in California, both were born in Iowa, George Freeman Gray in 1858 and Harry Nathaniel Gray three years later. During the 1880s they were in the business of making artificial stone — a novel material at that time, but today it's just "cement." The Gray Bros. Artificial Stone Paving Company, incorporated July 21, 1887, built many sidewalks and curbs, and even today some of the older sidewalks in San Francisco bear the company's mark. Until 1900 the firm had branches and offices in Los Angeles, Oakland and Alameda, but the brothers' activities centered around their San Francisco quarries, particularly the one on the east side of Telegraph Hill.

January 1894 was an unusually rainy month, as the Brown family would long remember, after an early morning rockslide upset their duplex house at 312½ and 314½ Vallejo Street. By a miracle no one was injured, and neighbors extracted the family from the wreckage. The slide which so rudely awakened them had originated 150 feet away in the Gray Bros. quarry and was caused by the combination of rain-soaked ground and a heavy blast two days before. Ernst Buchel, owner of the house, won a court judgment of $3000 damages from the Grays.

The blasting continued despite the protests of neighbors, and the only concession the quarrymen made was to schedule their explosions, giving parents time to grab their children and seek refuge from the flying rocks and breaking glass. Near-by homes became more endangered with each blast and soon one kitchen floor was carried down the Hill.

Bernard Pos, a peppery little Frenchman ordinarily engaged in making shoes for the City of Paris, became concerned when his house at the southeast corner of Union and Calhoun slipped off its foundations. Hauling the Grays into court, he sought to enjoin their blasting. In the course of the trial Judge Hebbard went to Pos' house to determine for himself the effects of a sample blast. The shock was surprisingly mild, but when the judge learned that he had been tricked — the contractor had loosened the earth around the charge to lessen the shock — he remarked in his decision that the "experimental blast [was] not a fair test of ordinary operations." He also noted that the blasting was a "serious interference with the comfortable enjoyment of life and property" for Telegraph Hill residents, and so on September 11, 1895, he granted a permanent injunction against blasting.

For the moment the Gray brothers were stymied, but they were getting ready for bigger things. On August 10, 1897, they incorporated The Gray Bros. Crushed Rock Company, with a larger capitalization than the old firm. They purchased property on Corona Heights, near Twin Peaks, only to find that the rock was unsuitable for quarrying. Then, as a rescue operation, they formed the San Francisco Brick Company on May 19, 1898, to manufacture bricks from this native stone. The quality of their brick was in-

The little girl by the fence and the person on the balcony of the house will have a splendid view of the launching of the *Monarch* (page 54), soon to take place. The tug is located near the intersection of Kearny and Francisco streets. (—*San Francisco Maritime Museum*)

ferior but the lower price made it competitive, particularly on larger jobs. However, after about ten years of operations the brick works was closed due to smoke complaints.

In appearance and character George and Harry Gray were remarkably different. Unpleasant divorce proceedings had involved George in extended litigation, his ex-wife having charged him with "kidnapping" one of their two children on a Sunday afternoon visit. The matter was aggravated when her mother named George Gray as executor of her estate two years after the divorce and just five days before she died. Each event became a matter for lawyers, and commanded regular space in the press.

On the other hand, debonair Harry Gray cut a wide swath in the fancy social circles of San Francisco. His Sunday afternoons were spent dashing through Golden Gate Park. He was married to a beautiful young widow of Denver society, Mrs. Persis Wilson, in January 1898. When the elite San Francisco Club was dedicated in that same month, A. B. Spreckels of the sugar family was elected president and Harry Gray was named secretary. That summer, when the Republicans opened their campaign with a meeting at the Palace Hotel, Harry Gray and J. B. Spreckels were there along with Abe Ruef, the infamous political lawyer. Harry associated with good company, which quietly redounded to the benefit of the quarry operations.

The annihilation of Telegraph Hill was one of George Gray's publicly declared goals, and the brothers had taken a step in that direction when they bought the old castle property in January 1899. It seemed that they would be thwarted again when on August 3, 1903, the Board of Supervisors approved Ordinance No. 944, which prohibited blasting and quarrying in certain areas of San Francisco. But ignoring the new law, the Gray brothers set off blasts in their Telegraph Hill quarry on September 28 and October 8, according to local witnesses. The Grays denied that any blasting had been done and somehow were able to make amends with City Hall, and for a time afterwards they behaved quietly.

John Kelso, who operated a quarry with William Center near Lombard and Montgomery, was prying down rock for crushing. Although he was not blasting, he had violated the city ordinance and was arrested on December 28, 1903. He paid his fine of $25 but challenged the ordinance in the courts. The California Supreme Court ruled in August 1905 that the law went beyond the "legitimate exercise of the police power." Undoubtedly the Grays rejoiced at the news.

They resumed blasting at their Telegraph Hill quarry, a move which brought so many protests that Judge Seawell signed a restraining order on Monday, November 12, 1906. The Gray brothers were slow to respond, setting off two more blasts, and claimed that they had not received the order until Wednesday. However, local residents were incensed by the blasts and rushed into action, attacking the workers with a volley of stones and threatening to shoot anyone attempting to operate the quarry. Four policemen were detailed to protect the quarrymen — and to prevent further blasting.

But next spring the Gray brothers were at it again. On the morning of March 27, 1907, a particularly heavy blast on Telegraph Hill wiped out the northwest corner of Green and Calhoun, but even before the dust had settled, the rock crusher down on Sansome Street was grinding away as usual. The effects of the charge clearly demonstrated the wanton carelessness of the quarrymen. One house was hurled to the bottom of the cliff, almost sweeping a near-by 13-year-old girl to her death. The house, owned by Gray Bros., was rented to Mrs. J. F. Lawson and her sister, Mrs. Adam Weissel. Illness had caused Mrs. Weissel and her four children to move out temporarily, but Mrs. Lawson had only been away for a short time that day and returned to find her furniture, the house and the lot in a splintered mess down below. Other damage included Mrs. Ryan's house on Calhoun, which was so severely undermined that it was unsafe for occupancy, and the two-story flat of Mrs. Anna Redmond, the brick foundation of which was badly cracked.

Public attention was next focused on the Grays' operation around Diamond Heights, and Judge Frank Murasky issued a restraining order to pro-

Eadweard Muybridge (originally Edward J. Muybridge), whose 1872 photographs of a running horse, made for Leland Stanford, started him on his pioneer motion picture work, took many photographs of Telegraph Hill which recorded early quarry activity. (—Bancroft Library)

hibit the firm's blasting there. But George Gray could not change his ways: in April 1908 a large blast showered boulders on a near-by school, injuring three children, so the police moved in. Hauled into court by Assistant City Attorney Jesse H. Steinhart, Gray eluded jail only through the legal skill of his lawyer, Fisher Ames. But just as the trial ended Gray called Steinhart a "rattlesnake," at which point Ames hustled his client away.

While the two brothers were acquiring unsavory public images in the San Francisco press, Mrs. Harry Gray's activities as a socialite were another matter. Her appearance at fashionable events always merited a portrait, or at least a mention. "A merry dinner party at St. Dunstan's" (their apartment residence) and an afternoon bridge party a few days later were noted in the social pages — far removed from news of the destruction her husband's firm was causing.

In February of 1909 Judge Murasky confirmed and strengthened the court order directing Gray Bros. to cease blasting on Telegraph Hill. Jesse Steinhart thought that the legal battle was over, and so it appeared to be — until Independence Day, which in 1909 was celebrated on Monday, July 5. Using the booming Presidio cannons as a shield, the firm set off its blasts, but a shower of rocks on the roofs of houses on the Hill brought an instant reaction from irate neighbors, who descended on the Sansome Street quarry. The workers wisely dropped their tools and ran from the mob. Harry Gray later denied any knowledge of the explosions. With a look of innocence he told the aroused public, "We would never think of violating the terms of the injunction. We ordered no blasting at the quarry on the Fourth and do not believe any of our workmen set a blast off. Boys in the neighborhood may have been responsible for the explosion. It does not seem possible to us, however, that stones were hurled from the quarry to the top of the cliff, as has been described."

True, there were "boys in the neighborhood," but they were witnesses rather than participants in the blast. One 12-year-old, Henry Casanova, was almost hit by a three-pound rock. Other witnesses provided City Attorney Percy V. Long with information, and again Jesse Steinhart was assigned to the case. "This firm is absolutely unscrupulous in its dealings," Long announced. "This time, however, we believe we have sufficient proof to show they have been flagrant in their violation of the law and we will push the case." At the trial, local witnesses confirmed both preparations for the blast and the detonation itself, but again Ames managed to keep his clients out of jail.

For future blasting operations the Gray brothers' lawyers proposed another scheme. Back in September of 1905 the Grays had organized the Golden Gate Tile Company; from its plant, at the northeast corner of Bay and Powell streets, their common and ornamental brick found its way into many buildings, including the General Hospital and Lowell High School. After one legal battle the quarries were sold to the tile company, which then leased them to the Western Development Syndicate. Although the latter was organized in the interests of the Gray brothers, only the names of their attorneys appeared on the papers that were filed in Nevada on September 22, 1908. Again the brothers were back in business, as the new firm had not been named in the previous court injunction.

But the Grays were having other troubles; ever since the 1906 fire the firm had been on the verge of bankruptcy. Subcontractors were forced to take their fees in crushed rock instead of cash, and regular paydays for the workmen became only a memory.

Instead of receiving a pay envelope bulging with gold and silver coins, a Gray Bros. employee had to go through a long process full of devious delays before collecting his wages. First he went to the company office in the Wells Fargo (Express) Building, at Mission and Second streets, and presented his time slip and numbered tag to the cashier, Miss Caroline Brasch. In exchange he received a draft from the firm — actually, a promissory note — payable in sixty days. As the drafts were unacceptable to banks, the employee simply had to wait, unless he sold the draft to a collection agency at a twenty per cent discount.

After working several weeks at a Gray Bros. quarry during April of 1909, James Edward Cunningham took his time slip to Miss Brasch, but she told him to return on the next payday, May 18. When he came back for his money, he had

At the crest of the Hill above the Wetmores' quarry, the false-front building is at the corner of Montgomery and Greenwich streets (the present site of Julius' Castle). The four buildings to the right, northward along Montgomery Street, have long since vanished with the underlying ground.

Taken in the same area four months later, but looking northwest, the photograph below shows the demolition of the buildings along Montgomery Street (upper left) already begun. The handsome two-story house (at the far right) fronts on Winthrop Street. (—*Both photos, Society of California Pioneers*)

WETMORE'S QUARRY,
MONTGOMERY ST. BET. LOMBARD & GREENWICH STS. OCT. 11, 1904.

to accept a check for $15.35 and a draft for the same amount, payable in sixty days. Planning to leave the city, he instead appeared on June 30 and demanded immediate payment of the draft. After Miss Brasch refused he argued heatedly, then drew a pistol and killed her.

Cunningham ran and went into hiding. However, when another employee named Novak, who had similar paycheck difficulties, was arrested and charged with murder, Cunningham courageously stepped forward and made a full confession. While languishing in jail, he told reporters:

> I trust the crime that has put me here will wipe out the paycheck system. I did not have this in mind when I shot down the girl but I have since come to the conclusion that I probably emphasized the evils of the system in a way that will not be forgotten.

Two months later Cunningham was ruled insane and on October 11, 1909, he was committed.

This tragic episode did result in a city ordinance requiring the prompt payment of wages, but the lot of the Gray Bros. employees failed to improve. In September of 1910 some Russian workmen filed charges after they had reported to the company office eight times and still had not been paid. Arrested and hauled into court, the Grays quickly found the necessary funds to pay them. But then, only a few months later, fifty men at their brickyard sued for back wages.

The firm was in a financial quagmire. In March 1910 a local bank had seized the two rock crushers at the Telegraph Hill quarry and the equipment in the office to force settlement on a $12,000 note. Part of the Gray brothers' problem was that they were constantly in litigation — it has been said that they were involved in 52 lawsuits in five years — and therefore had no money for more mundane things like wages and bills. Their attorneys, Fisher Ames and J. E. Manning, should have been wealthy men, provided that their fees were paid.

Their long battle with City Hall and the crusading Jesse Steinhart culminated in a lengthy action which began in the fall of 1911. Steinhart was the victor when Judge Murasky issued his opinion on June 13, 1913; both the Gray brothers and their family of corporations, as well as quarry operator John Kelso, were "restrained from removing any rock, dirt or stone" from the Lombard-Montgomery streets quarry, except for loose material in a very limited area, but that without the use of explosives.

Things had gone from bad to worse. George Gray filed a petition in bankruptcy on October 30, 1914. His liabilities totaled $163,948.24, including old debts going back to 1909. Even the firm of J. B. Spreckels & Bros., whose owner was a long-time associate of Harry Gray's, held an unpaid judgment of almost $16,000. But there were other lesser claims against George Gray.

Joseph Lococo had emigrated from Sicily in 1902, taking a job with Cadillac in Detroit. Poor health and the search for a milder climate brought him to San Francisco, where he settled on Potrero Hill. In October 1914 he worked ten days for the

(—Society of California Pioneers)

The telephone pole silhouetted against the sky marks the end of Green Street as it was in 1927. Though the Grays had ceased quarrying here some years before, there were still landslides (note the fences to retard falling rocks), a situation which continues to the present time. To the right, out of the picture, are Calhoun Terraces. (—*Dept. of Public Works*)

Gray brothers, until his condition forced him to rest. Recovering slightly, he went to see George Gray about his wages, explaining that there was nothing to eat in the house and his two infants needed milk. Gray told him to return on payday.

After that, Lococo went to the company office almost every day, trying to get his wages of $17.50. The cashier would never say exactly when payday was, but Lococo found out the hard way. After illness had confined him to his bed for two days, he went to the office, where the girl smiled sweetly and said, "It was payday yesterday. You got to wait another month."

Appeals to the authorities brought sympathy but no action. Kindly neighbors kept the family alive, and their crippled landlord withheld eviction, but that was not enough. Sometime before, Lococo had bought a gun for protection and now was the time to sell it. On November 10, 1914, on his way to sell the pistol, he stopped at the quarry at 29th and Castro streets to plead his case with George Gray once more. Again Gray ignored his request, then looked back, waved his arm and told Lococo to go away. Infuriated, and thinking that Gray was about to strike him, Lococo fired two shots. Gray died on the way to the emergency hospital.

Frightened, Lococo ran off and boarded a passing streetcar. William Jurgens, a policeman who happened to be in the neighborhood in his car, learned about the shooting and chased the streetcar for eight blocks, calling for the motorman to halt. Lococo was arrested without resistance and taken to jail. Never was an unknown stranger treated so kindly; the police knew about George Gray's business ethics.

The stern-wheeler *Centennial* (155 feet long) enters the harbor with Telegraph Hill in the background. Above the bow is Union Street; the large building to the lower left is the sugar factory. Filbert Street is in the middle of the photo while Greenwich Street, crowned by the castle, is over the paddle wheel. The time is about 1890. (—*San Francisco Maritime Museum*)

As soon as the story appeared in the headlines, all kinds of people were moved to help. Food and money were showered on the destitute family, and one person offered to pay the $5 monthly rent indefinitely. A cash collection was even sent from the mountain town of Truckee. The International Workers' Defense League scheduled a dance at Dreamland Rink to raise funds for legal expenses. Lococo was tried on April 6, 1915, and acquitted, a verdict that brought cheers from the spectators. Then he was taken home in an automobile, a new experience for him.

The late George Gray continued to be in the news, as all kinds of claims were filed against his estate. It was alleged that he had had hidden assets of $1,000,000 in spite of the bankruptcy. There was also talk of a mysterious tin box; finally found, it was brought into probate court to be opened in the presence of the attorneys, both equally anxious and tense. The box contained practically nothing of value.

Just before the Christmas of 1915 Harry Gray also went into bankruptcy. His indebtedness was larger — $185,627 — but many of his creditors were the same ones that his brother had failed to satisfy. From then on Harry received less notoriety. In 1925 he was arrested when a charge was set off without a license in his Diamond Heights quarry; accordingly he was fined fifty dollars. But Harry lived a full life and survived his wife, who died suddenly in 1937.

The blasting and quarrying of Telegraph Hill had finally ended by 1914, after two deaths, bankruptcy and mounting public pressure. But the work of the incredible quarrymen will not be forgotten since unexpected reminders — roaring landslides, usually prompted by a spell of rain — continue to this day.

In 1927, instead of the castle with houses below it, there was only a flagpole rising above the trees and the scars of abandoned quarries. In more recent times the two piers, Nos. 27 and 29, have been combined to accommodate the ships of the Pacific Far East Line. (—Dept. of Public Works)

The Wetmore Brothers Quarry

Charles Abbott Wetmore and George Peabody Wetmore were born of a New England background, in 1867 and 1870 respectively. When their large family moved to California, some of the brothers went into the fruit-and-produce commission business under the family name in San Francisco, while a distant cousin was the pioneer California viticulturalist who founded the Cresta Blanca winery. Livermore

George Wetmore left his draftsman's table on January 25, 1895, to join Sidney B. Cushing and others in forming the Cushing-Wetmore Company, manufacturing crushed rock and cement. Cushing was also president of the Mill Valley and Mt. Tamalpais Scenic Railway and had had previous experience in the rock crushing business. Horace B. Sperry, of the flour milling family and also one of the incorporators, owned the fifty-vara lot on the south side of Lombard that would provide rock for the 180-ton crusher.

The business was a success because, if all the allegations are true, the Gray brothers were so concerned with the competition that they took steps to restrain the Cushing-Wetmore operations. Access to the latter's plant was by way of Lombard Street; so when the Grays, who had been acquiring the adjoining property, dumped a load of rock on Lombard on May 3, 1899, the rival company considered it an unkind act. Two days later the Gray brothers set off a large blast which threw down 5000 tons of rock on Lombard, bringing the Cushing-Wetmore business to a halt. More intolerable acts followed until finally Cushing-Wetmore sued for damages and in March 1900 was awarded $5000. Though the Grays appealed the decision, the case progressed slowly.

Around 1902, when Cushing stepped out of the picture, Charles A. Wetmore came in as superintendent and the firm was then known as the Wetmore Brothers Quarry. Back of the Vulcan Iron Works, at Francisco and Kearny streets, the Wetmores also operated the Vulcan Quarry, using carts to haul this rock to their crusher on Lombard Street. In May 1907 the Globe Grain & Milling Company obtained a permit to lower the level of its block to the "official level" of the adjoining streets and employed the Wetmores to do the job.

It was not until October 1907 that the Supreme Court rendered its opinion in the damages suit, reversing the lower court and wiping out the $5000 award. But by that time the whole issue was academic, as Sperry had sold his Lombard Street lot to the Gray brothers that year, and two years earlier the Wetmores had sold two other lots to the city. The Wetmore brothers then moved their operations to McNear's Point, near San Rafael. In September 1913 George Wetmore was driving back from San Rafael when he went off the road in the dark and was killed.

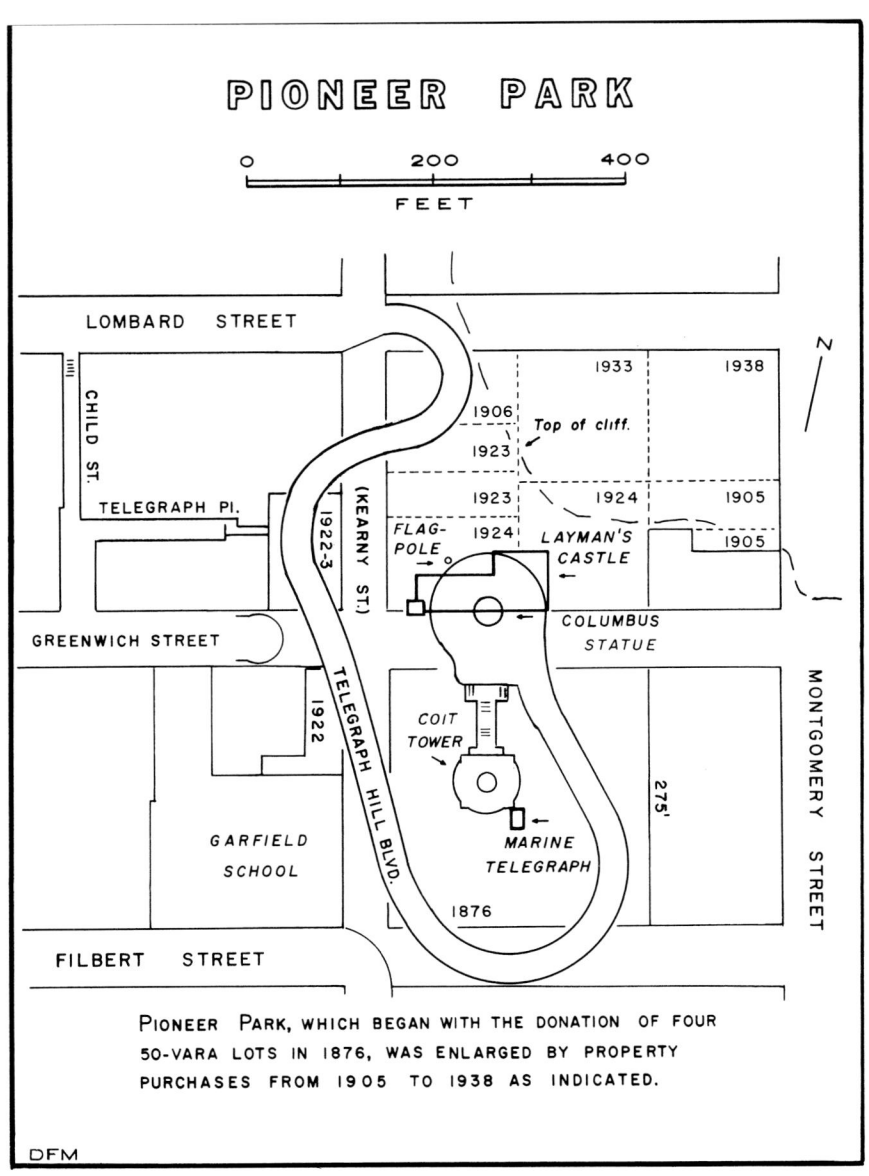

PIONEER PARK, WHICH BEGAN WITH THE DONATION OF FOUR 50-VARA LOTS IN 1876, WAS ENLARGED BY PROPERTY PURCHASES FROM 1905 TO 1938 AS INDICATED.

After Pioneer Park (below) was donated to the city, a retaining wall was built as part of a soon-forgotten plan of development. The camera faced south; Montgomery Street is at the far left. (—*California Historical Society*)

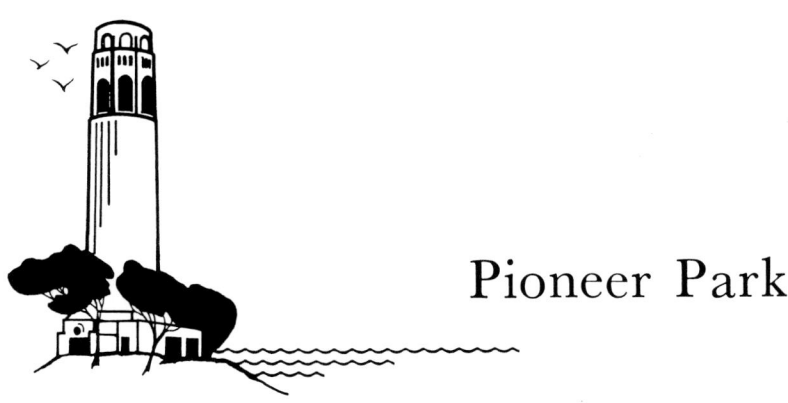

Pioneer Park

After the great storm of 1870 destroyed the old signal station, the four 50-vara lots at the top of Telegraph Hill remained vacant. Concerned that someone might use the land for personal gain, a group of 22 businessmen purchased the site in February of 1876 for $12,000, intending to preserve it as a park. Their spokesman, mining stockbroker J. M. McDonald, donated the land to the city through the Board of Supervisors the following May; the only condition was that the lots be maintained forever as a public place, under the name Pioneer Park.

The supervisors directed the street superintendent to prepare plans for improvements. In the next year $4354 was expended on a retaining wall around the top of the Hill; smaller amounts were appropriated in the following two years, for other parks, particularly Golden Gate Park, corralled all available funds. It was thought that the construction of the German castle and the cable car line in 1884 would spur improvements for Pioneer Park, but official interest continued to wane.

In the 1890s people began to realize that Pioneer Park and the whole of Telegraph Hill were endangered by the quarrymen, who continued to blast and gouge away the hillside. The Gray brothers favored leveling the Hill completely so that the land could be developed commercially, after they had harvested the rock. Opposed to this notion were the Hill residents themselves and the California Club, an early environmental group composed of ladies involved in civic and charitable causes. The North Beach merchants were divided on the issue: while sympathizing with their neighbors, they also wanted easier access to the northern water front.

The California Club became interested in the matter just after the Christmas of 1899, when an investigating committee of 15 members prowled around Telegraph Hill and found the quarrying so far advanced that immediate action was necessary. The North Beach Improvement Club joined the California Club in its effort to "do something," and at a mass meeting in Washington Square Hall the ladies secured support for their resolution protesting the destruction of Telegraph Hill. In response to the pressure from this group and others, the Board of Supervisors ordered City Engineer C. Ewald Grunsky to prepare a study of the Hill's future.

The first of Grunsky's two reports appeared on May 20, 1901. He deplored the conditions caused by the quarry operators, who had ruthlessly ignored the official street grades. It would be unwise to remove the Hill, he felt, since it acted as a windbreak, protecting shipping along the water front from Lombard to Market Street "to no inconsiderable extent." However, in answer to the North Central Improvement Association's request for direct access to the North Beach, Grunsky suggested a tunnel under Telegraph Hill along the course of Montgomery Street. It would be 30 feet wide and 2415 feet long, plus approaches of 260 feet, beginning between Jackson and Pacific and terminating north of Greenwich. The cost was to be $360,000, but the tunnel would alleviate congestion along East Street (the Embarcadero) for traffic moving to the north side of the city. A possible alternative was the

Telegraph Hill Boulevard in the early 1920s. The apartment house on Greenwich Street and the Garfield School still stand, but in five decades there have been many changes: the road is now paved, another floor has been added to the apartment and trees and shrubs almost block the view. (—*Gabriel Moulin Studios*)

lowering of Sansome so that it would pass under Broadway.

In his second report, issued on March 29, 1902, Grunsky listed 14 combinations of improvements for Telegraph Hill. He suggested a shorter tunnel than the one mentioned in his first report, 950 feet long and terminating at Vallejo. Or a new street could be laid along the east face of the Hill. Another proposal was the enlargement of Pioneer Park, with a winding road graded to the summit.

While Grunsky fiddled with his various proposals, the Merchants' Association of San Francisco, which supported the work of the California Club, undertook its own study through a small committee. The group included Robert H. Fletcher, curator of the Mark Hopkins Institute of Art, as chairman; John McLaren, superintendent of public parks; Bruce Porter, a San Francisco artist; and Gelett Burgess, originator of the small, whimsical magazine *Lark,* best remembered for its classic verse, "Purple Cow."

The committee's report, which came out on April 3, 1902, echoed prophecies of the Hill's destruction and then pointed to the San Francisco residents' general lack of appreciation for their hills. The committee cited James Bryce, who had compared San Francisco to Mediterranean cities, their hills crowned with an acropolis or with feudal castles. But, the report went on, "the stranger does not find our hills Acropolis crowned, on the contrary he finds one of the most prominent, one of the most artistic and one of the most intimately connected with the early history of the place, Telegraph Hill, situated on the very front of the city's fair face, scarred, gashed, dismantled and forlorn." In conclusion they recommended more land for the park, the planting of trees, and a winding road from Greenwich to the summit.

Interest in the preservation of Telegraph Hill was gaining. The *North End Review,* a neighborhood weekly, issued a progress edition in May 1902 which focused on the district's future. Three months later the California Outdoor Art League was incorporated by prominent San Francisco women dedicated among other things to preserving the Hill.

City Engineer Grunsky's several proposals were finally narrowed down to one, the purchase of land for the park, and one of the propositions submitted to the voters on September 29, 1903, was a bond issue of $597,000 for this purpose. Despite the campaigning of the North End Protective League and others, the bond issue was narrowly defeated — ironically because of a technical change in the city charter on voting matters.

In the fall of 1905 the Burnham Plan provided new support for the beautification of Telegraph Hill. Daniel H. Burnham, the highly regarded Chicago architect, said that the Hill "has the great advantage of overlooking the docks and shipping. Advantage has been taken of this feature in many cities of the Old World, notably Genoa and Budapest." His plan contemplated enlarging Pioneer Park and dividing it into two terraces, with a drive around the Hill at the lower level. Two approaches to the terraces would sweep around the slope in long curves, while the summit was to be topped with a "monument symbolical of some phases of the city's life." Winding paths and small terraces were proposed for the eastern face of the Hill.

After the 1906 fire the Burnham Plan was set aside in the city's haste to rebuild, but the Outdoor Art League continued its efforts. Mrs. Lovell White, president of the league, officiated at the flag raising in Pioneer Park on July 4, 1907, during which Mrs. Alexander D. Sharon compared 1776 with the battle to save the Hill.

It was an afternoon about 1920 when this pastoral scene was recorded. The carpenter Gothic houses are on Montgomery between Alta and Union streets. In the background are the Ferry Building and the Southern Pacific General Offices. (*—Bancroft Library*)

On May 6, 1908, when the Great White Fleet returned to San Francisco from its trip around the world, thousands lined the city's northern hills to greet the U. S. warships. A huge sign had been put up on Telegraph Hill for the occasion; though it contained only seven letters, W-E-L-C-O-M-E, it was rated the largest sign in the world, as each letter was fifty feet high. The materials included 20,000 electric lights (the sign was visible for thirty miles), 18,000 feet of wire for bracing and 48,000 board feet of lumber, which in later years ended up as houses on the Hill, particularly The Compound owned by Harry Lafler.

A second attempt to win voter approval of a $250,000 bond issue to purchase land for Pioneer Park was defeated on June 22, 1909. But it was

Though it was sunny, the winter chill made overcoats necessary in this picture, just before Christmas in 1923. To the left of the touring car are the poles of the short-lived radio station, KFDB. (—*Dept. of Public Works*)

not alone, for all but one of the other propositions went down as well.

Much credit for the ultimate preservation of Telegraph Hill rightfully belongs to the Outdoor Art League, which continued to arouse public interest. When the league celebrated the Independence Day of 1909 in Pioneer Park, the speaker was Father Terence Caraher, the crusading priest of St. Francis Church. A new flagpole, installed that year for the Portolá Times celebration, was used in the July 4th ceremony. The pole had originally been 106 feet tall, put up at California and Market streets by Frederick W. Van Sicklin, a commission merchant, when the California troops left for the Philippines during the war with Spain. Van Sicklin's office was swept away in the 1906 fire but the pole was undamaged, except for a hole 12 feet above the ground. Shortened to 86 feet, the flagpole stood like a sentinel on the Hill for many years.

A committee of the Outdoor Art League, headed by Mrs. George T. Marsh, brought bushels of yellow poppy seeds to the Hill in March of 1912. Hundreds of people of all ages scratched at the earth with rakes and trowels, and in one day most of the land was seeded. Superintendent of Parks John McLaren praised the work and declared that Telegraph Hill could be made beautiful despite the depredations of the quarrymen. One of his ideas was a series of man-made waterfalls to cover the barren cliffs on the east side.

A few months later Richard de Fontana, the Greek consul general, proposed that a replica of the Parthenon be built on the Hill to complement the forthcoming Panama-Pacific International Exposition. While approval was sought from the king of Greece, the necessary $350,000 could be solicited from the 400,000 Greeks living in the United States. But the idea aroused little enthusiasm and nothing came of it.

The quarrymen's activities had diminished by this time and the preservation of the Hill was no longer in doubt. Still, there were many improvements needed for Pioneer Park, and from 1914 to 1916 the North Beach Promotion Association took up the cause.

In 1917 engineers began planning the proposed road to the summit, following the serpentine pattern that was finally adopted. Perhaps to publicize the project, the first automobile was driven to the top of the Hill on March 10 of that year. According to one report, the assault of "the powerful car," a Jeffrey Six, was "both dangerous and thrilling." The cable line's approach from Greenwich

A Saturday afternoon early in October 1971 found these cars standing still on Telegraph Hill Boulevard, not far from the apartment house pictured on page 70, patiently waiting to go to the summit.

Street, long obliterated by the elements, was the chosen route and as the steepest part was covered with grass, the car spun its wheels until chains were installed. Then, after a great mass of rusty barbed wire was pulled aside, the auto shot up to the summit.

Superintendent John McLaren announced plans for the road in January 1921 and condemnation suits were filed in November of the following year. Since some picturesque artists' shacks would have to be torn down, there was an outcry at this "rude interruption to the traditions that have grown up on Telegraph Hill." But the job went ahead and the road was graded in 1923, to be paved later. McLaren's plans had included not only a road, but an esplanade, terraces, and a concrete balustrade, designed by architect G. Albert Lansburgh, to surround the automobile parking area. In June 1925 the construction contract for the balustrade was awarded to Paul E. Denivelle at a bid of $14,450.

When Sunday drivers arrived at the top of the Hill later that year, they found the view from their cars obstructed. The balustrade, nearly four feet high, was bad enough, but the "unlovely funeral urns" added another three feet. Although there were grumblings, nothing was done until January 1931, when the Park Commission was planning an extension of the balustrade down the road. Then the commissioners found themselves dodging a barrage of critical editorials in the *Chronicle* and sharp comments from local civic clubs, who not only wanted the balustrade removed but also sought implementation of John McLaren's plan for a waterfall — this time with night lighting. The commission declined to build a waterfall, but it decided not to extend the balustrade and ultimately removed the existing vases and railing around the parking area.

The ornamentation of Telegraph Hill was the goal of many groups during the 1920s. In October 1925 some people wanted to restore the Column of Progress from the 1915 Exposition for a "monumental treatment of Telegraph Hill," but the idea did not find support. In May 1929 the North Beach Merchants' Association announced a contest to select a design for a treatment of the Hill's summit; hopefully the $1000 in prizes would be donated by generous contributors, but there was little interest in the plan.

Then, later that year Lewis F. Byington, a prominent attorney, was appointed by the Native Sons of the Golden West to head a committee that would plan a statue "of more monumental proportions than the Statue of Liberty." The base of the monument would include a museum of historic artifacts, and Telegraph Hill was chosen as the site. Pioneer families were expected to supply the necessary funds and in that way "perpetuate the names and deeds of their illustrious forebears." But the cost of vanity seemed too high, particularly after the 1929 market crash. Still, this proposal for Pioneer Park stayed alive for some time, until it was eclipsed by another. Unlike earlier plans, this new one was from the beginning backed by enough money to become a reality.

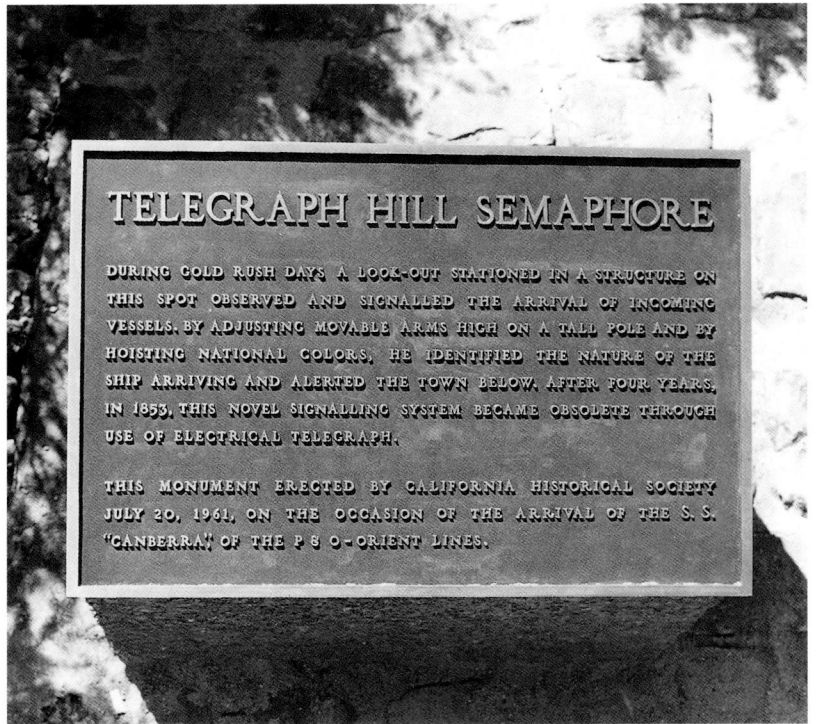

Coit Tower and Telegraph Hill Boulevard from the northeast. In the foreground next to the quarry site is the Paul Smith House, and in the background are Columbus Avenue and Washington Square. (—*Gabriel Moulin Studios*)

When the S. S. *Canberra* arrived in San Francisco, the event was celebrated by appropriate ceremonies on Telegraph Hill (page 33). The monument, placed near the edge of the circle pictured above, is no longer there, having been the victim of nefarious hands. (—*San Francisco Examiner*)

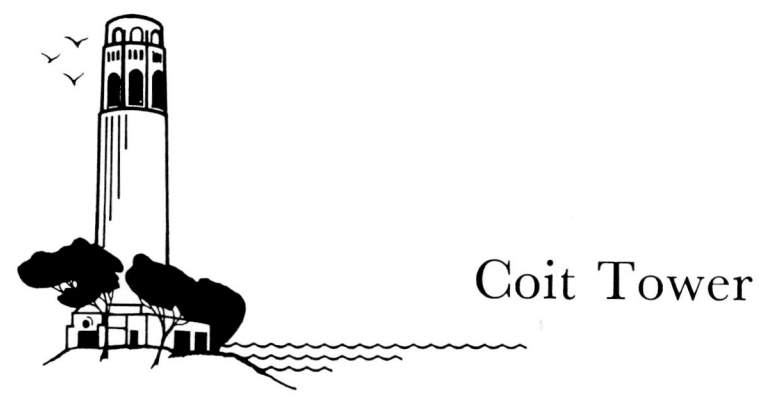

Coit Tower

When a little old lady died on July 22, 1929, in the Dante Sanatorium on Russian Hill, a chain of events was set off that would revise the profile of Telegraph Hill.

Lillie Hitchcock Coit was one of the many characters out of San Francisco's golden past. Independent by nature, she was a controversial person. Born in 1842 at West Point, where her father, Charles M. Hitchcock, was a physician, Lillie came with her family to California while she was still a child. In San Francisco the dashing firemen and their gleaming engines delighted her but it was Knickerbocker Engine Company No. 5 that especially caught the girl's fancy. Whenever that volunteer group went to a fire, Lillie slipped out to cheer the brave men on; eventually they made her an honorary member of that company and she always displayed her badge proudly. Her marriage to Benjamin Howard Coit, a handsome Arizona mining man and later a caller on the San Francisco Stock Board, was a social highlight of 1869, but the couple was soon separated and Lillie never remarried. Instead, she found diversion in playing poker and smoking cigarettes, and much of her life after 1903 was spent in Paris. Soon after her return to San Francisco in 1924 Lillie suffered a crippling stroke that made her an invalid for the last four years.

Lillie Coit's will indicated that she thought well of many people. To each surviving member of the Knickerbocker Engine Company she left $5000, while about two dozen other individuals were remembered with smaller amounts. Relatives in Texas received a cash bequest and her property in that state. One provision directed her executors "to engage the services of a competent sculptor (preferably Mr. Haig Patigian, if possible) to create . . . an artistic monument . . . to the memory of the original Volunteer Fire Department," and $50,000 was left for this purpose. The residue of the estate was divided evenly among the University of California, the University of Maryland (in both cases honoring the Hitchcock family), and the City and County of San Francisco "with the request that the Supervisors thereof shall expend the same in an appropriate manner for the purpose of adding to the beauty of said city which I have always loved."

An advisory committee was formed in April 1931 to handle the two bequests to the city. It immediately commissioned Patigian to create the statue of the firemen, and after approving Patigian's model that fall, the committee agreed to place the finished work on Telegraph Hill. However, the statue eventually ended up in Washington Square.

That Mrs. Coit failed to specify a use for the larger bequest to the city was not an oversight on her part. Shortly before completing her will in October 1924, she had contemplated leaving the money for an observatory on Telegraph Hill. To refresh her memory of the Hill she asked Lucius E. Greene, a trust officer of the Wells Fargo Bank, to accompany her in a taxi to the summit. There, Greene recalled, she "spent some time . . . talking animatedly about the idea she had in mind." But realizing that the attitude of city officials might be uncertain after her death, and that the residue of her estate might not be sufficient, she abandoned definite plans for an observatory.

It was on this site that Coit Tower was erected in 1933. In the background are the Matson and Pacific Gas and Electric buildings (left) and the Fairmont Hotel (right). (—*Gabriel Moulin Studios*)

The city received $118,731 from Lillie Coit's estate, and the Park Commission proposed that the money be used to build a tower on Telegraph Hill. Accordingly, in September of 1931 the commission appointed the architectural firm of Arthur Brown, Jr., to prepare plans for such a tower, following preliminary sketches previously submitted. Brown was best known for classical buildings such as the Opera House.

At that time Supervisor James B. McSheehy, who was a member of the advisory committee, introduced an ordinance to rezone part of Telegraph Hill "so that the skyscrapers of the future would not interfere with the view or detract from the beauty of Coit Memorial." The matter came before the Board of Supervisors on June 20, 1932. By then the tower had become a highly controversial subject; many artists had ridiculed the general design, and Lewis F. Byington was insisting on a structure at least 250 feet tall. But at this meeting the artists, led by Albert W. Barrows, joined with Byington to attack Herbert Fleishhacker, president of the Park Commission and chief proponent of the tower. After several hours of debate, all but one of the supervisors voted for the rezoning. Allegedly it was Fleishhacker's strong position in the city that caused three supervisors to switch their votes, and the lone dissenter, William P. Stanton, later remarked,

"Mr. Fleishhacker ought to come up here often. He can put a lot of things over because they all tumble to him."

The newly created Art Commission had been empowered to review the design of public buildings and so appointed a small committee, consisting of sculptor Edgar Walter and architects John Blakewell, Jr., and George W. Kelham, to examine the tower plans. The committee suggested several modifications, which were incorporated in the design, and then the Art Commission met to consider the revised plans on August 18, 1932. The commission voted seven to four to accept the altered design, despite a petition of 464 names protesting the tower and the comment of one minority member, author Gertrude Atherton, who felt that "it looked like the remnants of an old ruin." Among other changes, the height of the tower had been increased, which pushed the construction cost up by $27,000 to $104,307. With architectural fees and landscaping, the final bill would be $124,605 — more than the Coit estate had provided, but the city made up the difference.

Much thought had gone into the design of the Coit Memorial, and various forms were considered: a low mass, a large statue or a single column. Since the Hill is asymmetrical, with its long axis running north and south, a monument pleasing to the eye from one direction might look

Slowly the tower rose to its full height of 180 feet. (—San Francisco Examiner)

clumsy from another. Therefore, only a polygonal form approaching the round would present the same profile in every direction. Prevailing public opinion called for the monument to be utilitarian, and so in keeping with Telegraph Hill's history the structure should be an observation tower.

Henry T. Howard, an architect with the firm of Arthur Brown, Jr., had more to do with the design than anyone else, except possibly Brown himself. Howard explained his thinking in 1933 when he wrote:

> The silhouette was studied most carefully. Account was taken of the foreshortening from points below, particularly as one approached up the hill, as well as of the elevational effect which would be obtained from a distance. A massive base was provided to raise the shaft above the trees and to carry the eye upward.

The tower would rise 180 feet above the base and have an observation deck 32 feet below the top. Rather than being a single shell, the structure would be three cylinders, one inside the other. The outside wall, decorated with 24 vertical flutings in the manner of a column, was to be approximately eight inches thick in the concave part of the flutes. Between the first and second walls a stairway would wind its way to the top, while the innermost cylinder would house an elevator. So that the tower might appear vertical to the human eye, the outer wall would taper inward slightly until the diameter at the top was 18 inches smaller than that at the base.

Young and Horstmeyer, contractors with many years' experience in San Francisco, were the successful bidders and construction began early in 1933, during the cold and windy part of the year. The excavation work and the ground floor were completed in two months, and the tower itself was expected to be finished within the next four months. Every other day cement was poured around the steel reinforcing rods between the plywood forms, and the tower rose another four feet. The eight-foot forms were staggered to prevent the formation of horizontal rings marking the end of each pouring. As soon as the concrete had set, the forms were removed and a plasterer applied the "dash finish." The plywood molds were used again and again, but each time they were trimmed slightly with a band saw to create the tapering effect.

The huge scaffolding that was built around the rising tower formed its own impressive silhouette as it crisscrossed the white concrete. A tremendous amount of lumber, 350,000 board feet, went into this structure, and the contractors had a lucky break when wholesale lumber prices went up during 1933, so the used wood could be sold to another builder for more than its original cost.

By early August the scaffolding was dismantled and the job neared completion. On the windy afternoon of Sunday, October 8, 1933, the Lillie Hitchcock Coit Tower was dedicated. The program included speeches by Mayor Angelo J. Rossi and Supervisor McSheehy, but most of the 17 events were musical solos, and the Municipal Band, with a touch of narcissism, concluded the festivities with "I Love You California."

The Coit Tower Murals

Artists had a particularly difficult time during the depression of the 1930s. The federal government had found employment for about sixty San Francisco artists on public projects sponsored by the Civil Works Administration, but when that agency was scheduled to terminate on February 15, 1934, the artists could again look forward to hard times. Hopefully another program would follow, but that of course depended on Washington.

While everyone waited for the official word, the San Francisco Art Commission appointed a small committee to approve art projects suggested for federal funding. Dr. Walter Heil, the eminent director of the Legion of Honor Museum and later of the de Young Museum, would head the committee, which included sculptor Edgar Walter and Charles Stafford Duncan, an accomplished artist as well as an advertising art director.

Just before the Christmas of 1933 Duncan told the Art Commission that one of the new projects, if Washington approved another agency to fund it, would be decorations for the interior of the brand-new Coit Tower. While the idea was still very tentative, a sampling of the San Francisco art community was invited to the de Young Museum and the proposal was explained. When it was announced that to be truly representative the project would include both established artists and younger but talented painters, some of the

The view looking north to Alcatraz and Angel islands in 1927 included the balustrade and "funeral urns." Continued public protests brought about removal of these obstructions. (—*Dept. of Public Works*)

Dedication of the Columbus statue in 1957 was a formal occasion in which the naval forces of several nations took part. (—*Special Collections, San Francisco Public Library*)

Behind these windows on the south side of Coit Tower are some of the murals.

An elevator ride and a few stairs bring visitors to the viewing platform.

senior artists had reservations, but Bernard Zakheim finally persuaded them to participate. Ralph Stackpole, however, was one of the accomplished artists who supported the idea from the beginning.

The whole plan hung in limbo while the federal government made up its mind, and the artists grew frustrated as the C.W.A. deadline approached. Finally, at the home of Maynard Dixon they held a strategy meeting and passed the hat to collect sixty cents for a night telegram to Edward Bruce, an artist-banker friend of Stackpole's who had influence in Washington. A few days later came the happy reply that the Coit Tower murals were approved as the first proposal under the new Public Works of Art Project.

During January of 1934 there was a flurry of activity in the workrooms of the de Young Museum as the artists sketched their ideas about contemporary life in California, including business, agriculture and recreation. Although the senior members of the group would be allotted the largest spaces, all received the monthly salary of $94.

The Coit Tower murals sparked the renaissance of fresco painting in the United States. Many of the artists, such as Mallette Dean and Gordon Langdon, had studied under Ray Boynton at the California School of Fine Arts or at the University of California, while others had worked with Diego Rivera in Mexico. Of the thirty murals, only four are oil, one is egg tempera and the remainder are frescoes.

In the fresco technique, paint is applied to wet plaster; the lime provides the binding agent and the pigment becomes incorporated with the plaster as it dries. The artist works from a sketch, prepared on tracing paper in the studio, which he transfers to the wet plaster. With close moisture-content tolerances, only enough plaster is put up for a single day's painting. As the nature of the medium dictates irregular hours, night work was not unusual at Coit Tower, and sometimes work went on until dawn. Two skilled plasterers were assigned to the job under the direction of Mathew Barnes, a plasterer by trade and "a beautiful artist."

In spite of varying backgrounds, political views and expertise, the artists, helpers and plasterers managed to create a co-ordinated series of murals. Dr. Heil was in charge, but once he had approved the sketches he left the artists pretty much to themselves. One of the trustees occasionally showed up to make sure that everyone was working rather than enjoying a prolonged drunk; his characteristic pose — thumbs stuck in the top of his vest — has been immortalized in one mural. However, throughout the project the experienced artists served as assistant directors, quietly advising the younger men; Victor Arnautoff is particularly remembered for his help.

Except for Ralph Stackpole, Otis Oldfield and Mallette Dean, most of the artists lived off Telegraph Hill. Still, they were all sociable and had fun both on and off the job. After hours there were parties and exhibit previews, and at work the artists enjoyed including the faces of friends in the murals. Maxine Albro portrayed Stackpole as a perspiring farm laborer, while in Zakheim's

Many artists helped with the larger murals. Here one young painter is working on part of the Victor Arnautoff mural, *City Life*, which measures 10 x 36 feet. (*—National Archives*)

On another part of Arnautoff's mural, below, the street signs read "Montgomery" and "Washington." In the corner at the left is *News Gathering* by Suzanne Scheuer.

In the lobby of the elevator are two oil paintings entitled *Bay Area Hills* by Rinaldo Cuneo, a long-time resident of Telegraph Hill. (—*National Archives*)

Below, Coit Tower is framed by the rigging of the *Balclutha,* a sailing ship museum near Fisherman's Wharf. (—*Southern Pacific*)

library scene he reads a newspaper. Zakheim's work also depicts Colonel William J. Brady (then the tower caretaker) and Lucien Labaudt. Labaudt had chosen the stairway for his Powell Street epic — partly to get away from the crowded working conditions — but once he was there he thought of many people he admired, so Charles Stafford Duncan, Dr. Heil, Edgar Walter and even Mrs. Roosevelt will be found in his mural.

Where the political views of certain artists had entered their work, there was so much criticism that the Art Commission postponed the unveiling in 1934 from May 1 to October 12. During the interim the more sensitive aspects of some murals were revised at the commission's direction. Still, a few remaining items — such as the tome of Karl Marx's in the library scene — upset some individuals long after the unveiling. After the water-front strike of 1934, followed by a general strike in San Francisco, no objective appraisal of paintings with political overtones was possible. As late as August 1941 a formal complaint was filed about the subject matter in certain murals.

Some of the murals were damaged by water, despite repeated efforts to halt the leaks in the roof. Even more damaging have been the tourists who scratched their initials in the frescoes. In March 1960 Mrs. Dorothy Cravath undertook to restore the murals with acrylic paints; whenever possible she arranged for the original artist to do the work, but most of it she had to do herself. After she had worked several days a week for two years, there was a long hiatus but the restoration was finally completed in 1968.

At present the murals are not accessible to the public. Perhaps when adequate protective arrangements can be devised the rooms will be open again, but with large murals — some are forty feet long — displayed in small rooms, the solution to the problem is difficult. Still, thousands of tourists annually (160,000 in 1971) pay a quarter each to take the sixty-second elevator ride to the main landing then walk up 37 steps to the observation deck for a spectacular view of the San Francisco Bay.

Many proposals have been made for decorating the Coit Tower's exterior. At times a forty-foot gas flare has been suggested for the top, and in 1954 the United Crusade campaign varied the night lighting with colored floodlights. For the Christmas of 1971 the crew of the U.S.S. *Coral Sea* and others provided colored lights for the tower and, at the very top, a simulated Christmas tree.

Christopher Columbus

When a change in plans sent Haig Patigian's statue of the volunteer firemen to Washington Square, the thirty-foot circle in the parking lot on Telegraph Hill was vacant, except for flowers. Then in October 1956 Pierluigi Alvera, the Italian consul general in San Francisco, suggested that a statue of Christopher Columbus might be placed there. Contributions financed the commission of Italian sculptor Vittorio de Colbertaldo to create a standing figure of the Genoese navigator. Complications arose when Ugo Graziotti, a local sculptor and a leading proponent of the idea for the monument, presented his own model of a free-form statue interpreting the spirit of Columbus. However, in spite of the controversy, the de Colbertaldo figure was accepted, and in due course the 12-foot bronze statue left Italy for San Francisco. It arrived in time to be set in the circle for the dedication, which appropriately enough was held on October 12, 1957.

COIT TOWER ARTISTS

Elevator Lobby:
  Rinaldo Cuneo
  Otis Oldfield
  Jose Moya del Pino

First Floor:
  Maxine Albro
  Victor Arnautoff
  Ray Bertrand
  Ray Boynton
  H. Mallette Dean
  George Harris

  William Hesthal
  John L. Howard
  Gordon Langdon
  Suzanne Scheuer
  Ralph Stackpole
  Frede Vidar
  Clifford Wight
  Bernard B. Zakheim

Stairway:
  Lucien Labaudt

Second Floor:
  Jane Berlandina
  Ralph Chesse
  Ben F. Cunningham
  Parker Hall
  Edith Anne Hamlin
  Edward T. Terada

Outside:
  Robert B. Howard

A Scene from the 20th Century-Fox Production
"HOUSE ON TELEGRAPH HILL"

In September 1950, Twentieth Century-Fox was on location filming *The House on Telegraph Hill*. Considerable stage scenery was necessary; here Montgomery Street near Julius' Castle has been embellished to take on the appearance of part of a formal garden. (—*Twentieth Century-Fox Film Corp.*)

One morning in April 1971 Telegraph Hill people walking to work were surprised to see the handsome gate at right, which suddenly appeared across Union Street by the Ice House. Inquiry revealed that it was built for a scene in *The Organization*, starring Sidney Poitier. At the same time *Dirty Harry*, with Clint Eastwood, was being filmed on the other side of the Hill.

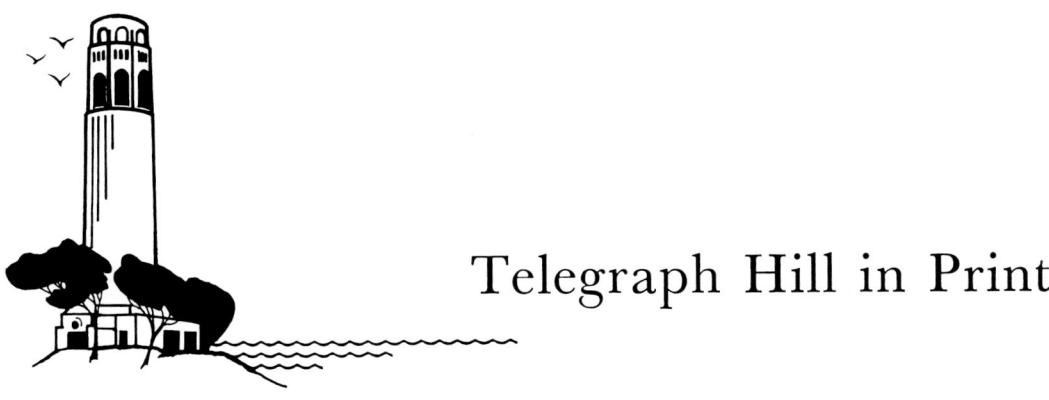

Telegraph Hill in Print

"Of all the noted hills in the United States, probably the most famous next to Bunker Hill is Telegraph Hill in San Francisco. . . . Telegraph Hill has always held an air of mysterious fascination about it." So wrote Leon J. Pinkson in the Sunday Automobile Section of the *San Francisco Chronicle* for May 23, 1920.

And it is true. The little streets — there are almost forty short streets on the Hill — the isolation of times past, the tales of local characters and the Bohemian life all combine to create an aura of mysterious enchantment.

Most books on San Francisco accord Telegraph Hill only a nod or two, while a few will devote a chapter to the Hill. Of the dozen or so books for which Telegraph Hill is the setting, the most delightful is Margaret Parton's *Laughter on the Hill* (1945). The Hill also sets the scene for novels, some with historical content, and children's stories. But Telegraph Hill is most often represented in artists' sketches of the city and in photographic works. Travel folders, posters and even shopping bags depict scenes identified with the Hill. One collector has gathered fifty post cards dealing with Telegraph Hill, including a dozen varied portraits of Coit Tower.

On the local scene, neighborhood newspapers have always contributed to the Hill's community spirit. Beginning in 1898, the *North End Review* blossomed for a few years with L. Achille Rea, a Stockton Street paint dealer, as its publisher. In the late 1920s and early '30s Mike Parsons' *North Beach Record* appeared sporadically. North Beach is considered almost a separate city, and from 1940 to 1969 the *Little City News* was published weekly by Armond De Martini and Mario Cugia. Of course, Italian-language newspapers have abounded and one, *L'Eco d'Italia,* is still issued every Thursday.

But the most unusual newspaper appeared unsolicited on doorsteps along Montgomery Street on February 6, 1928. Those who picked up and read the two-page mimeographed sheet were introduced to *The Telegraph Hill Alarm*. The masthead featured an alarm clock set on a hill with its hands pointing to three o'clock, and the prologue announced:

> With these lines you share in our nativity and we hope the rudiments of this natal speech are of consequence sufficient to merit your anticipated favor. We feel the purpose of fair, yet fearless discussions will mother our growth to solid manhood. So, the policy of this blur [sic] will be to promote the welfare of art expression on what may be said to be God's gift to San Francisco — "Tel'. Hill" . . . "Conscience" hokus will never be featured. We will reflect the clean, ambitious life of the Hill. Breathing the charm of the bay beneath us, we pause to say, sight-seeing expeditions, Sunday necking parties, rooming house extortionists are to be panned as the vile abominations of elect Hill folk. . . .

The weekly publication soon grew to eight pages, keeping the residents informed of pleasantries on the Hill. Some local advice and advertising, together with a one-act play and poems — including two previously unpublished verses by George Sterling, "who found solace in the haunts of Tel. Hill" — filled out the subsequent issues. Each week John G. Prendergast of 1347 Montgomery Street, a pleasant person and a newspaperman by trade, turned out the chatty paper. Circulation rose to 75 copies, then suddenly, after only seven issues, the *Alarm* ceased. Some rowdies had invaded the Telegraph Hill Tavern on Alta

Street where Prendergast was having his dinner; the trouble quieted down after he came to the aid of the proprietress, but then one of the malefactors smashed Prendergast's head with a bottle, rendering him unconscious and inflicting permanent brain damage.

Many years later, in May 1956, the *Telegraph Hill Bulletin* made its appearance with David F. Myrick as editor and publisher. Issued several times a year, it was the brainchild of Kenneth Evers, who as president of the Telegraph Hill Dwellers desired to keep the membership better informed. With the twenty-sixth issue (February 1966) it became the *Telegraph Hill Semaphore,* and in recent times Evers himself has taken over its editing and publishing.

Telegraph Hill has not escaped the whims of various poets, although most of the poems have been lost with the passage of time. "Telygraft Hill" by Wallace Irwin (1875-1959) is the best-known verse extant, published in *Sunset Magazine* for May of 1904. Irwin lived on Russian Hill with a view of Telegraph Hill from his home, but the only clue to the date of the work lies in the editorial comment that "the old castle has been destroyed by fire [July 1903] since this ballad-epic was written." Later the verse was set to music, in waltz time, by John Milton Hagen and was published in *Songs of San Francisco* by the Remick Music Corporation in 1939.

TELYGRAFT HILL
By Wallace Irwin

O Telygraft Hill she sits mighty and fine,
    Like a praty that's planted on ind,
And she's bannered wid washin's from manny a line,
    Which flutter and dance in the wind.
O th' goats and th' chickens av Telygraft Hill
    They prosper all grand and serene,
For when there's short pickin' on Telygraft Hill
    They feed their swate sowls on the scene.

For the Irish they live on the top av it,
And the Dagos they live on the base av it,
And every tin can in the knowledge av man,
Is scattered all over the face av it.
Av Telygraft Hill, Telygraft Hill,
Nobby owld, slobby owld Telygraft Hill!

O Telygraft Hill she sits proud as a queen
    And th' docks lie below in the glare
And th' bay runs beyant 'er all purple and green
    Wid th' ginger-bread island out there,
And the ferry boats toot at owld Telygraft Hill,
    And th' Hill it don't care if they do
While the Bradys and Caseys av Telygraft Hill
    Joost sit there enj'yin' th' view.

For th' Irish they live on th' top av it,
And th' Dagos they live on the base av it,
And th' goats and th' chicks and th' bricks bats and shticks
Is joombled all over the face av it,
Av Telygraft Hill, Telygraft Hill,
Crazy owld, daisy owld Telygraft Hill!

Sure Telygraft Hill has a castle from Wales
    Which was built by a local creator.
He made it av bed-slats wid hammer and nails
    Like a scene in a stylish the-ay-ter.
There's rats in th' castle o' Telygraft Hill,
    But it frowns wid an air of its own
For it's runnin th' bloof that owld Telygraft Hill
    Is a sthrong howld of morther and shtone.

For the Irish they live on the top av it,
And th' Dagos they live on the base av it,
And th' races they fight on the wrong side and right
To th' shame and onendin' disgrace av it,
Av Telygraft Hill, Telygraft Hill,
Windy-torn, shindy-torn Telygraft Hill!

And Telygraft Hill has an iligent lot
    Of shanties and shacks, Hivin knows!
An' they're hangin' on tight to the jumpin' off spot
    Be th' grace av th' Saints and their toes;
And th' la-ads that are livin' on Telygraft Hill
    Prefer to remain where they're at,
And they'd not trade a hen-roost on Telygraft Hill
    For a mansion below on th' flat.

For th' Irish they live on the top av it
And th' Dagos they live on th' base av it,
And th' owld sod-gossoon sits as high as th' moon
And there's nawthin he'd take in th' place av it,
Lumpy owld, bumpy owld Telygraft Hill!

On the stage and in motion pictures, Telegraph Hill has been represented many times. The Telegraph Hill Players, successor to La Vero Players, was intermittently active between 1924 and 1927. The group was organized and directed by Ben Legers, former director of the Greenwich Art Theater in Connecticut. The Players' headquarters were at 1413 Montgomery Street, but the performances were given in downtown theaters.

One of the most entertaining plays about life on Telegraph Hill was *Under the Yum Yum Tree*, written by Lawrence Roman. It opened in June of 1962 at the Off Broadway Theater and ran for several years with Edmund Johnson playing the part of Hogan, a lecherous man who made life trying for his pretty neighbor. However, when the play was made into a movie, the setting was a university rather than Telegraph Hill and local appeal vanished.

But many movies and television shows have been shot on the Hill. Scenes from *Dark Victory,* with Lauren Bacall and Humphrey Bogart, were filmed in 1947 on the Filbert Steps and in an apartment at 1360 Montgomery. Ten years later *Pal Joey,* with Kim Novak, took over Pioneer Park. After that a long procession of film crews came to the Hill, often with so much equipment that residential parking was made even more difficult.

The only movie in history which called the Hill by name was *House on Telegraph Hill,* based on the novel by Dana Lyons and starring Richard Basehart and Valentina Cortesa. Although their stay was brief, the Twentieth Century-Fox people made good neighbors. The owners of Speedy's grocery were delighted when Miss Cortesa was filmed buying fresh vegetables there — in all the production company spent $100 here — and Julius' Castle was also well patronized. One man lent them his garage and returned to find that the prop men had cleaned it up and painted the front door. Such were the public relations of the movie industry in those days!

The location of this tense scene is Montgomery Street at Montague Place. (*—Twentieth Century-Fox Film Corp.*)

A scene from the Twentieth Century-Fox Production
"HOUSE ON TELEGRAPH HILL"

Steps are a way of life . . .

Greenwich Steps: wooden stairs up from Sansome (Julius' Castle is now on the foundation), stone steps from the park and new stairs down to Sansome. (—*Upper left, Bancroft Library*)

steps line streets

and reach for houses

and climb to apartments

as they used to

Romolo Place (upper left) and apartment stairs at 425 Greenwich (below). Pardee and Gerke alleys today (above); Filbert Steps long ago. (—Lower right, California Historical Society)

Gardened steps crown a metropolis

Filbert Steps: cement steps up from Montgomery; wooden stairs down to Sansome (above).
(Right) A tribute to Grace Marchant, and the new steps under construction (center) and completed (below).

Through the gardens down to Sansome and the warehouses (above), and up from Sansome the Filbert Steps climb with twists and turns — a revised pattern (see page 89). (—*Bancroft Library*)

At Napier Lane it is still a long climb to Montgomery.

The old bag factory casts morning shadows across Sansome. The two-story building under the eucalyptus trees was the site of Farnsworth's initial television success, and years before, the location of the Gray Bros. rock crusher.

The Ice House (below, with pipe railing on roof), now occupied by interior decorators, is the large building at Battery and Union. The corner of Green and Battery (left) was the site of Fort Montgomery.

Part 2
NORTH AND SOUTH STREETS
Sansome and Battery Streets

If today's San Franciscan were to hear Sansome Street described as climbing a steep hill, he might wonder if he were hearing about the same low-level street that skirts the eastern base of Telegraph Hill. Yet, at one time both Sansome and Battery streets did climb over a shoulder of the Hill, for four blocks and one block respectively — until the quarry operators got to work. Battery Street was even named for a gun emplacement, Fort Montgomery, which perched on the Hill at what is now the northwest corner of Green and Battery.

One of the earliest pictures of Telegraph Hill was painted in 1850 by an unknown artist. This classic work, now hanging in the Wells Fargo Bank History Room, gives prominent attention to the red-roofed Fremont Hotel at the base of the Hill on Battery north of Vallejo. Some idea of the advantages offered by this Clark's Point establishment can be gleaned from the following advertisement, appearing in *The Pacific News* during April 1850:

> Fremont's Family Hotel — There are a few rooms remaining unoccupied at this popular hotel. Those persons who are desirous of enjoying one of the healthiest situations in this city, combined with the most beautiful view of the harbor, ought to make early application. Terms, $40 per month, for furnished rooms; board $18 per week.

Aside from this soft-sell advertising, various reasons might explain the hotel's failure to achieve a reputation as the great hostelry of the new city; the shrinking of the North Beach boom and the lowering of Battery Street in 1852 may have contributed to its lack of popularity. However, the structure was acquired by Drs. H. and W. P. Gibbons. With a card in LeCount and Strong's 1854 city directory they announced their San Francisco Private Hospital, one of two in the city, but this enterprise, too, was short-lived.

Much of the land between Telegraph Hill and the water front was given over to warehouses, whose solid brick construction suggested immobility and perpetual strength. But this general impression was undermined on April 12, 1854, when two walls of the United States Bonded Warehouse, at the corner of Battery and Union, suddenly fell with a loud crash and several men narrowly escaped becoming patients of the good Drs. Gibbons. Portions of three floors were carried to the ground and, sad to relate, a large amount of liquor stored in cases and casks ended up in a "confused mess." The accident was traced to repairwork then under

The Fremont Hotel on Battery Street offered its guests a fine view of the harbor. (—*California Historical Society*)

San Francisco Bay following an afternoon storm. In the string of houses along Alta Street, most prominent is the two-balconied house with the present address of 31 Alta. (—*Bancroft Library*)

In 1914 the Terminus Saloon was at the corner of Sansome and Chestnut. Fronting on Sansome was the North Point Dock (Grain) Warehouse; next was the Sea Wall Warehouse. Above are some of the dwellings along Montgomery Street. (—*San Francisco Maritime Museum*)

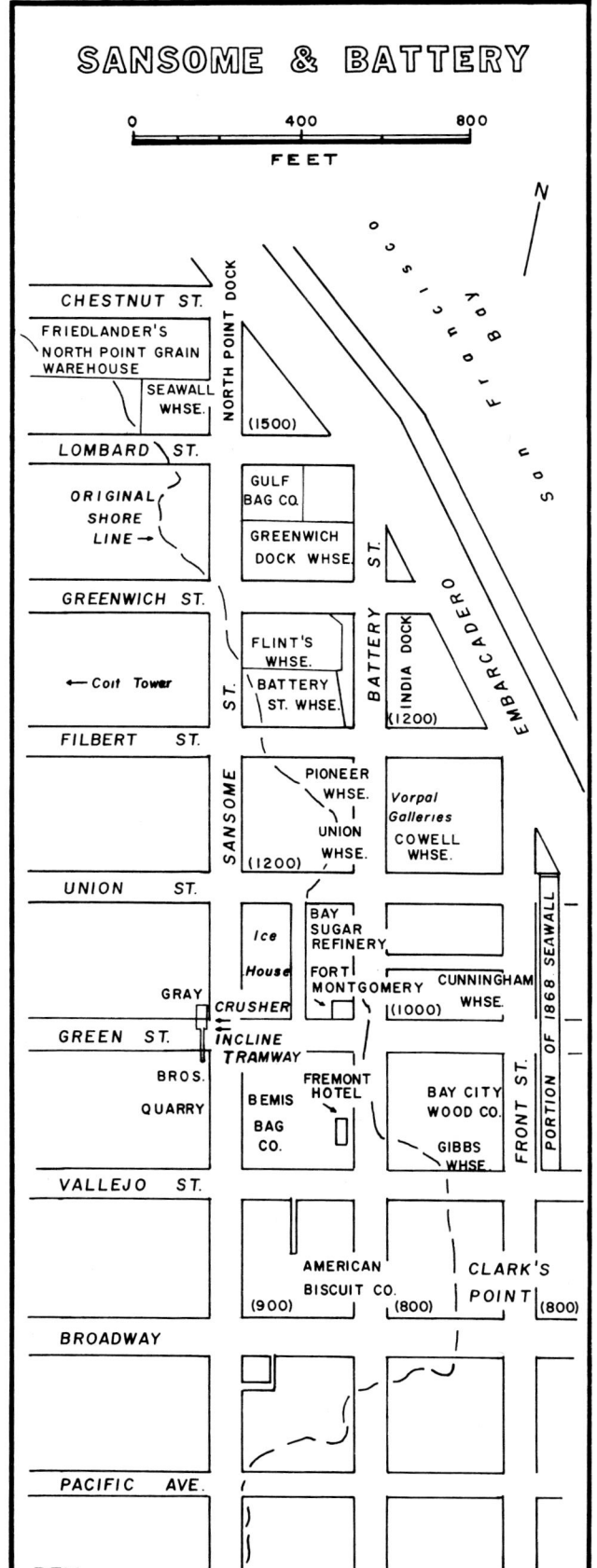

way: some of the floors had previously settled four inches and were being raised; in the process the weight of the stored goods put lateral pressure against the walls, and down they went.

Farther up the Hill, Sansome Street at that time — and for the next thirty years or so — was clustered with small houses and a few stores. In 1859 Mrs. S. Kelly operated a grocery at Union and Sansome, while half a block away, at Gaines Street (now Icehouse Alley), Christian and Doscher had another. Ten years later John O'Connell's grocery on the north side of Union near Sansome was struggling to make ends meet; by 1876 he had departed and at the northeast corner of Sansome and Union was John Tully, with A. Brumwell on the opposite corner competing for the limited hilltop trade. North of Filbert Street, Sansome in its original state descended sharply as it approached the shore line, and here in 1869 John Gibney operated a grocery on the west side of the street, while on Battery that same year there was a grocery store at Green and two more at Vallejo.

As the quarrying continued, more businesses took advantage of the new, flat land; one of the earliest important concerns was the Bay Sugar Refinery. Built at the southwest corner of Battery and Union in the 1860s, the plant was used by Claus Spreckels in 1868 to conduct experiments in refining sugar beets. Considering the rivalry between cane and beet sugar, it is interesting that Spreckels was at that time the head of the California Sugar Refining Company, which had been processing sugar cane in its plant at Eighth and Brannan since 1865. The Bay Sugar Refinery changed hands many times, by 1882 becoming the American Sugar Refining Company, for years headed by Robert Oxnard, one of three brothers engaged in sugar manufacture (the California city is named for one of them).

The Bemis Bros. Bag Company had employed Telegraph Hill breadwinners since 1897. Immediately after the 1906 disaster, in which the firm's factory on Front Street was destroyed, Judson B. Bemis came out from St. Louis to establish temporary quarters in Oakland and plan for a larger factory. After purchasing the fire-gutted ruins of L. G. Sresovich's coconut works at the corner of Sansome and Vallejo, he cleared the rubble and

Frank Iacopi sold hay, grain and feed just across Sansome Street from the Bemis Bag factory. Wash hangs on the line along Vallejo; the Sterling Laundry wagon came all the way from the Mission District to make a delivery. Houses on the Hill (center) are on Union Street. (—*Roy D. Graves collection, Bancroft Library*)

The North Point Dock (Grain) Warehouse extended along Chestnut from Sansome to Montgomery. On the Hill, where there were elegant houses before the fire, there was little rebuilding by 1914. At the right of the trees is the Grosso house on Chestnut Street. (—*San Francisco Maritime Museum*)

From time to time different route numbers were assigned to the white-front cars operating on Sansome Street. Poised at Chestnut Street in 1939, the trolley is ready to roll southward to the Third and Townsend Station. (—*W. C. Whittaker photo*)

Front Street divided part of the city from its harbor until the 1880s. The building on the right is on the site of the former Cunningham Warehouse while to the south (ahead) are the Broadway ramps of the freeway and the dark Alcoa Building.

(Left) At the turn of the century, railroad tracks along the Embarcadero included a third rail to accommodate the narrow-gauge freight cars of the North Pacific Coast Ry. which arrived on the Sausalito ferry. Long unused, this remnant still remains on Front Street, and in the picture above a portion is under the pickup truck.

began construction. Five months after the quake Bemis was operating again; other buildings were added the following year. As manufacturing methods changed, the plant became obsolete, and in September 1960 Bemis Bag moved to a new facility across the Bay at Newark.

To take workers to and from their jobs, the Market Street Railway Company operated the No. 34 streetcar line from south of Market, through the central business district and along Sansome to Chestnut Street. When the regular carmen went on strike in the early part of this century, non-union employees operated the streetcars. Telegraph Hill children, whose family sympathies were with the strikers, felt no compunction about expressing their views by hurling rocks at the streetcars passing down below on Sansome. In the fall of 1941 operations of this double-track line were discontinued and buses were substituted.

Probably the most famous—and easily the most detested—enterprise on Sansome Street was the Gray Bros. quarry. In 1898 their buildings extended along the west side of the street from Vallejo to Green, where an inclined tramway carried large rocks across Green Street to the crusher.

Today a variety of businesses are located along Sansome and Battery streets, ranging from the cluster of interior decorators near The Ice House (once a cold-storage warehouse), to advertising offices, a hardware store, the Vorpal Galleries, the Cargo West restaurant and the multi-story warehouses that still dominate the scene.

By 1862 Calhoun had become a pleasant residential street with homes surrounded by picket fences and gardens. Long before August 1904, below, virtually all the houses on the east (right) side of the street were gone; of these houses flanking Union Street some remain today. (—*Top, Bancroft Library; bottom, Society of California Pioneers*)

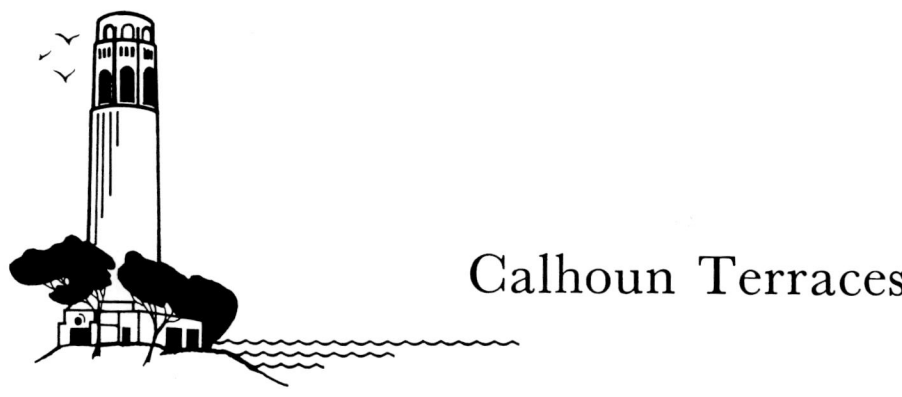

Calhoun Terraces

Calhoun Street was one of the earliest short streets on Telegraph Hill and dates back to 1851, when it originally connected Union and Green. In the early times of San Francisco people both famous and infamous lived in this area, the latter including the Sidney Ducks, tough Australians who made life miserable for those living on the west side of the Hill. Edward H. Coe, a member of the board of education in 1868 and, ironically enough, later a jailer at the County Jail down on Broadway, lived at 10 Calhoun Street. Many prominent businessmen also lived here, or along Green and Union.

The quarrying of Telegraph Hill has left its mark most deeply here. In 1877 convenient access between Green and Calhoun was still possible; indeed, a Norwegian named Erick Olsen Berg operated a small grocery at 218 Green and lived just around the corner at 2 Calhoun Street. Now only Union Street connects with Calhoun.

In 1880 there were five houses on the west side of Calhoun and seven on the east. By 1899, as the quarrying continued, all of the houses on the east side had vanished, except for the Nightengale house at the corner of Union, but the ground was soon cut from under it, too.

The only old house remaining on Calhoun is at No. 9. This white, two-story structure with a peak roof was built in 1854 by Dr. David G. "Yankee" Robinson, a popular theater entrepreneur and performer. One of the house's distinguishing features was a large circular stairway inside, but it was removed many years ago. Around 1870 this house came into the possession of the Bacigalupi family. Mrs. Rosa Bacigalupi, a widow, had moved to Filbert Street by the 1890s, but her son Louis, a tile setter by trade, continued to live in the family home. According to Telegraph Hill folklore, when the fire of 1906 was marching up the Hill and sparks threatened to set fire to the roof, Louis and his friends actively pursued errant sparks with wine-soaked rags, thus saving his Calhoun Street home from destruction. Some of the family still live there.

Probably the most memorable structure in the history of Calhoun Terraces is The Compound, once located at the southwest corner of Union and

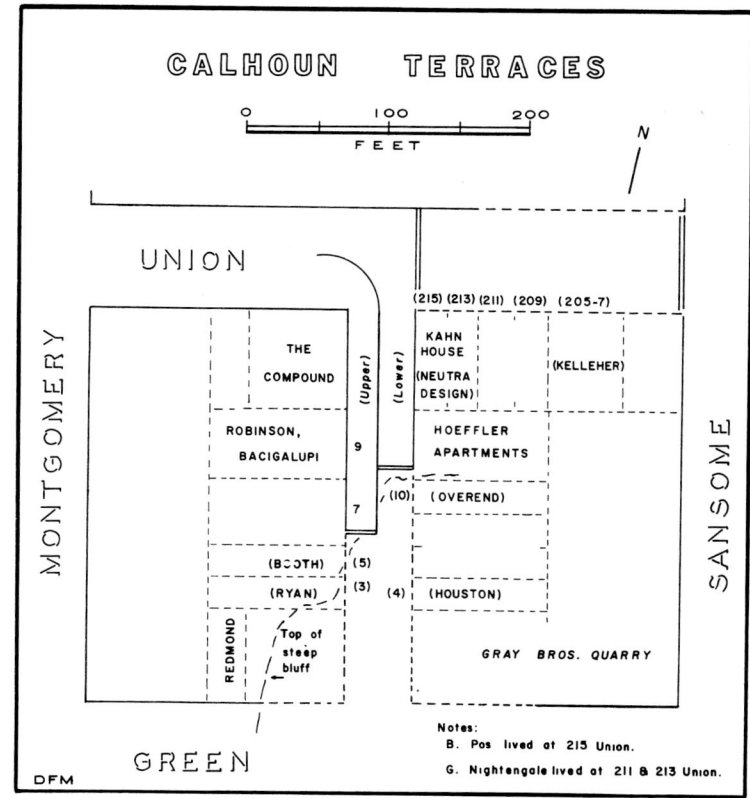

While the present apartment house at the corner of Calhoun and Union was under construction early in 1962, the old Robinson house at 9 Calhoun stood out boldly against the sky.

Calhoun. There have been several compounds on Telegraph Hill; each has its own story and its own loyal supporters who refer to their place as *The* Compound.

Separation of fact and fiction poses a problem in considering The Compound on Calhoun; even its beginnings are shrouded by a variety of opinions. Some say it originated in the last century, but a detailed 1899 map contradicts this allegation, since much of the lot was then vacant. According to local tradition, the place had been everything from a den of prostitution to a Salesian (Catholic) Boys' Club — although obviously not at the same time. Artists, writers and musicians of varying ability and productivity made this their home for several decades. Peter Macchiarini, the well-known Grant Avenue jewelry designer, once lived here, as did a German artist named Wolo. Right after the fire Rudolph Friml made his home in The Compound, although most of his popular operettas did not appear until several years later.

For many years the "true Bohemians" lived almost as one big family in the "rabbit warren," as some outsiders disparagingly called The Compound. Then, in 1937 Ian Hoeffler bought the property and strived diligently to improve the appearance of this corner. Although the informal atmosphere continued after World War II, the dozen studio apartments were more frequently occupied by lawyers, engineers, secretaries and airline stewardesses than by artists. Most winter weekends found the tenants skiing in the mountains, while in summer they were either out sailing or gathered on the sun deck.

In the late 1930s the inevitable automobile was beginning to make its appearance on Calhoun. In

The tall buildings of the Golden Gateway later took over the area used by the produce market (center) and drastically changed the scene shown here in 1955.

The Sidney Kahn house had just been completed but much remained to be done on Calhoun Street. (*—Dept. of Public Works*)

By August 1940, even though the paving of Union and Calhoun had been completed, there was still ample parking space. To the right of the fire hydrant being tested is Hoeffler's famous Compound. (*—Dept. of Public Works*)

Part of Calhoun was extremely narrow when this picture was taken in November of 1938. However, the new street was anticipated by two garages — one on the left and the doors in the wall of Hoeffler's new apartments on the right. (—*Dept. of Public Works*)

Another view of Hoeffler's apartments cascading down the slopes below Calhoun Terraces.

1939-40 the street was paved and the south end shored up with an impressive concrete cantilever structure, done partly as a W.P.A. project. Even with this bit of Twentieth-Century engineering Calhoun Street still lacks 115 feet of forming a connection with Green Street. As part of the project, Calhoun was split into upper and lower levels. Appropriately enough, in 1942 the name of the street was changed from Calhoun Street to Calhoun Terraces.

On several occasions members of The Compound formed the nucleus of a street dance on "upper" Calhoun Terrace. Arrangements were made to rope off the street, engage a dance band and spread the pavement liberally with dance wax; then everyone hoped that the evening would be warm and pleasant. Of course, indoor hospitality and refreshments were readily available should the weather be adverse.

Before work had begun on the new street, Ian Hoeffler, owner of The Compound, completed a series of apartments which cascaded down the Hill on five different levels, just above the sheer cliffs. Because of the building's symmetric form, with San Francisco Bay in the background, this structure has been the subject of many photographic essays.

On the Union Street side of these apartments is a three-story house designed by Richard Neutra, a well-known modern architect. Built in 1939 for Sidney Kahn, an investment banker, the house's simple outside lines, full-length decks on the Bay side and wide use of glass afford expansive views. Neutra placed the kitchen and dining room on the first floor by the street-level entrance, with the bedrooms on the floor above and the living room on the top floor; all floors were served by an elevator. The house has passed through several hands since the original owner, and in recent years it has been separated into two flats, with the smaller occupying the first floor.

The days and nights of great parties at The Compound came to an end in 1961 when Hoeffler sold the property to an outlander, who razed the structure and replaced it with a boxlike building containing a garage and three floors of apartments. Just before he issued the eviction notice, Hoeffler painted the old building a shocking pink. Although the tenants of The Compound had been given ample time to vacate, they hated to leave their homes and postponed the departure until the last minute. After a great two-day party over the last weekend of July, everyone departed but with a melancholy feeling. Remarked one pretty blonde, "I've had the best time of my life here." Another girl, reaching back to the post-fire days for a San Francisco tradition, took the doors of her apartment with her, declaring, "They'll be my portals to the past."

In the fall of 1954 the street dance was announced by this handbill. Heading the sponsors was "Mayor" Harry Stearns of Montgomery Street.

Montgomery at Union, a century apart. The corner building has been plastered and rearranged, and the road to the telescope has been rebuilt to serve Coit Tower. (—Bottom, *Society of California Pioneers*)

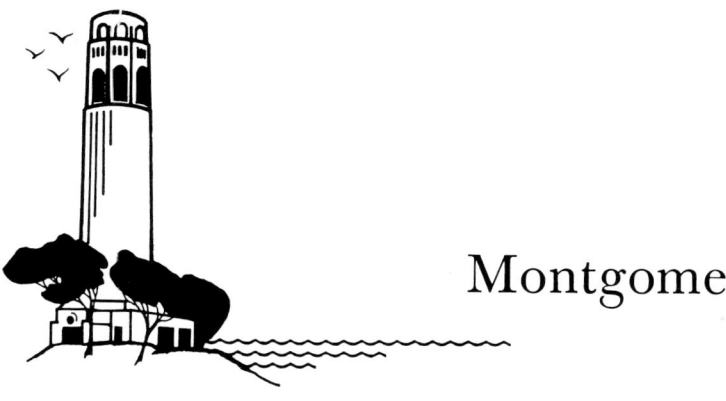

Montgomery Street

Montgomery Street in San Francisco is well known as one of the world's leading financial districts, but although the street stretches a full nineteen blocks, the financial district encompasses only the five between Market and Sacramento streets. The intervening five blocks to Broadway contain a variety of businesses: office buildings with lawyers, travel agents and interior decorators, along with restaurants, places of entertainment and one vine-covered building rich with the aroma of wine vinegar.

Above Broadway, Montgomery Street's steep climb begins, cresting near Union and terminating at a steep cliff north of Greenwich. In these five blocks crossing the Hill the character of the street undergoes such a marked change that one might wonder if this is indeed the same Montgomery Street of the busy downtown section. Beyond Greenwich, the street resumes at the bottom of the Hill and continues for several blocks to the Embarcadero amid large warehouses and manufacturing facilities.

Lining the two blocks between Broadway and Green are the standard bay-window apartments, so alike in design that the effect is monotonous. However, the street is brightened each morning and evening by the parade of girls going to and from their offices in the business district. The more sure-footed girls stepped down the sidewalk in high heels, when they were in style, while others walked down the Hill with flat shoes on their feet and a shoe box in hand. At the bottom of the Hill the flats went into the box and the girls proceeded in high heels as typical, well-dressed San Franciscans. Observant men agree that this uphill climb almost invariably ensures attractive legs.

At the corner of Vallejo the girls used to pause on their way home to buy groceries or ice cream at Fred Varrachi's store at 1100 Montgomery. But in 1970 the grocery closed after forty years of operation. On the southwest corner of this intersection lived the Marianetti brothers, for many years associated with the Fior D'Italia restaurant, located down the Hill and around the corner on Broadway.

Telegraph Hill has had its share of kept women, mistresses, shady ladies, bordellos and call houses, but one of the fanciest establishments of recent times was at 1090 Montgomery. There an enterprising girl named Lori conducted quite a business from her apartment until the police closed in on her in the summer of 1964. An eight-year veteran in the trade since she was twenty, Lori had had some trouble with the police, and accordingly her telephone had been removed. She solved this problem by moving from the third to the second floor of the building. Then, a month later, one of her girls was surprised in a downtown hotel and "sang like a canary"; the police moved in and the whole business folded like a tent. Officers discovered five address books and a revolving index, all of which listed 500 names, including some prominent people. (Undoubtedly Lori employed the old trick of recording the names of innocent political figures to prevent public disclosure of the list.) The police were impressed by the establishment. "You could call it a ritzy operation," declared the inspector, "the ritziest we've found here in a long time."

Half a block above Green Street a formidable concrete barricade, built in 1928 when this section of Montgomery Street was graded and surfaced, necessitates a long detour for automobiles, but pedestrians, after negotiating a modest flight of

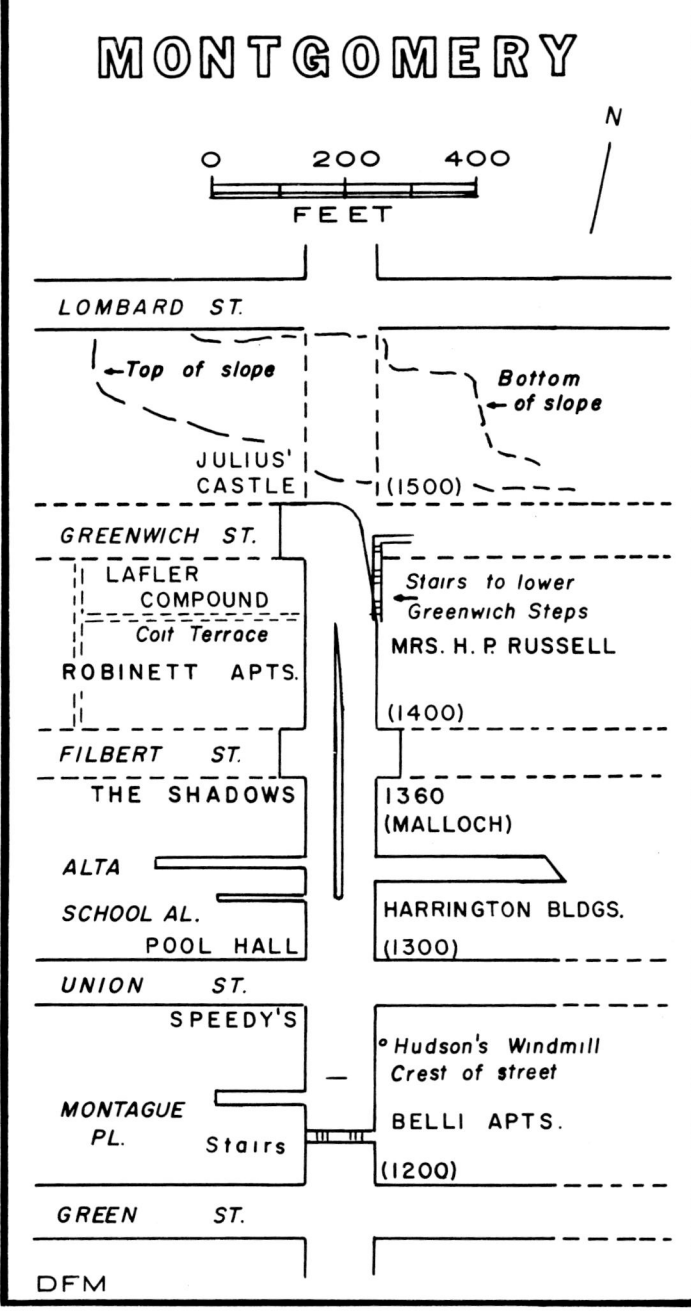

is sometimes known as the King of Torts. Belli's extensive outdoor Christmas lighting makes the building a nocturnal landmark each December. Another landmark, known to a smaller and more select circle, is Belli's penthouse, where illustrious guests join for fun and conviviality at his parties.

In the building next to the Belli apartments Robert O'Brien once lived. His column, "Riptides," was a regular *Chronicle* feature in the 1950s, and his books on San Francisco and California history are well known.

Almost at the crest of the Hill was the house of Benjamin Shellard, a pioneer organ builder who came to Telegraph Hill from Ireland via New York, where his daughter Helen was born. The family settled on the Hill in 1851 and kept the house for over half a century until Helen's death. Subsequently it was converted into two flats, 1248 and 1250 Montgomery. In 1967 Harold Weise, an attorney, erected a new dwelling on the site of the Shellard house.

The large two-story structure at the southeast corner of Montgomery and Union, old as it is, was not the first but probably the third building erected on that site. An old sketch, printed in London in November 1851, shows the harbor as seen from Telegraph Hill and includes a small windmill that powered the grinders of Mr. H. C. Hudson's coffee mill. Sometimes referred to as the spice mill, Hudson's building was a short distance south of Union Street, close to Montgomery, and took advantage of prevailing winds around the southeastern knoll of Telegraph Hill. How long Mr. Hudson's mill remained in operation has not been established, but it was probably between 1851 and 1855. While the structure at the corner of Montgomery and Union was still a single story in height, it became the property of Vincenzo Davalle, one of the owners of the Toscana Hotel at 619 Broadway. The building, altered to become several flats, passed through several hands and by the 1920s came under the ownership of Nich Cella, a stonemason by trade.

One of the building's occupants fifty or sixty years ago is remembered as a rough character, Mrs. Baumgartner, who wore a gingham dress and apron and embellished her language with choice swear words. She was frequently observed sitting

stairs, soon arrive at the next level. From there it is only a short walk to the ancillary summit of Telegraph Hill, and then Montgomery slopes downward to Greenwich Street.

On the east side of Montgomery at this barricade are several pre-fire structures and an apartment house that was built by the Ferreti family around 1920. This apartment house has since passed into the hands of Melvin Belli, a colorful and highly successful personal-injury lawyer who

From the Bay, Telegraph Hill displayed many houses. Over the bow of the *Delphine Melanie* is Crowley's store (now the site of Julius' Castle). In the 1870s houses lined Montgomery all the way to Lombard and beyond. (—*San Francisco Maritime Museum*)

Below is Lafler's Compound about 1920. On the right was the home of A. L. Marsten (oilman); in the lower center house lived Dr. Herb Darling, whose garden included a small waterfall. Architect Clarence Tantau's house, beside it on the left, was later destroyed by fire. (—*California Historical Society*)

Looking down to the financial district about 1921. The children have grown and moved away but the house on the right, although now over a garage, still remains.

A quiet neighborhood (below). A lady proceeds cautiously down the plank walk by Meisel's store; a kite has been abandoned in the overhead wire. Though trucks were found on the Hill, their travel on Montgomery was limited. (—Both, *Special Collections, San Francisco Public Library*)

Small children, above, are on their way to the two groceries on Montgomery, one at Alta and the other at Filbert. (—Bancroft Library)

The Welsbach gas lamp was a welcome guide home when Darrell Place, at right, was only a dirt path. Gas Street lamps served San Francisco until 1930. (—Bancroft Library)

Many houses were for rent or for sale, left, in 1929. No. 1325, the store at the end of the rickety plank walk, is now The Shadows. "Upper" Montgomery terminated just beyond the touring car. (Dept. of Public Works)

"Lower" Montgomery, when graded all the way to Julius' Castle, was equally narrow. The turntable at right was the only practical way to turn cars around. (—Dept. of Public Works)

The solution to grading Montgomery Street was to divide it into two levels, which involved major construction in 1931. (—*Dept. of Public Works*)

in the window of her flat, sometimes remaining in the same spot all night long. To break the monotony she would occasionally go on a real bender, terminating her spree only when her funds were exhausted. Before she became a widow, she and her husband ran a saloon on Davis or Drumm Street; as the story goes, this was one of those legendary establishments with a trap door for shanghaiing sailors.

Measuring some 900 feet, the two and a half blocks of Montgomery, from near Montague Place to Greenwich, with their byways embrace most of the older part of Telegraph Hill, although the buildings along the west side of Montgomery between Green and Union were built after the 1906 fire. The estimated population of this part of the Hill is about 450 people.

For those who lived on the Hill before the era of the automobile there were compensations to offset the isolation. In the course of time groceries and liquors were sold at ten different locations along the two blocks of Montgomery between Union and Greenwich, although there were never more than half a dozen stores in operation at any one time. By the 1920s the groceries had narrowed down to Speedy's and from time to time one or two others one of which was in the building now occupied by The Shadows. The number of stores dwindled as residents gained increasing mobility, and after 1933 only one remained.

Along the east side of Montgomery, between Meisel's grocery and Alta Street, were six houses, of which four faced Montgomery, and all were owned by James Harrington for several decades. In 1880 Harrington, a widower, lived in the house at 33 Alta with his seven children, aged four to eighteen years. The family's movements are traced in the children's birthplaces — Ireland, Massachusetts and California. Annie, the eldest, kept house while Harrington worked as a night watchman for the Union Iron Works, some distance away in the Potrero District. Subsequently the family moved around the corner to Harrington's house at 1308 Montgomery, and he became a mounted policeman in Golden Gate Park. After 1914 the six houses were occupied, then purchased, by Spanish people who had emigrated from their homeland via Hawaii. These houses, with bargeboards under their gables, were splendid examples of carpenter Gothic, but all that was stripped away when the

Looking north along "Upper" Montgomery past the iron-balconied apartments and Julius' Castle to Angel Island and Red Rock.

houses were converted to flats. In 1969 the house at 1306 Montgomery was dismantled and a new structure was built in its place the following year.

The building at the southeast corner of Alta and Montgomery, No. 1310, was once a grocery store, and in more recent times it was the home of Mary Erckenbrack, the accomplished San Francisco sculptress. But back in the 1920s the upstairs flat was the home of a woman about whom a local version of the Lady Godiva story evolves. Although Prohibition was in force, this woman — once married to a member of a socially prominent San Francisco family — managed to secure all the alcohol she needed, plus some to spare. One day, running out of the house in her nightgown, she unhitched a horse tied to a wagon and, stripping off her raiment, galloped up and down Montgomery Street. Another and more plausible version has it that the lady was overcome by patriotism and alcohol one Fourth of July. Striding out into the street in a loosely woven net gown she loudly shouted "freedom is wonderful" and "everybody should be free!" Spying the milkman's delivery wagon, with the horse waiting for the driver's return, the woman liberated the steed and dispatched it down the street with a slap on the rump.

Stepping across Montgomery Street and returning to the corner at Union, one finds a venerable structure, its brick walls long ago covered by plaster. Formerly the property of Meisel and now containing apartments, the building was once the local pool room — located upstairs when operated by Frank Diaz, and downstairs in the 1920s when under the direction of Juan Ortega of the Filbert Street steps. Pool was popular with the young neighbors, while the older generation met there to play Pedro (a card game). Sales of soft drinks helped support the operation.

To the north is a double apartment house which was the property of Mrs. Marion Montague. (The short street in the last block honors her husband's family.) Better known as Yureska, she let her artistic talents come forth in carved redwood miniatures, particularly when she lived near Santa Cruz. Her property terminated at School Alley, a name which usurped "Montgomery Place" because children made their way through the alley to the school fronting on Union Street.

On both sides of Alta were small groceries and, though cash customers were limited, people were drawn to this spot. One pastime was leaning back in comfortable chairs and shooting rats as they appeared on the plank sidewalks.

Today tourists flock to The Shadows, a well-known restaurant specializing in German cooking. The old building in which it is housed had been used for a temporary school, artist's studio and grocery, and has been remodeled many times since

The Shadows took it over, greatly changing its appearance. Rafael and Antonio Herrero, after operating a grocery here for several years, closed the business in 1921 and moved to Sunnyvale, where they achieved considerable success as sausage manufacturers. Four years later Alphonse Caberillo tried his hand in the grocery business but gave up after a year. From time to time after that the place provided a home for impecunious artists, and when Jackson Novak was looking for a place to live on Telegraph Hill in the early part of 1932, he found that the owner, Mrs. Mary Heffernan, was delighted to let him have it for $15 a month, with all of its artistic and primitive charm and an absence of electricity.

Friends suggested to Novak that by opening a tearoom perhaps he could realize more income than he could from his writing. The tearoom expanded into a tiny restaurant with a diminutive menu; there were never more than two choices and the price was always 35 cents. Flickering candlelight casting shadows around the room provided the name, and guitar players offered occasional entertainment. An article by columnist John Bruce helped to boost Novak's business; so after a year he applied for a business license—only to be turned down because of zoning restrictions. When Carl Rebmann approached him and told him that he could secure a license, Novak accepted the suggestion that the two men form a partnership. Within a short time the partnership was terminated and Rebmann became the proprietor.

The popularity of the restaurant brought more patrons; their cars added to the parking problem for patrons and neighbors alike. So, after an early morning fire on December 1, 1950, gutted the interior and necessitated nearly $10,000 worth of repairs, neighbors protested the application for a permit to rebuild. They pointed to the fact that the whole area had been zoned for residential use since 1921, but Rebmann squeaked by with a three-to-two decision after promising that attendants would park patrons' cars off the Hill. (Rebmann died in the spring of 1971 at the age of 70.)

Across the Filbert intersection was another grocery in times past. Though that building has been replaced by one of Spanish-style architecture, the next buildings date back to the early days.

Narrow stairways lead to a back row of apartments separated by small courtyards from the buildings fronting on Montgomery. Two of the frame structures appear prominently in old photographs. Upstairs at 1405 Montgomery lived Otis Oldfield and his family during the late 1920s and 1930s; his studio with its view of the Bay enabled him to sketch various types of sailing craft as they entered the harbor. Downstairs lived artist Helen Forbes until a legacy enabled her to build a home on Alta Street.

The two buildings to the north (1407 and 1409 Montgomery) are the products of considerable remodeling by Clyde Robinett, who died in 1955, and the present owners, Dr. and Mrs. Stanley Burton. Robinett, an Oriental art dealer, furnished his apartment with some of his most treasured art objects. One unusual feature of his home was a bathroom with all fixtures in jet black. Later changes by the Burtons included the installation of a glass-lined hydraulic elevator. Margaret Chung, who lived at 1407 Montgomery, was a Chinese lady doctor known for her cuisine. Dr. Chung had a wide circle of friends, and a 1939 article said that "perhaps she was the most outstanding hostess on the hill," a tradition she carried on for servicemen during the war years.

The Compound, occupying the fifty-vara lot at the corner of Montgomery and Greenwich, quietly slipped into oblivion years ago. Harry Lafler, an artist and newspaperman, who at times garnered moderate wealth selling industrial real estate in Oakland, built five cottages on this land around 1920. Building materials came from various sources; Harry salvaged lumber from the "Welcome" sign of 1908 for the top house. During its heyday in the 1920s, this was perhaps the most interesting place to live on Telegraph Hill. Poet George Sterling was a frequent visitor, and a young bachelor, now a distinguished South American diplomat, was once a resident. Locally admired was another resident, painter Pat Leahy, who set up scaffolds and cheerfully painted houses singlehandedly, never deterred by the absence of one leg.

Mary Lafler, still remembered for her kindness and her remarkable beauty, was married to Harry for ten years. Subsequently she married Otto Winkler, an architect associated with Richard

Three little houses on Montgomery were well planted with shrubs and vines in 1956. Their future was to be short-lived.

Melvin Belli's apartment at right is built around a tree-filled courtyard.

Neutra. The building at 1441-45 Montgomery was designed by Winkler.

At the other corner of Montgomery and Greenwich is Julius' Castle, a restaurant known far and wide for its view. In 1889 Michael Crowley sold groceries and liquors on this site; around the end of World War I, when John B. Mini made his home here, his house was destroyed by fire. Julius Roz came to San Francisco from Turin, Italy, in 1898 and worked in Bigin's Restaurant on Columbus Avenue. His regular patrons included Harry and Mary Lafler, who encouraged Julius to build an eating place on the Hill. Julius' Castle was built on the old concrete foundation of the former Mini house, and Roz began serving in 1922.

Until the Castle opened, there was no Montgomery Street north of Alta, only a trail. A road was put in, but motorists were bewildered when they arrived at the Castle after an uneasy drive to find no visible place for their cars. Just when all hope seemed lost, a teen-age boy would dash out with the reassuring statement, "I'll park your car." And indeed he did, turning it on the turntable. Many years have gone by but Victor Merrill, the former boy, still parks cars there at noontime.

Julius Roz, who is remembered standing in front of his restaurant flanked by his two collies, passed away in December 1943 at the age of 75, shortly after one of his dogs died.

The east side of Montgomery Street between Filbert and Greenwich is now lined with substantial apartments. The three buildings closest to Greenwich were built before World War II; the one at 1460 Montgomery, completed in 1936 with a bridge to the garage, was the first.

Mrs. Henry Potter Russell, a member of the Crocker family, lived at 1440 before building the apartment house at 1420 Montgomery in 1960. The structure, strengthened by steel girders, was designed by Gardner Dailey, while the mosaic mural

The three little houses shown on page 113 gave way to a large apartment building (above) in 1960.

(Below) Sgraffito wall decorations, etched glass and glass bricks are identifiable features of the apartment building at 1360 Montgomery. To the right are the apartments at 80 and 90 Alta.

in the lobby was designed by Mrs. Russell's cousin, Marie Anne Poniatowski, and executed by Alfonso Pardinas. Mrs. Russell, who died in the summer of 1966, was an active member of numerous cultural and charitable organizations. Her strong support of the San Francisco Museum of Art, giving of both her time and money, contributed much to its success; the same observation could be made about the Symphony, Opera and so on.

For many decades the site of this building had been filled by three small, wooden houses. Before additions were made, these houses were so tiny that it was hard to find tenants, even with a monthly rental as low as three dollars prevailing during the First World War; impecunious artists and would-be artists then made their homes here. Helen Morgan, the blues singer, was an occupant at one time. A woman living here once gave a little girl a dime to run an errand at Speedy's. Returning with a loaf of bread, the girl was greatly surprised when the front door opened. "She had nothing on but the door," the child explained to her mother. From 1937 to about 1960, one of these houses was the home of a kindly hospital nurse, Miss Eda Hoelscher, and her many cats, while in another lived Harry Stearns, one-time unofficial mayor of Telegraph Hill.

Compared with the neighborhood houses, the building at 1360 Montgomery, at the corner of Filbert, was so large that there were many protests during its construction in 1936. To bring a halt to later vandalism, owner Jack Malloch found it necessary to employ a night guard. Finally completed, the building's sgraffito wall decorations (created by scratching through several layers of cement) established it as a convenient landmark. Apartment dwellers here have included theatrical producer Randolph Hale and Senator Hiram Johnson. After the little house next door was torn down, a vegetable garden occupied the lot until it became a parking lot and still later the site of an apartment house (80 and 90 on Alta), whose roof too is adorned with television antennas.

These two blocks of Montgomery have undergone many changes with the passage of time. The biggest change came in 1931, when the street was graded and paved, a process that seemed interminable as dust and noise filled the air for months. Late in 1954 a narrow walk was placed along "lower" Montgomery, and a few months after that trees were planted in the dividing strip. An even greater improvement came in the early part of 1958 when all the utility wires were placed underground in this area.

Walking to work down Montgomery now affords this fine view of the city.

At Portsmouth Square, Coit Tower is presented in a double image in this photograph of Kearny Street. The Bella Union is an old theatrical name in San Francisco's history. Another link with the past is the Columbus Tower where "Boss" Ruef wheeled and dealed in post-fire politics.

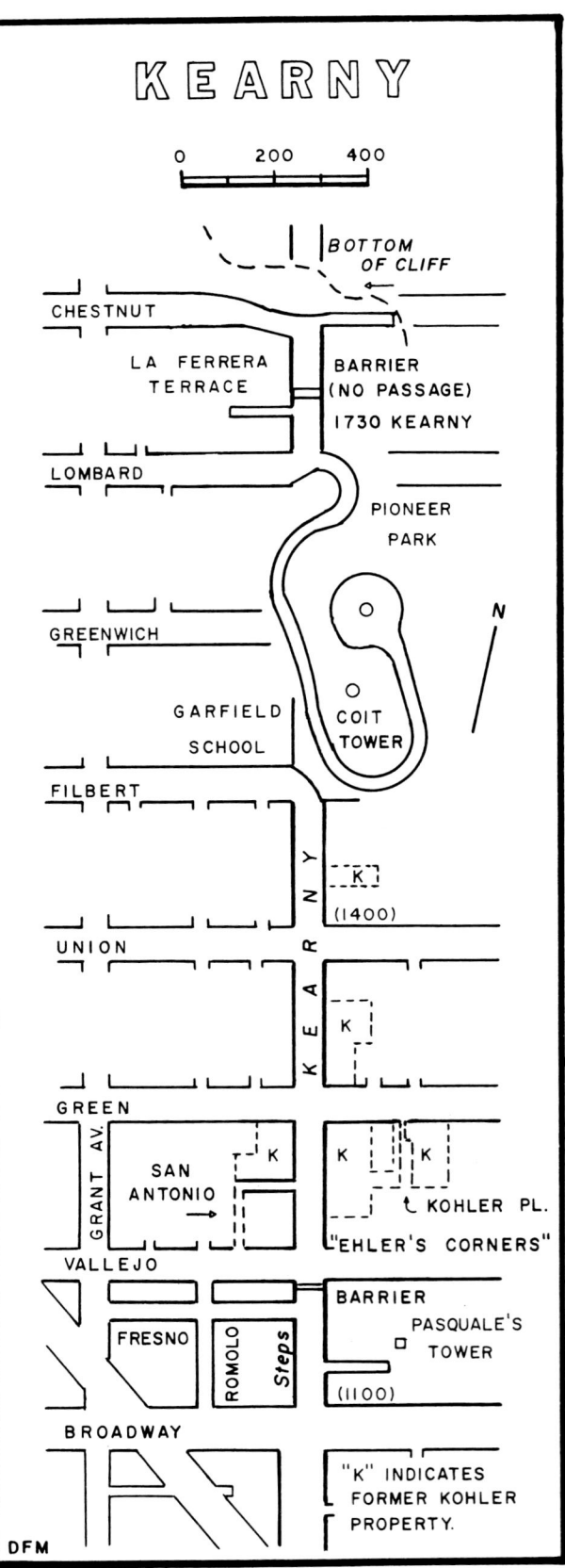

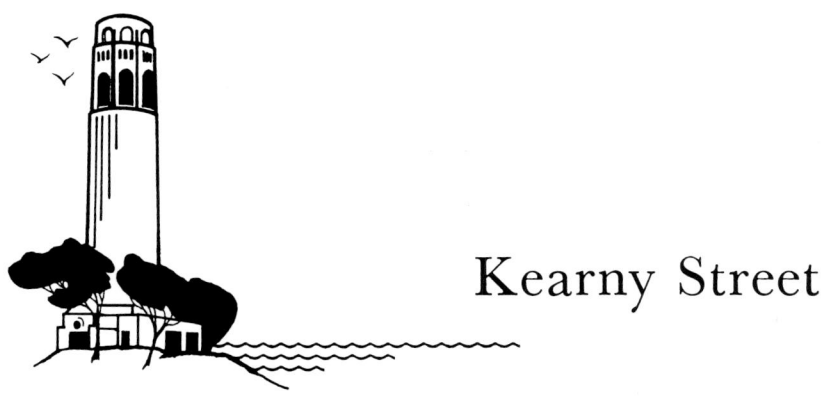

Kearny Street

Climbing the awkward concrete steps from Broadway up Kearny has often evoked a secret prayer from pedestrians for a cable car line. It will never happen, but if the neighbors back in 1882 had not protested so vigorously, Layman would have built his line here instead of along Greenwich Street.

In the first block of Kearny is Dunne's Alley, which rises to end near the base of a tall, slim building. The dome on top, said to resemble a Genoese structure, arouses much interest and several tales of the tower's origin circulate on the Hill.

Romantics say the builder was a young Italian fisherman who came to this country determined to erect a dream house and then send for his waiting fiancée. Avoiding the *dolce vita,* he saved his money, built the tower and sent passage money to his sweetheart. The great day came when she stepped off the ferryboat into the arms of the waiting fisherman, who triumphantly led her to their future home. "I don't like it," she said, throwing up her hands in horror. The entreaties that followed were useless; the prospective bride detached herself from the engagement and returned to Italy. The saddened man closed his castle.

So much for the romantic. The bureaucratic version is that the city building inspector, on seeing the plans, refused to issue a building permit, but the tower was built anyway. Without a permit no utilities could be connected, which made the tower uninhabitable.

Actually, Pasquale Gogna built the house in 1930. Arriving in San Francisco in 1907, he worked as a baker and through frugality he was able to join his brother in purchasing several small hotels in the city. The tower consists of four square rooms directly above each other, with access provided by an enclosed stairway on the west side of the building. In the northern corners of each room are two alcoves which collectively house the usual appurtenances found in kitchens and bathrooms. With the sink in one corner, the stove in another and so on, this arrangement offered some inconveniences, but the spectacular view offset these minor annoyances. Mr. Gogna must have enjoyed the house, for he lived there comfortably — with all utilities — until January 1956, when his arthritic condition caused him to move into his brother's home on Russian Hill, after which the tower was rented. As the tower attracts much attention, a wrought-iron gate — with the name GOGNA in black metal letters on the top of the grill — has been erected to keep out trespassers.

From the west side of Kearny, Fresno Street runs one block to Grant Avenue, intersecting Romolo Place along the way. Originally these two byways were known as Hinkley Street and Pinkney Place respectively, the latter being one of the oldest short streets on the Hill. Like the through streets, these two lanes contained lodging houses, hotels, flats and groceries.

Weichen Ehlers came to this country from Germany in 1852 and subsequently opened a grocery in partnership with Frederick Rose at the southeast corner of Hinckley and Pinkney. Competition appeared by 1859 with the store of Carsten Hildebrandt and Henry Knop across the street; ten years later Ehlers, then sole owner of his store, faced competition from a second store and conceded by moving his operations to 1127 Kearny.

Pasquale's tower from the south shows off its balconies.

The No. 15 streetcar line crosses Pacific on Kearny in the spring of 1939. At that time the International Settlement was not yet the active night club district; rentals were available. (—W. C. Whittaker photo)

In the 1870s Marie L. Roncovieri, a widow, operated a lodging house at 33 Hinckley, supporting herself and her son Alfred. He was then a student and later a musician, subsequently becoming superintendent of the San Francisco schools. On these streets in older times were a number of permanent guest hotels; today only the Basque Hotel at 15 Romolo Place remains.

Trouble brewed in this neighborhood in March 1903. A woman, known only as Canuta, invited Ignacio Sanchez for an indefinite stay in her flat at 17 Hinckley while her husband was out of the city. One night, out for a breath of air at 4 a.m., the intoxicated Sanchez paused to greet two friends at the corner. That was the last time they saw him alive. Ignacio was abducted by several men, carried to the end of Green Street and hurled off the cliff. So great was the force of his 150-foot fall that when he was found the next morning, his head and shoulders were imbedded in the soft ground. According to his brother, two men had been jealous of his cozy living arrangement and threatened to kill him.

One evening in the summer of 1963, police became suspicious when they saw 27 men entering and leaving the flats at 15-17 Romolo Place. After a week of surveillance, the police broke down the door, ignoring the usual protocol of smiling

Afternoon shadows darken Kearny's steps. At the bottom of the climb is Broadway; beyond is Columbus Tower.

Looking east from Grant Avenue, the quiet appearance of Fresno Street in 1971 belies its active past. Fresno Street crosses Romolo Place and terminates at Kearny. On the left is the Eng Bros. Sheet Metal Shop.

At right the buildings along Kearny Street, north of Lombard, welcome the sunrise. The tall building is at 290 Lombard (corner of Kearny); to its right the address is 1730 Kearny. The building with the mansard roof is at the corner of Chestnut and Winthrop streets.

Side streets offer many surprises in the way of gardens and decorative sculpture. At the left San Antonio turns into an area of gardens.

through the peephole and waiting for the buzzer. Once inside, they arrested a number of people on prostitution charges.

Moving his grocery a second time to 1201 Kearny, Weichen Ehlers profited by his new location on the corner of Vallejo and was able to purchase property on all four corners of this intersection. After the 1906 fire he rebuilt "Ehlers' Corners" with a new store, a duplex home and two apartment houses, all with similar cornices and dentils. He lived in the duplex and kept an eye on the other properties until his death in 1916. In 1958 the apartment building at the northeast corner was purchased and extensively remodeled by Dennis Flynn, a real estate man and long-time treasurer of the Telegraph Hill Dwellers

Just north of Ehlers' Corners is San Antonio Street, a small lane running west from Kearny and turning south to pass through a garden of ivy, flowers and succulents before terminating at Vallejo. In the 1950s the interior portion of this block was vacant except for foundations of buildings lost in the 1906 fire; now the shadows of apartments almost hide the streets.

Just after the fire, most of the property on both sides of Kearny between Vallejo and Green that was not held by Ehlers was owned by Henry Kohler (1829-1914). Kohler, a German immigrant, managed his real estate operations from his office at 1221 Kearny. He also owned the adjoining fifty-vara lot at the crest of Green Street in which was incorporated Kohler Place, a short street since absorbed by adjacent lots.

At 1220 Kearny lived Milanelli Cosenza, "the goat lady," and her husband Angelo. She sold fresh goat milk on the Hill — fresh because she performed the milking right at the customer's door. Each day she led her herd through a back lot, over to Castle Street and up to a foraging place on Montgomery Street, returning for them in the evening. This procedure did not please Mary Lafler, for the goats strayed into her flower garden and feasted on the blossoms. On April 1, 1928, an ordinance banished goats from certain areas of the city, including Telegraph Hill, and the goat ladies, calling out the melodious Italian names of their charges, became just another bit of Hill folklore.

Passing a building of flats once called Overbearing Manor, Kearny points upward from Union before its identity is usurped by the boulevard in Pioneer Park. Kearny Street begins again at Lombard.

At No. 1730 is a large apartment building that replaced a smaller house dismantled in the summer

of 1955. When Dr. Collin H. Dong proposed the new structure, neighbors objected because of inadequate garage space for his tenants. Although the plans were modified to provide sufficient spaces for automobiles, Dr. Dong's original proposal and the contemporary apartments at 40-50 Alta Street sparked the reform in city planning laws which resulted in the one-for-one offstreet parking law.

One of the newest street names (adopted in 1933) on Telegraph Hill is La Ferrera Terrace, which extends 137 feet west from this part of Kearny. Several years ago a prospective builder went to a tax sale and bought a lot occupying the middle eight feet of this street, which itself was only sixteen feet wide. Not knowing of the easement over this lot which provides the only access to many garages, the purchaser planned to build a house on his narrow property. When protests from neighbors were heeded by the authorities in 1969, the building permit was denied and La Ferrera Terrace was saved.

From the other side of these apartments (at left) on La Ferrera Terrace are fine views of Marin County.

(Below) Kearny Street near Broadway in 1971. The "Off Broadway" has since moved to the corner at the left, opposite Enrico's.

Characteristic of Grant Avenue today are colorful names ranging from the Chelsea Bird to the Coffee Gallery. The 1972 Grant Avenue Street Fair (below) was a happy occasion.

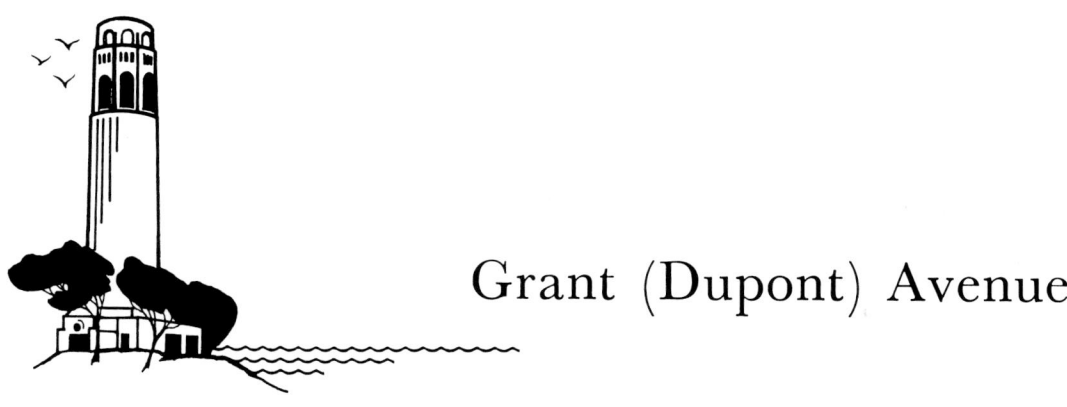

Grant (Dupont) Avenue

From Market Street, Grant Avenue passes through a stylish shopping area to Bush Street and into Chinatown. Above Broadway it continues through the commercial district along the west side of Telegraph Hill to Filbert Street, after which Grant is largely residential in character. Prior to 1908 that part north of Bush retained the early name of Dupont Street.

Dupont was busy in the early days. For example, in 1876 there were twenty groceries on this street north of Broadway, often several at one intersection. In contrast, Stockton and Kearny Streets each counted but a third of that number. Usually these stores sold liquor, but spirits could also be purchased by the glass from other purveyors.

Above Vallejo the commercial section of Grant prior to World War II was markedly different from its character today. The carriage trade liberally patronized the Costa Brothers' fancy grocery and the fruit and vegetable store of the Di Grazia Brothers. In the same block, Nicola Capurro left his hardware business sometime around the First World War to run the Sempione Hotel, only a few steps away at 1347 Grant Avenue. The hardware store was taken over by Louis Figoni and, in spite of the surrounding changes, it is still there. There were four men's clothing stores in this vicinity, and at 1361 Grant was Guillo Pera's popular Italian restaurant, where dinners began with a big tureen of soup. In the next block, at the corner of Green was the Grannucci Grocery, another carriage-trade establishment, and at 1453 Grant the Telegraph Hill Cafe served meals in the late 1930s.

Of the nineteen macaroni-ravioli factories around North Beach in 1917, four were located on this part of Grant Avenue. Ten years later, only nine were operating, including the Canal Exposition Ravioli Factory and, just a few doors away at 1358 Grant, the Panama Canal Ravioli Factory, which is one of the few left in the distirct today.

At present there are Chinese-operated groceries and laundries on Grant Avenue as well as the Italian French Bakery, one source of San Francisco's famed sour dough bread. An old store at Filbert now houses the City Lights Publishing Company. Of the restaurants, there is a wide assortment ranging from the New Pisa to The Savoy-Tivoli and Mooney's Irish Pub, recently the site of a yo-yo contest. The trend, however, has been oriented toward shops featuring local works of art such as jewelry, paintings, prints, leather clothing, sandals and metal sculpture. Some of the participants have only brief experience in these arts, although one exception is Peter Macchiarini, who has designed and made avant-garde jewelry for over thirty years.

Beginning in 1954, the Grant Avenue Street Fair provided a place for artists to show their wares and for patrons, spectators and other artists to buy or just gawk. One weekend each June, the two blocks between Vallejo and Union were closed to autos, and exhibits of all kinds lined Grant Avenue. Attendance grew over the years and so did complaints; after several years of ambivalence, the police declined to close the street in 1971. A general open house was substituted but the spirit was lacking and the crowds were disappointing. In 1972 the police relented and the fair was reinstated, this time extending three blocks to Filbert.

During the 1950s the artists and art shops along Grant Avenue attracted Bohemians to the area, but

Clothes and sandals, food, drink and entertainment draw both natives and tourists to Grant Avenue.

it was not until the summer of 1958 that their dress and way of life captured the public's attention. Feature stories in newspapers and magazines, the publicity arising from Jack Kerouac's novel, *On the Road*, and some of the local poetry were responsible, particularly when police tried to suppress Allen Ginsberg's poem, "Howl." All this attention drew many young people to Grant Avenue in an attempt to escape the fearsome routine of the nine-to-five, gray-flannel syndrome.

This was the time of the beatniks. Some were artists, actors or poets, but of all the Bohemians the actual number of producers was sadly small. Living above the shops, the beatniks — men wearing long beards and the women dressed in black — made the scene each day at the coffeehouses to exchange philosophy, news and gossip. In 1958 their appearance was still novel and tour-bus drivers delighted their passengers by gleefully pointing out real, live beatniks. Even "squares" in casual clothes felt the concerted stares of the gaping tourists.

The tourists' invasion of Grant Avenue was tolerated because they bought trinkets and jewelry or patronized the coffeehouses. But one night in August 1958 the beats decided to turn the tables. Hiring a sight-seeing bus, about 100 beatniks toured downtown San Francisco to study the life style of the outside world. Arriving at one large hotel with bagels, flutes and bongo drums, they startled both management and guests, who failed to reciprocate the cordial reception usually accorded visitors to Grant Avenue. However, except for some frayed nerves no damage was done.

Beatnik activity generally centered around Green and Grant, the drawing card being the Co-existence Bagel Shop at the southeast corner. Jay Hoppe, the owner, had more than his share of problems: allegedly a black patrol wagon parked in front of his establishment intimidated patrons; other harassments came from letters threatening to blow up the building. These threats were partially fulfilled on July 14, 1958, at 2:30 in the morning when an unknown party blew up the plumbing in the ladies' room. The composure of a roomful of customers was shaken but physical damage was limited. The reason for the blast remains a mystery; perhaps it was a Bastille Day prank.

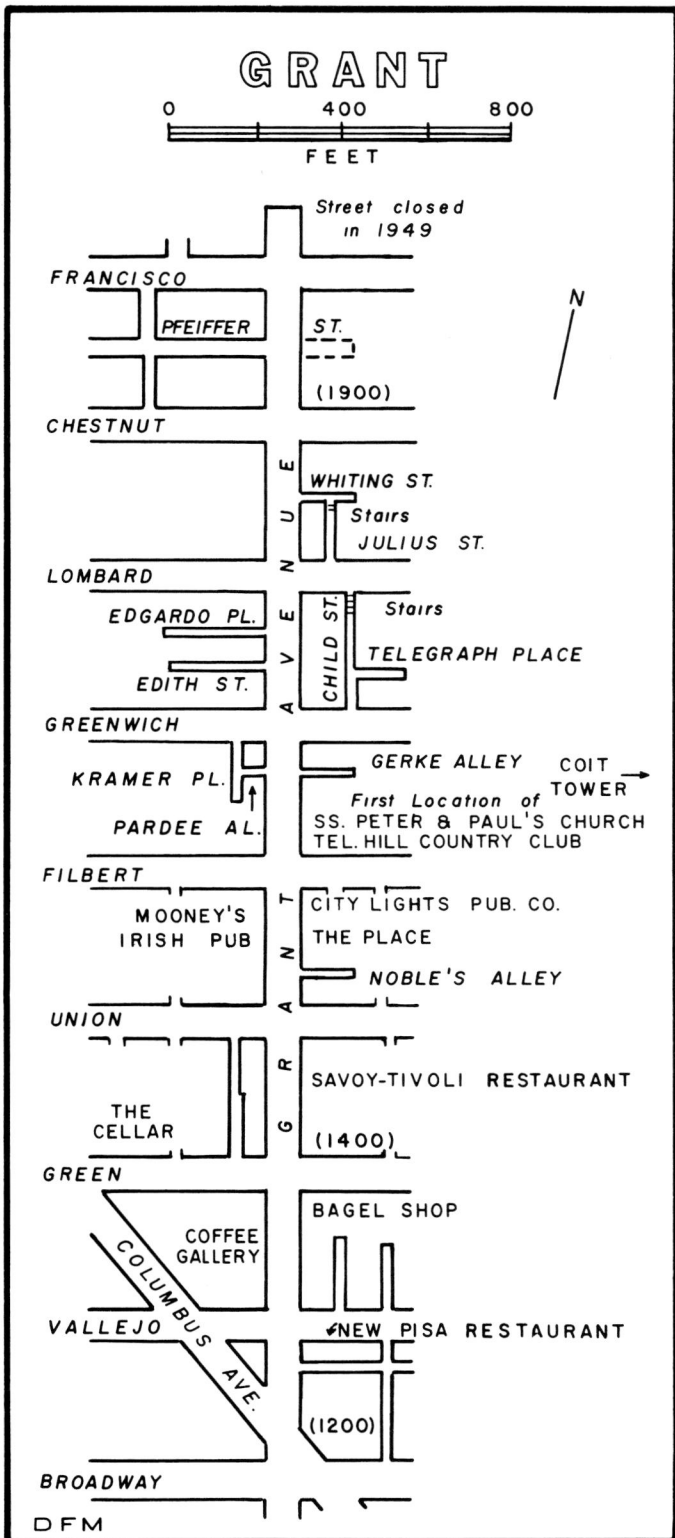

Looking down Grant Avenue to Bay Street in 1915 where the stacks of lumber indicate a remodeling is underway. (—Ted Wurm collection)

Leo Krikorian's coffeehouse near Filbert Street was known simply as The Place. The décor relied heavily on sawdust floors and black walls covered with local art. Mondays were especially popular as that was Blabbermouth Night and crowds jammed The Place to hear a series of speakers expound briefly on any topic they chose; a bottle of champagne went to the speaker rated best by the audience. The evangelist Billy Graham once considered participating, until his scouts returned with a negative report. Probably the most popular speaker appeared in 1965 (by then Blabbermouth Night was held at The Coffee Gallery) when Baby Jane Dunn, wearing a fetching costume, took a few minutes off from her act at Big Al's to defend topless dancers. Her audience was easily convinced.

Other spots on the beatnik circuit were The Cellar, on Green Street, featuring subterranean poetry readings and jazz; Miss Smith's Tearoom at 1353 Grant, operated by LaVeta Margaret Smith, who also ran the Old Jazz Record Shop in the next block; and the Party Pad, an informal club upstairs on Oregon Street in the former produce district, managed by Eric Nord. Standing 6'7" and weighing 300 pounds, Nord had run the "hungry i" night club and later was night manager of the Bagel Shop. A confidant of many young Bohemians, he was affectionately known as Big Daddy.

In June 1958 a young saxophone player died when he fell off the roof of the Party Pad, and a few days later his girl friend, who had a long history with the bottle, was strangled near the Presidio. Both events commanded considerable newspaper space. Whatever good feelings had existed between the old-time neighbors and the beatniks were breaking down. Street noises late at night — shouting, breaking windows, rolling beer cans down the street — resulted in complaints to the police and increased surveillance. The coffeehouse clientele began to drift away; some sought the new Cassandra Coffee House on Columbus Avenue; others moved to Potrero Hill, to Nepenthe at Big Sur or to Greenwich Village. Early in 1960 The Place closed its doors and later that year the Bagel Shop folded up. Grant Avenue, once described as "an open-air mental hospital three blocks long," was being vacated.

By 1962, without the beatniks and the wide-eyed tourists, stores and cafes along Grant Avenue fell upon hard times. Some became only a memory. Meanwhile the Haight-Ashbury district and the hippies provided a substitute tourist attraction. Grant Avenue, however, has made a comeback with many productive artists and craftsmen enlivening the scene.

North of Filbert

Apartment houses, occasional grocery stores and laundromats line Grant Avenue north of Filbert, but the neighborhood is not without tales to tell.

The Telegraph Hill Country Club flourished briefly at the northeast corner of Filbert and Grant. Membership was open to anyone willing to pay the greens fee to play on the miniature golf course managed by Harry Sweet. SS. Peter and Paul's Church, now at Washington Square, was once at this corner, and its foundation, flooded by a spring, was the neighborhood swimming hole before the golf course became active in 1931.

At or near this site many years earlier was the Third Baptist Church, organized in 1854. By 1862 the membership of this Negro church totalled 82 under the Reverend Charles Satchell; five years later the church moved to Powell Street on Nob Hill.

In this block is Gerke Alley, one of the shortest streets on the Hill. Henry Gerke, in later years a wholesaler of native wines and brandies, was listed by the *Alta* in November 1850 as one of the largest taxpayers in San Francisco — his total payment was $755 — and perhaps this was sufficient to perpetuate his name on this short street.

Long ago, at the northeast corner of Grant and Gerke was a restaurant and a rooming house. The house at the end of the alley, No. 6, was built in 1884 and later became the property of Frank Bacigalupi. When the house next door was for sale, Bacigalupi withdrew $2000 in gold coin from his savings on April 17, 1906, to buy the building the next day. Of course the sale was not consummated; instead Bacigalupi joined the other refugees trudging out to the Presidio. Guarding his suitcase full of gold, he was able to act quickly after the fire had been subdued. Instead of buying the property next door, he used his money to purchase 18-inch redwood boards which the army had brought in to help rebuild the ravaged city. Brushing aside the still-warm embers and using the old foundations, Bacigalupi built two houses on his lot within a week. These structures, one fronting on Greenwich and the other at 6 Gerke Alley, were among the first post-fire buildings on Telegraph Hill. To be sure that his wooden houses would withstand future earthquakes, he used a great many nails in their construction, apparently forgetting that the fire did the damage.

Grant Avenue and adjoining streets offer varied architecture. The striking tall building on Edith Street (formerly Church Street) carries out its wooden theme with a wine press over the doorway.

In 1951 landscape architect Douglas Baylis bought one of the Bacigalupi houses and remodeled it. The old church lot back of the house was vacant except for a chicken coop, so Baylis bought the property and converted the old basement into a delightful garden. Various trees now bloom there, including a Japanese maple, lemons and even a fig tree which somehow survived the fire although it no longer bears good fruit. The garden is so expertly planned that each year the landscaping classes of the University of California make a pilgrimage to study it.

Kramer Place, just west of the corner of Greenwich and Grant, probably took its name from Jacob Kramer, who operated a grocery store here as early as 1856. After his demise his family continued the business until the fire.

Edith Street and Edgardo Place contain a number of recently constructed, attractive apartment

From Chestnut to Francisco, Grant Avenue descends rapidly. Just beyond Francisco — the bay-windowed, shingle apartment house marks the intersection — Grant Avenue was closed in 1949. In the distance is Angel Island.

houses which belie the troubles of the former residents during the Gay Nineties.

In the wee hours of January 5, 1894, a fire broke out in the Edith Street flat of Pacifico Biagini, of the family of wagon manufacturers, causing the family to flee in their night clothes. Within minutes buildings on both sides were in flames, six horses were burned fatally and seven carriages went up in flames. Four other structures were scorched, including the home of Dr. Henry D. Rogers, a long-time resident of Greenwich Street.

Then, in the summer of 1895, a sewer main was being laid along Edith Street, which required heavy blasting. Mrs. Ercerlia Cazneau, a widow with six children, lived at the south corner of Edith and Grant and supported her family by sewing and taking in boarders. The contractor, Dan O'Connor, set off his charges in the narrow street not five feet from her house. Soon her home was hanging precariously over a 15-foot chasm; after the bottom of Mrs. Cazneau's kitchen fell out she had to stop taking in boarders.

O'Connor put in temporary props to support the house and then coldly informed Mrs. Cazneau that all repairs had become her responsibility. He even threatened to remove the props if she did not arrange for the repairs promptly, and when she remonstrated he dared her to sue him. How-

The quiet residential part of Grant Avenue begins at Filbert, only a block away from Greenwich where this picture was taken on a spring afternoon in 1972.

Endangered by excavations, this building was ordered demolished. After the last major support had been removed, a professional wrecker pushed the building with his foot and over it went, providing afternoon entertainment for 300 spectators.
(—San Francisco Examiner)

ever, the lady was not unresourceful. She managed to discover that he had been working without a license and then got her side of the story in the *Call*. The San Francisco supervisors ordered a committee to find out what was going on and to arrange for repairs, but whatever work was done was swept away by fire 11 years later.

The weed-covered slope at the southeast corner of Grant and Lombard presents a quiet scene now, but in the fall of 1964 it was considerably livelier. The ground supporting the foundations of several buildings at the corner of Lombard and Child streets was considerably higher than the level of the lot on Grant Avenue; consequently, excavations for a proposed 28-unit apartment house on Grant could well undermine the foundations of the buildings above. And that is exactly what happened. Late in October 1964 the occupants of two buildings, one being at 373-75 Lombard and 55-57 Child streets and the other at 43-45 Child Street, were ordered to leave their homes when the foundations began to crumble.

The unusually heavy rains that swept Northern California that season further weakened the foundations, and on December 27 the buildings started to crack. Early the following morning half of the building at the corner of Lombard and Child snapped and collapsed with a roar, bringing hundreds of neighbors from their beds to survey the damage. Chairs, beds, tables and other furnishings that the evacuated tenants had not been allowed to retrieve were scattered over the hillside. Acting on emergency orders from the mayor, a wrecking company pulled down the remaining half of the corner building and the apartment house at 43-45 Child Street. Four other structures, including two east of Child Street, were ordered evacuated; their tenants joined the others in seeking shelter from the storm and could not return to their apartments for several weeks.

How and why the situation was allowed to develop has never been adequately explained. Mrs. Elvetzia Airoldi, an 81-year-old widow whose late husband had built the house on Child Street in 1910, had on November 24 sought a court injunction to halt the excavations until proper precautions had been taken. The court had failed to take affirmative action during the four weeks preceding the collapse of her apartment house

Since 1949, Grant Avenue has no longer connected with Bay and North Point streets, as it terminates just north of Francisco Street. The installation of a large sewage-treatment plant is responsible for closing the street.

Looking up Stockton Street to North Beach and Telegraph Hill around the 1860s. To the right, the Lutheran Church on Greenwich forms part of the skyline. Alcatraz Island, with only a few structures, is in the left background. (—*Society of California Pioneers*)

From August 1907 until May 1954, the present Maybeck Building at 1734-36 Stockton Street was the home of the Telegraph Hill Neighborhood Association until new quarters were established on Lombard Street.

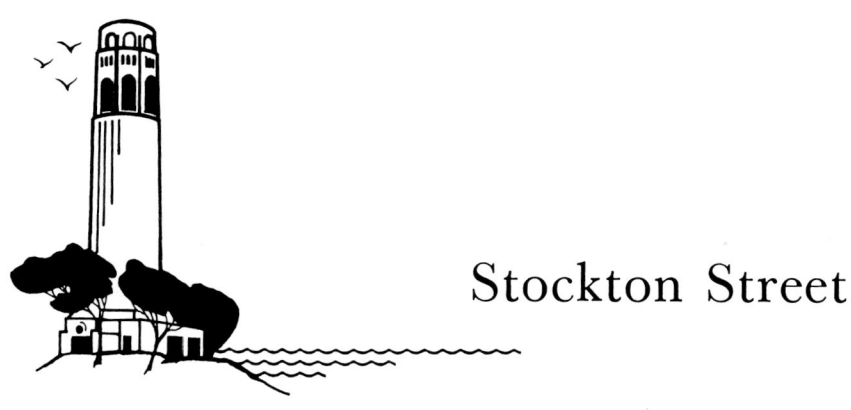

Stockton Street

Stockton Street was important in early San Francisco because of its pioneer hospitals and other institutions. Taking over the former American Hotel, the State Marine Hospital opened its doors on June 30, 1853. The name was later changed to the Hospital of the Sisters of Mercy and its renumbered address was 1316 Stockton. About 20 sisters cared for some 35 patients each month. In December 1861 the hospital moved to Rincon Hill to become St. Mary's, a hospital which now operates at a different location.

It was at the American Hotel that the Reverend Dr. Ver Mehr, the first California missionary of the Episcopal Church, preached his initial sermon in September 1849. Subsequently services were conducted for a few months at Frank Ward's "palatial residence," also on Stockton near Green. Near-by at 376 Stockton, now the 1500 block between Green and Union, was the San Francisco Bible Society, which had "issued" 8594 Bibles in various languages in the five years after its founding by John M. Finley and others on October 30, 1849. By 1861 it had become the California Bible Society and was at 20 Montgomery Street.

Near the corner was Washington Square Hall, erected in the 1890s by the Italian Bersaglieri Mutual Benefit Society, which was used for local meetings. During the Prohibition era several night clubs were flourishing in this vicinity, so the police declared "open war" on them in March 1927. Raided were the Silver Slipper at 1516 Stockton Street (rated the "swankiest," as its patrons were in evening clothes), The Studio around the corner at 683 Green Street and several others.

Beyond Filbert Street, almost in the middle of the block, is the Maybeck Building, a two-story frame office building which for many years was the home of the Telegraph Hill Neighborhood Association.

The association had its beginning in 1888 when two ladies set out to help impoverished immigrants in the city. Elizabeth H. Ashe, the daughter of a North Carolina doctor (Asheville is named for his grandfather) who came to California in 1849, was born twenty years after his arrival. Strong and full of ideas, Miss Ashe was a very dynamic person who started talking when she entered a room, with the result that no one else had a chance. Her associate, Alice S. Griffith, a lady of firm convictions, was born in San Francisco in 1865. Her father, Millen Griffith, also arrived in San Francisco in 1849. Capitalizing on the needs of the harbor, he operated a lighter business which soon branched into a fleet of tug boats, eventually becoming part of Goodall, Nelson & Perkins (Red Stack Tugs). In addition he was a partner in the Pacific Steam Whaling Company.

In February 1890 Alice Griffith, Elizabeth Ashe and eight other ladies formed the Willing Circle, which shortly became the City Front Association, offering housekeeping classes at the Pioneer Kindergarten in Silver Star Hall at Sansome and Pacific. A few years later the City Front Boys Club was established in rooms over the Ghirardelli Chocolate Co. on Sansome Street.

The war with Spain, while disrupting the club, persuaded Miss Ashe to study nursing at the Presbyterian Hospital in New York. On her return, the Telegraph Hill Neighborhood House was established in December 1902 at the crest of Vallejo (No. 427) with Miss Griffith in charge. Initially only first-aid treatments and housekeep-

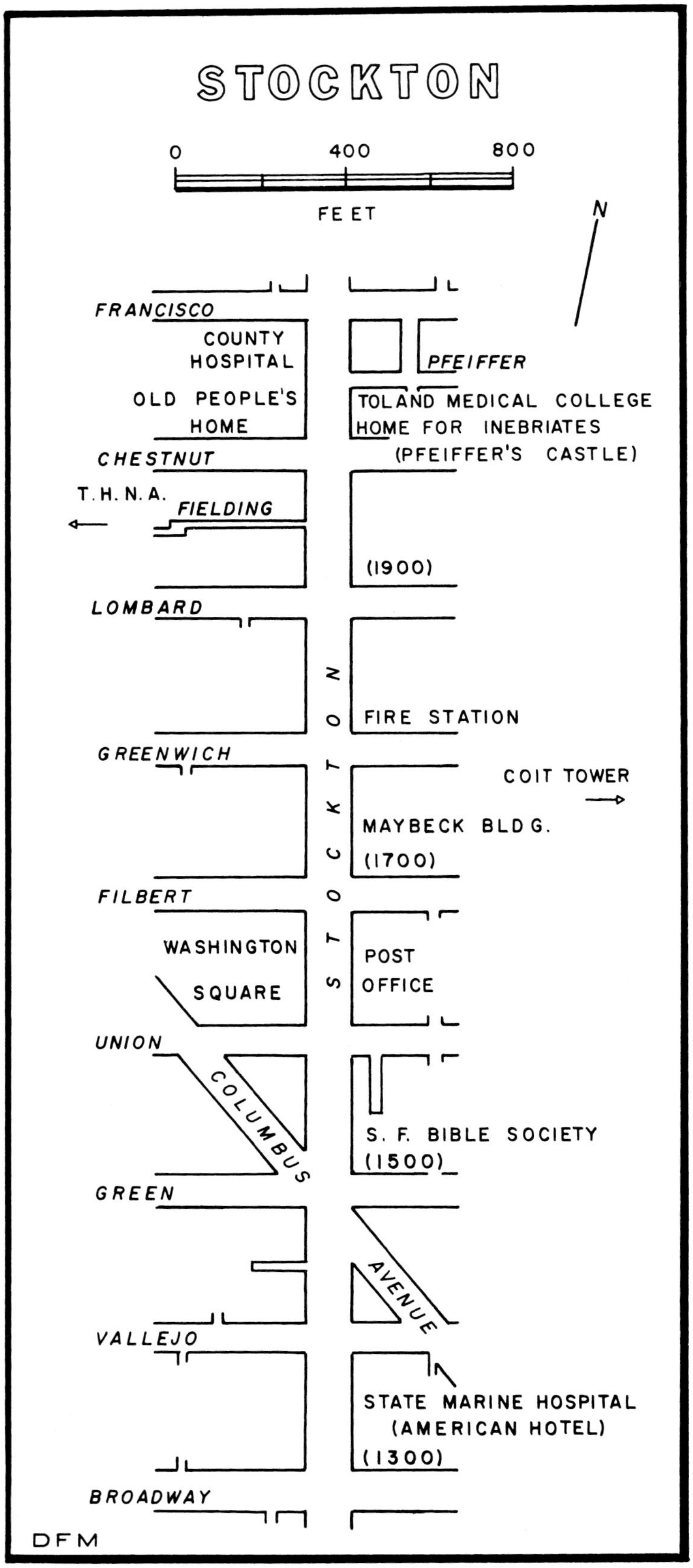

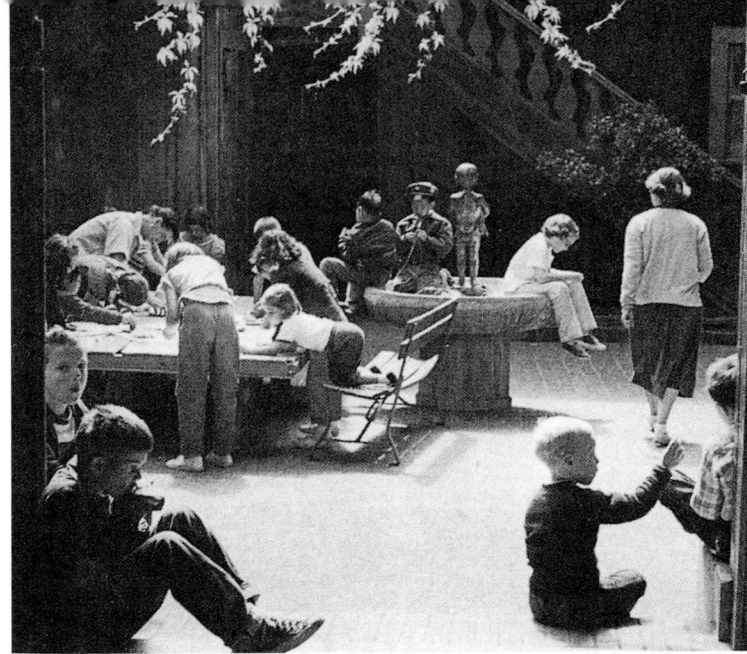

Children play around the fountain in the court of the Neighborhood House on Stockton Street in the summer of 1953. (—E. M. Griffith collection)

ing classes were conducted here, but gradually all activities were transferred from Silver Star Hall.

Once their suspicions had been overcome, people responded to the Neighborhood House. Gifts of all kinds appeared, principally fish, fruit and vegetables. Impressed by the work of this settlement house, Miss Daisy Johnson became the second trained nurse. She asked no compensation but allowed she would need a little help after her $600 savings were exhausted.

Mrs. Norman McLaren, a board member and Miss Ashe's sister, was shocked to learn that the new nurse was to work without pay. As there were no funds available, she wrote a cookbook of receipts gathered from Telegraph Hill kitchens. The book, *High Living — Receipts from Southern Climes*, was published in 1904 and raised $1080.54 the first year, thus providing for Miss Johnson's modest salary. Reprinted after the fire, the cookbook sold regularly for many years and Miss Johnson, a slim little woman, continued to work until shortly before her death at the age of 82. Mrs. McLaren raised funds in other ways for the association, which for the first few years had an annual budget of about $4000.

Many activities such as the Telegraph Hill Sorosis Club, an evening club for working girls, were held at the Neighborhood House, and chil-

Stockton Street just north of Filbert. In the middle of the block on the right is the Maybeck Building.

dren went to the country under the association's auspices. Sixteen boys established a model town called City of Telhi when they were sent to the summer resort of Glen Ellen in 1904. Government consisted of eleven rules, including "No spitting or swearing in the tents" and "Everybody who is not pleased with the meals must appeal to the Council or Mayor." For the next several years, Henry E. Bothin generously made available the Hill Farm, near Fairfax in Marin County, for a summer camp. Here many children experienced country atmosphere for the first time.

A new Neighborhood House was built at 650 Filbert Street (Washington Square), although the dispensary remained at 536 Green Street, and in April 1905 the five Girls' Clubs were the first groups to use the new facility. As the stature of the Telegraph Hill Neighborhood Association grew, it attracted greater interest from well-known San Francisco families and its volunteer medical staff included such men as Dr. Langley Porter and Dr. Walter Scott Franklin. Although the 1906 fire swept away all material accomplishments, the spirit remained alive, and the staff and volunteers were active in rehabilitation work both in Washington Square and Pioneer Park. In the latter place the city Board of Health erected a small shack for use as a dispensary under the direction of Miss Ashe, not an easy assignment after the fire: "on the summit of the hill congregated many of the worst elements from the narrow streets and alleys of Telegraph Hill," wrote Alice Griffith in the 1907 report of the association.

Looking to the future, the directors bought a lot on Stockton Street in August 1906 for $5000, of which $4000 was borrowed from the Donohoe-Kelly Bank. Donations from the East and more loans from the bank enabled the association to erect a Neighborhood House and dispensary at 1734-1736 Stockton Street. Architect Bernard Maybeck drew the plans and the facility was completed in 1907 for $19,000 including lot.

After the temporary cottages were removed from Washington Square that same August, the association moved ten cottages to the former church lot at Filbert and Stockton, which it had leased for three years for this purpose.

The activities and services of the Telegraph Hill Neighborhood Association were varied. In addition to homemaking classes and the health clinic (over 7000 cases were recorded in 1913, including 2152 house calls), vigorous efforts were made to combat bad housing conditions. Mrs. Maud M. W. Clark organized the Neighborhood Improvement Club in October 1907 to interest mothers in civic matters in the neighborhood.

Stockton and Powell streets frame Washington Square in this picture taken from Coit Tower. Columbus Avenue is the only diagonal street in this part of the city. To the right are the spires of SS. Peter and Paul's Church on Filbert Street.

Social activities for boys and girls were conducted, sometimes under trying conditions. During the first two years after the fire, "the boys were absolutely lawless . . . wantonly destroyed everything in sight, stole whatever they could lay their hands on." It was necessary to expel one club of forty members and refuse reinstatement in spite of pleas for another chance. This firm action worked; gradually the realization spread that good conduct was a prerequisite for participation in the Neighborhood House activities.

In 1909, thanks to a generous donation from Mrs. William Irwin, wife of the author, a library was added — again designed by Maybeck — and the next year a miniature hospital was established in the dispensary.

In 1920, the organization was amalgamated with The People's Place, a settlement house at 555 Chestnut, to become briefly the San Francisco Neighborhood Association until reverting to the former name.

The Neighborhood House continues its services, supported by the community and by annual domino tournaments, fashion shows and other money-raising events sponsored by the Telegraph Hill Neighborhood Association Auxiliary. Lack of funds delayed the long-anticipated construction of larger quarters and a gymnasium on the enlarged lot extending from 555 Chestnut across the block to 660 Lombard Street. Elizabeth Ashe died only a few months before the new building was opened in May 1954, but Alice Griffith was there. Unusually strong for a lady in her later years, she walked downtown almost every day until shortly before her death at the age of 94.

Some eighty years ago a cautious person crossing Greenwich Street would have peered in both directions for cable cars; now one should watch for fire engines dashing out of Engine Co. 28. A fire house has been at this location since the early 1860s, when Crescent Engine Co. No. 10 moved its quarters from Pacific Avenue, east of Kearny, to Stockton Street, just north of Greenwich. Equipment consisted of a Second Class Engine, built by Cowing & Co. of Seneca Falls, New York, and a two-wheel hose cart, both housed in a two-story brick building. When the city fire department was established in December 1867, this station became San Francisco Hose Co. No. 4. Probably the firemen whiled away some idle moments chatting with neighbors in the grocery store at the southwest corner of Greenwich and Stockton when it was owned by John Puvogel in 1869.

Where Stockton crossed Chestnut, it entered the area of benevolence which prevailed on both sides of the street during the last century. True,

(Above) It is high noon on Stockton Street looking downtown. Filbert Street forms the first intersection.

Across Pfeiffer Street was the site of Toland Medical College. The four-story apartment stands where Pfeiffer's Castle once was.

the Barbary Coast was scarcely eight blocks away and there was an ample selection of saloons in close proximity, but in this area were a number of institutions with different objectives.

At the northeast corner was the Home for the Care of Inebriates, supported by civic-minded citizens who bought the former Pfeiffer Castle in July 1862. This organization, founded three years before, had the famed Unitarian minister, Thomas Starr King, on its board and had already treated 1200 people. The quarters were enlarged in 1877 and again in 1885, but about the turn of the century the building became the Pacific Hospital, operated by the Christian Hospital Association. Also facing Stockton on the adjoining lot, 42½ feet wide and terminating at Pfeiffer Street, was the only college in the Telegraph Hill-North Beach area.

Hugh Huger Toland (1806-1880) of South Carolina, received his medical training in Lexington, Kentucky, and Paris. Although he had built up a profitable practice in his native state, the lure of California gold was too much to resist, so he came to California in 1852. However, instead of being penniless, the newcomer's usual status, Toland arrived in Mokelumne Hill with enough money to buy a mine and had the foresight to arrange for a quartz crusher to be at the mine.

Toland soon recognized his inability at mining and returned to medicine before going through his fortune. Establishing an office and drugstore in Naglee's Building at Montgomery and Merchant streets, Dr. Toland arranged his schedule to see private patients in the morning, and in the afternoon his office became a clinic. Soon the word spread that no charge was made for clinical examinations and the doctor was busy every afternoon. Leaving the clinic, there was only one way out — through the Toland pharmacy. Partly because of its location and partly because no one else could read Dr. Toland's prescriptions, the drugstore enjoyed a booming business. By 1860 Toland was reported to have an annual income of $40,000 from his medical practice, for in addition to his office calls he did a thriving business by mail. From isolated mining camps in California and Nevada people wrote him describing their symptoms, and the prescribed medicines were dispatched express collect via Wells Fargo.

Behind this group, presumably the staff and perhaps the guests, the long stairway leads to the Inebriates home, the former Pfeiffer's Castle. (—*California Historical Society*)

With an income said to be larger than anyone else in the San Francisco medical profession, plus a prosperous ranch in the Sacramento River bottom lands, Dr. Toland was ready for other things. A medical school, initiated in 1858 under the auspices of the University of Pacific, was in the doldrums after the death of its founder in 1862. So when Dr. Toland began to formulate his plans for a medical school, the old facility suspended its operations while the staff joined the Toland Medical College. Financed by Dr. Toland, an imposing three-story structure rose on the narrow Stockton Street lot. A belfry on top added identification, and with that instruction began there in November 1864.

Things went well for six years, but then a difference of views on policy undermined the medical school and Dr. Levi C. Lane, in the role of Pied Piper, drew the entire staff and all but one of the students away from the Toland Medical College. Having personally put $75,000 into the school and now about to witness the entire project threatened with extinction, Dr. Toland took matters in hand, and after some persuasion a number of the defecting students and faculty returned. (Dr. Lane refused to return; eventually his Lane Hospital became part of the Stanford Medical School.)

The University of California, which opened its doors in the fall of 1869, began affiliating with Toland Medical College in June 1870. Dr. Toland was about to convey the entire property to the university, but the condition that the name remain unchanged was unacceptable to the latter. Finally in March 1873, after a compromise had been effected by which an academic chair was named for him, Dr. Toland turned the school over to the university. Until 1898 this was the medical school of the University of California; after that date it was moved to Parnassus Heights.

Although Dr. Toland was known for his competent bone surgery, he also wrote a prodigious number of prescriptions. Each of these was pasted in a book, and when that book was filled it was filed on a shelf in the pharmacy. Over a 15-year period, the count was a phenomenal 581,000 prescriptions. No wonder when Dr. Toland died, he left an estate of almost $2,000,000!

On the opposite side of Stockton Street were two more charitable institutions. At the corner of Chestnut was the Old People's Home of San Francisco, dating back to 1874. About the year 1900 the Home was moved to Pine Street near Pierce and so escaped the fire of 1906.

The playground at the corner of Francisco was once the site of the Fire Department Repair Shop (Corporation Yard No. 1) and, many years before that, was the location of the County Hospital. Established in 1857, it utilized the former school building, which was enlarged four years later to accommodate more patients. By 1862 the average number of patients was 212 with three being admitted each day. The needs of the growing city required still larger facilities; so in 1872 the hospital was moved to the west side of Potrero Hill.

Toland Hall, at Pfeiffer and Stockton streets, served as the medical department of the University of California. (—*From "Announcement of Lectures" for 1876*)

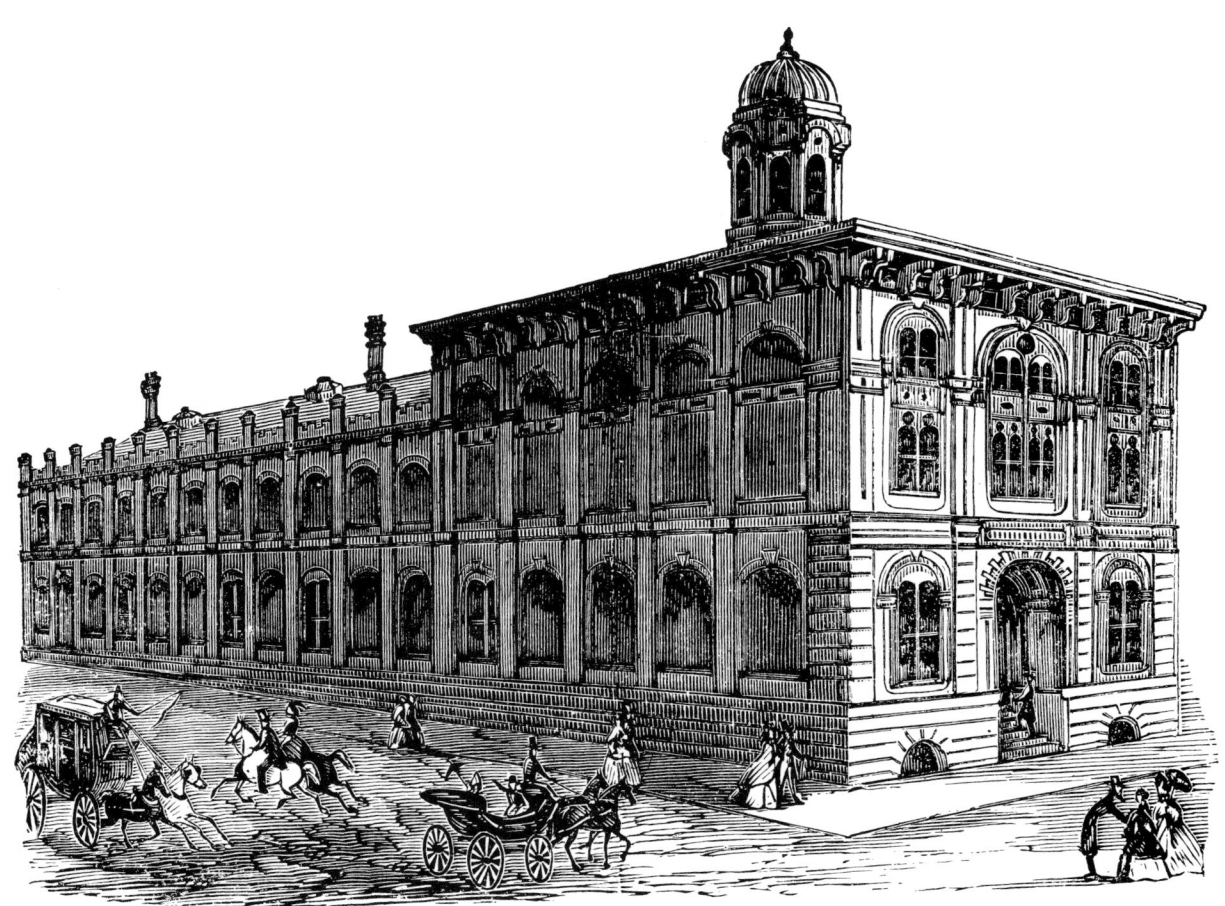

Washington Square (left) in 1865 was a neglected area bordered by fences. The unimaginative crossed pathways were later relandscaped into a pleasant park with trees. Russian Hill, in the background, had its own observation tower. (—*Bancroft Library*)

For about a year after the fire, these barracks-type buildings in Washington Square provided temporary shelter for hundreds of people. (—*Society of California Pioneers*)

Washington Square

In William M. Eddy's 1849 map, Larkin Street formed the western boundary of San Francisco. Besides Portsmouth Square, there were two unnamed public squares on his map: one became Union Square and the other, 14 blocks due north, Washington Square. The latter name was not always fully accepted; flanked by Columbus Avenue and surrounded by Italian households, it has been erroneously called Columbus Square. Adding to the confusion is a statue in the park, not of Washington but of Benjamin Franklin.

Executed by an unknown sculptor, the statue of Franklin was commissioned by an eccentric philanthropist, Henry D. Cogswell. Dr. Cogswell, who enjoyed an active dental practice in the early days of San Francisco and who then invested wisely and well, was able to found Cogswell College in 1887 and donate statues and drinking fountains — Dr. Cogswell was a teetotaler — to a number of communities. This statue and fountain, originally placed at Market and Kearny in 1879, was moved to its present location in 1904. Under the statue is a box which the dentist ordered remain sealed for 100 years.

While the contents of Cogswell's box will be a secret for several more years, the monument honoring the volunteer firemen is exposed for all to see — and criticize. A bequest of Lillie Coit, the bronze statue was executed by Haig Patigian and was dedicated on December 3, 1933, in Washington Square instead of being placed on Telegraph Hill as originally planned. The work received both praise and criticism from the art world. One critic called it an "unlovely group of three brave, bold, heroic firemen rescuing a damsel in a bronze nightgown from a fate worse than singeing, to wit: being caught in the merciless coils of hose that writhe, like Laocoon's serpents, through the piece."

In sharp contrast with the writhing hoses, a simple granite block reposes on the opposite side of the park. Placed there in 1869 as a survey station by Dr. George Davidson of the U. S. Coast and Geodetic Survey, it served its purpose for 11 years. Much later, about 1937, the latitude and longitude were carved on this monument.

Washington Square has a trim appearance today, but it was quite different in March 1855 when it was described as "the receptacle for all the vile compounds, dead dogs, cats and rubbish generally, which can be found in the whole city." One portion was then used for a stonecutter's yard. As Stockton Street was a favorite Sunday promenade of many ladies, remedial action was demanded.

A tint of green spread across the park following the spring rains of 1860, and a fence of rough slabs along Filbert, a ditch along Union and a sidewalk several feet above Stockton Street discouraged horses and carriages from running across the square. That summer, improvements continued as Captain Moore and his chain gang from the Broadway jail graded the park and watered the grass regularly.

Old pictures record changes in landscaping as trees were first planted and then removed. Montgomery (Columbus) Avenue clipped the southwest corner of the park when it was slashed through North Beach in 1873-75. For a year after the 1906 fire, a cluster of small houses filled the square, at one time sheltering almost 600 people.

The most recent revision of the park landscape came in 1958. Ten civic clubs, including the Tele-

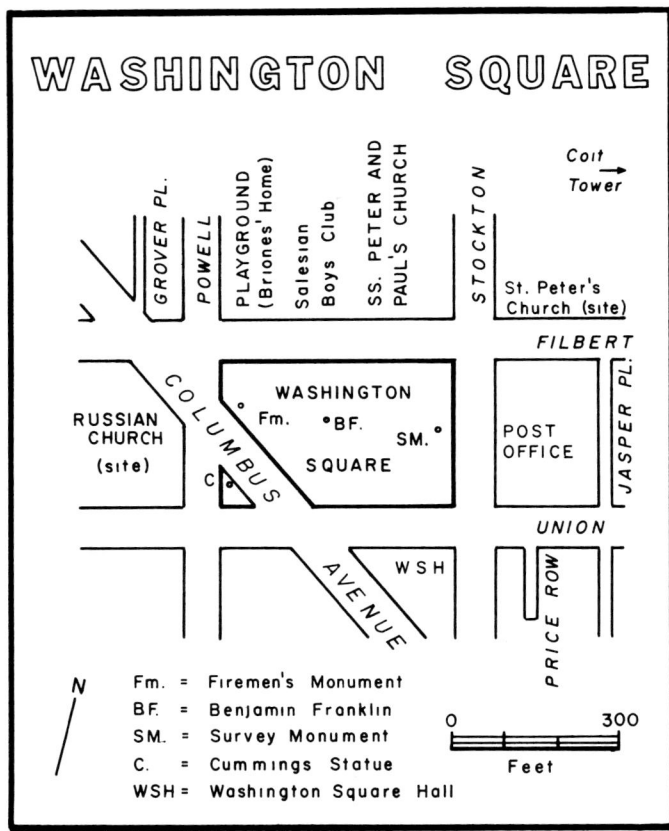

graph Hill Dwellers and several North Beach groups, had been working for two years as the Committee for the Beautification of Washington Square. Raising the necessary funds, the committee hired Lawrence Halprin to prepare a preliminary plan. Then Douglas Baylis, also an eminent landscape architect, completed the design for the Recreation and Park Department. Instead of breaking up the park with bench-lined walks forming the letter X, the walks and the benches were placed nearer the perimeter to expand the sweep of the children's playground.

As available city funds would not meet the renovation goals of the committee, the neighborhood raised additional money. Just before work began, a Martedi Grasso Carnevale was held on Saturday, February 15, 1958. Local businessmen and individuals pitched in to develop the program, and the staff of the Rudolph Schaeffer School of Design arranged for the decorations. A *bocce* ball game, a cheese-rolling contest and folk dancing took place in Washington Square in the afternoon. That evening, a costume parade wound its way through North Beach to end up

Playing games, strolling or just plain lounging are the typical ways of enjoying Washington Square. SS. Peter and Paul's Church and, to the left, the Salesian Boys Club overlook these pleasant pastimes.

at the dance in Fugazi Hall (678 Green Street). Adverse weather resulted in a smaller crowd than anticipated, yet $2300 was raised. With the $1000 previously raised through the efforts of Mrs. Dorothy Erskine, it was possible to provide new benches for the park; others were donated by individuals as memorials to friends and relatives.

No sooner had Washington Square been relandscaped than there was a move to tear it up, this time for an underground garage. Backing the proposal were North Beach merchants, but studies indicated that the proposed 535-car garage would not only be expensive but would also lose money. In spite of these findings, the supervisors passed the measure by a six-to-five vote. When it came to Mayor John F. Shelley, he said that the proposition was "ridiculous" and "had all the earmarks of skulduggery" and, noting that every city study of the proposal reported adversely, he vetoed the ordinance in October 1966. Two years later the scheme was revived for a brief period only to be reburied. Subsequently the 126-car parking garage and new police station on Vallejo Street were opened in 1969.

Cut off from Washington Square by Columbus Avenue is the small triangle which escapes public notice. Behind the iron picket fence is a bust of Frank Marini (1862-1952), a public benefactor of North Beach. Among the poplar trees in this diminutive park is also a bronze statue of a man drinking water from a small pool. It was created in 1902-04 by Melvin E. Cummings (1867-1939) while a student at the Beaux-Arts in Paris, using the same model employed by Auguste Rodin for his *St. John the Baptist*. Cummings donated his work to the city in 1905, and as a professor he taught sculpture for many years at the Mark Hopkins Institute of Art and the University of California.

Washington Square is the scene of many gatherings. In the 1920s the Unione Sportiva Italiano-Statuo Day was held every spring. More recently a concessionaire with a Ferris wheel and merry-go-round appears every Columbus Day, and at Easter children hunt for eggs. Political speakers find the square a convenient rostrum in their search for votes. Adlai Stevenson spoke here while seeking the presidency in 1956 but Pat Brown,

Though considerably remodeled, the Palace movie theater is still at the corner of Powell and Columbus, occupying the site of the Russian Church. Cummings' statue graced a larger pool in the early 1920s than today. (—*J. B. Monaco photo*)

later governor of California, made an important omission when introducing him; Brown paid due political homage to each of the many nationalities living in San Francisco save one — the Italians.

On the north side of Washington Square stands SS. Peter and Paul's Church with its twin spires. This is the second location; originally the church was established on the northeast corner of Grant and Filbert, where it was dedicated while still incomplete on June 29, 1884 — the same day the cable car line began operations. Initially referred to as the Italian Church, and later Sts. Pietro e Pablo Church, the large edifice was financed by contributions from the Italian community along the Pacific Coast. Judging from the elaborate dedication ceremony — even Archbishop Alemany gave an address in Italian — considerable importance was attached to this church.

Founded by secular priests, the church was taken over by the Order of Salesians of Saint John Bosco on March 12, 1897. Destroyed in the fire, it was replaced by a temporary church at the same site. The present property was acquired a few years later and excavations began in 1912. After two years the crypt was dedicated and finally, with sufficient funds available, the building was completed in 1922.

On January 30, 1926, the night stillness was broken when six sticks of dynamite were detonated at the church. The blast, set off at 11 p.m., shattered windows and shook up North Beach.

Three months later there was a second blast, then another in October and a fourth the following January — nearly all the blasts took place early Sunday morning. As police surveillance mounted, Detective Sergeant Louis de Matti and others were stationed in the church and in a near-by apartment.

Then, at 4:30 a.m., March 6, 1927, a man carrying a box approached the church. Police watched him place the box under the window, attach a fuse and stretch it out. The first match flickered out, but when the second ignited the fuse the bomber started to leave. Surprised when told to halt, he ran down the steps and reached for the pistol in his back pocket, at which time he was felled by police bullets. A second man, presumably a lookout, was wounded as he tried to escape.

Meanwhile the fuse was sputtering as the low flame crept toward the dynamite, which totaled 26 sticks this time. Joseph Gremminger, the detective standing just inside the doorway, grabbed the burning fuse and threw it into the street. He then took the dynamite sticks to the gutter to minimize the damage if they did explode. Thanks to his quick work, no one in the Sunday congregations was aware of what had taken place.

The mystery of the dead man made good copy; speculation as to his identity ran wild. The second man, disclaiming any knowledge of the bomber, died in the hospital some weeks later. Though the case was never solved, there was no further bombing.

SS. Peter and Paul's Church, with its altars of Carrara marble and its mosaics, was portrayed in Cecil B. De Mille's film, *The Ten Commandments*. Locally the church has received more recognition because of the Salesian Boys' Club. Organized in 1919 by Father Oreste Trinchieri to combat delinquency, it interested boys in games and sports. At first success was not easy, but 25 years and 132,000 boys later the group's contribution to the general welfare of North Beach was recognized. Among its former members are men who have done well in various professions and in sports; Joe Di Maggio is one fine example.

The monument to the volunteer firemen was executed by sculptor Haig Patigian. Below Coit Tower is the Garfield School.

Washington Square on a windy afternoon about 1934. Full-grown trees in the park contrast with recent plantings around Coit Tower. (*—Gabriel Moulin Studios*)

In 1979, when the secret box under the statue of Franklin is to be opened, Dr. Cogswell's selection of items for the future will be interesting to all.

Two other churches were within the perimeter of Washington Square. Old photographs show the dome of the Russian church on Powell Street. The first Eastern Orthodox church in San Francisco was begun September 20, 1868, at 504 Greenwich Street. Four years later, still under the direction of the bishop of Alaska, church services were held on Jackson Street and then on Pierce Street, until Bishop Nestor bought a house on Powell Street in 1881. This church was expanded and consecrated in the name of Saint Nicholas in 1888 only to be destroyed by fire the following year. Soon replaced, it was enlarged in 1897 and took the name of the Holy Trinity but was burned out again in the 1906 fire. The present church at Green and Van Ness Avenue was built in 1909.

When the vestry of Grace Church summarily abolished the well-trained choir, the men refused to disband and sang in other churches where they were cordially received. From this resulted the formation of the St. Peter's (Episcopal) parish on August 25, 1867. Four years went by before St. Peter's Church was erected on a leased lot at the northeast corner of Stockton and Filbert, where the Liguria Bakery is today. Dr. F. O. Barstow was the first minister of the small church, and though the vestry included some prominent businessmen, the church was confronted with financial difficulties. Accommodating 300 worshipers, the structure was reported to have cost a modest $4500. With ever-increasing numbers of Roman Catholics in the neighborhood, the ranks of Episcopalians grew correspondingly smaller and it was not until 1903 that St. Peter's became debt-free. Shortly before the fire the property was sold, and as the flames approached the helpless building the Reverend W. M. Bours resolved that if the structure was to go it was only fitting that the books and records of the parish should be consumed along with it. And so they were. When the fire was over, a temporary chapel was built on Russian Hill, but shortly thereafter St. Peter's was moved to a new church several miles to the west at 29th Street near Clement, where it is today.

Inviting and Varied Doorways on the Hill

Page opposite: Edgardo Place (top) and Vallejo Street. This page: Grant Avenue and Chestnut Street (top). Edgardo Place and Margrave Place. (Some house numbers on Edgardo Place follow the pattern of Lombard Street.)

Carpenter Gothic houses at Montgomery and Broadway in 1865. At the Broadway wharf a river steamer is ready to leave for Sacramento. In the distance is Goat Island.

The photograph below is probably the last one taken of the Broadway Jail, the temporary home for thousands of people during its fifty-year life. (—*Bancroft Library*)

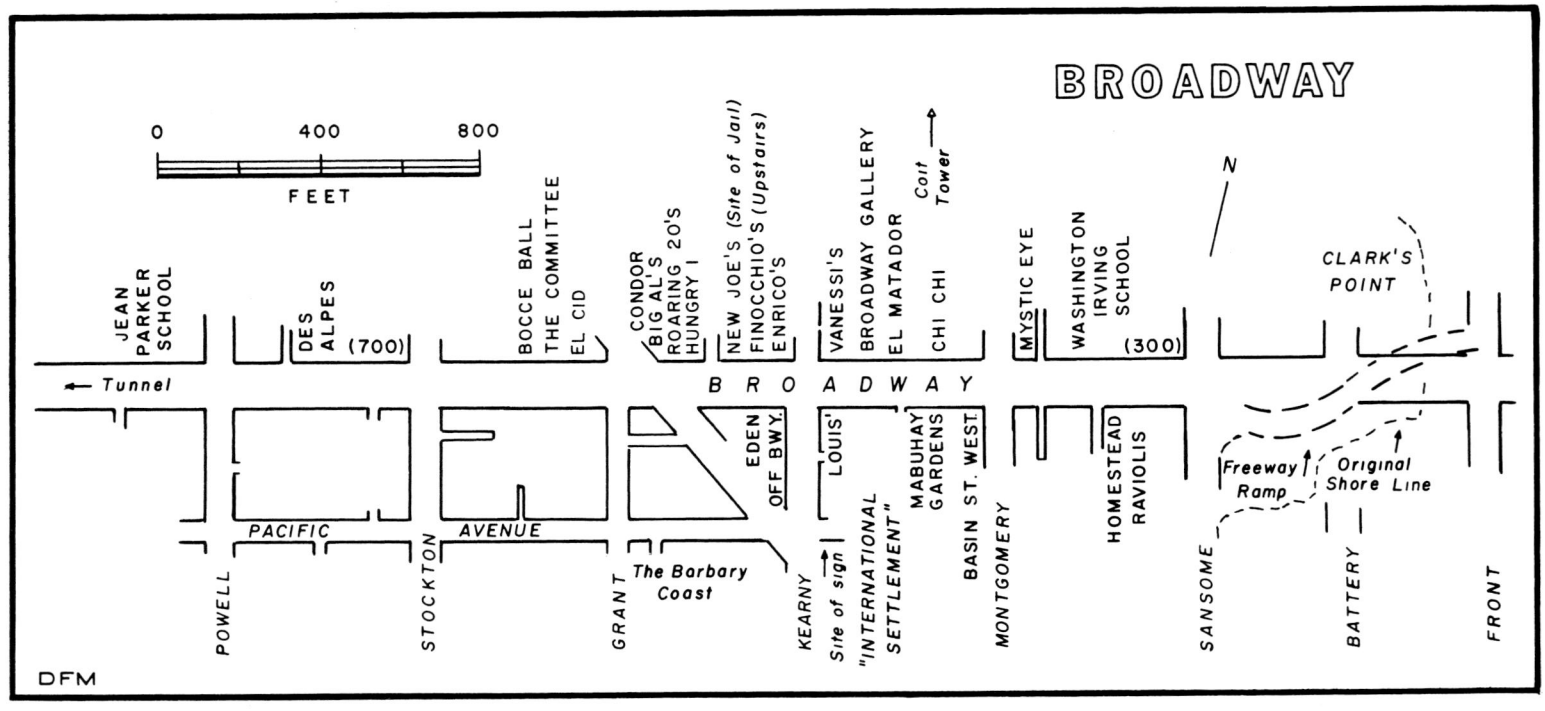

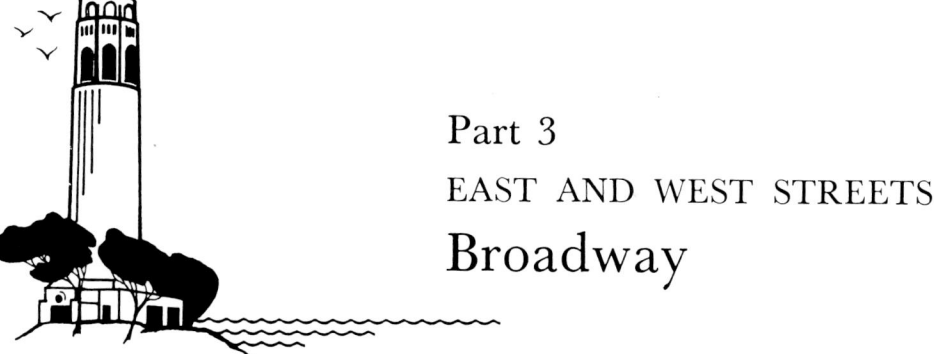

Part 3
EAST AND WEST STREETS
Broadway

Broadway — the very name suggests a wide street, whether it be in San Francisco or New York, and indeed Broadway is wide in both places. Excluding the Embarcadero, it is the widest street in northeastern San Francisco.

To the conventioneer Broadway has been known as the place of the "topless joints" since 1964, but to those living in Pacific Heights or across the Golden Gate Bridge, it is one route between home and the office. Auto traffic increased considerably after the Broadway Tunnel pierced Russian Hill in December 1952 and again in 1960 when the Embarcadero Freeway linked Broadway with the Bay Bridge and the Peninsula.

In the early days, a traveler arriving in San Francisco after a long sea voyage would step ashore at Broadway, which had the only stable pier, and then walk westward, passing sailors' boardinghouses and ship chandlers. He might have noted the house of the illustrious Henry Meiggs at the corner of Sansome, while further on the traveler would have seen men cutting a passage through the rocky shoulder of Telegraph Hill which then encumbered passage along both Broadway and Pacific Avenue.

The northeast corner of Broadway and Pinkney (now Romolo Place) was to be avoided since here was the famous Broadway jail, for years the only establishment of its kind in the city. The Hill behind had been chiseled away to allow for a building 137 feet long and 57 feet wide to be constructed. In November 1850, as the jail was nearing completion, an *Alta* reporter happened by, and he wrote of the Norman-style architecture that used brick faced with granite from China. To be more imposing, the three-story structure was embellished with cornices and friezes of freestone imported from Sydney, Australia. In total there were about sixty cells; quarters on the second floor were somewhat larger than those on the street level, which was in reality a basement as much of it was burrowed into the rock. Each cell was supplied with water from a cistern and waste pipes connected with the sewer. The jailer's room and offices were on the third floor.

Life in the Broadway Jail was rated particularly unattractive soon after it was opened in 1851. Grand juries, not noted for entertaining charitable thoughts about the plight of malfeasants, found the situation so bad that they regularly recommended construction of a new jail and, just as regularly, the suggestion was ignored. Sheriff John S. Ellis wrote in the *Municipal Report* of 1861-62:

> Briefly stated, the County Jail is a disgrace to this city. The lot having been excavated from the side of a hill, one-half of the prison is dark, and in winter dripping with moisture, and consequently unhealthy. On the other side a high, crumbling brick wall, worn away in places in the foundation, encloses the yard, and is liable to topple over at any time. . . .

Regular habitués included the Sydney Ducks, who migrated back and forth from Telegraph Hill to the Broadway bastille according to their recent conduct and the capability of the police. A review of the record of 1876-77 revealed that of the 3474 people incarcerated that year, almost one-third were arrested for drunkenness, a large number for burglary and larceny, 18 for murder, 35 for attempted murder, 169 for using vulgar language and so on. Four were jailed for "fast driving"!

As the city grew, other jails were erected, but until the 1906 fire the Broadway Jail was well patronized.

The Stella Pharmacy's wall made good reading as one climbed the Kearny steps around 1915. The Fior D'Italia, now on Union Street, was at this location for many years; Vanessi's is at this corner today. (—Roy D. Graves collection, Bancroft Library)

Contemporary views of Broadway: (Above) Looking west from Montgomery; the towering apartments are on Russian Hill. (Left) Pasquale's tower stands out against the sky in this view from Stockton, while under and beyond the Bay Bridge is Oakland.

During November and December 1850, San Francisco was swept by an epidemic of cholera, taking a dozen lives each day. The Board of Health met daily, but before the epidemic subsided, about 500 deaths were recorded. In spite of protests, a special hospital was established on Broadway between Stockton and Dupont. E. W. Kimball stepped forward at that time to offer the city a house on Dupont Street for another hospital. The price was right: $14,000, but the terms were stiff: city scrip payable in one year with interest at 3% *per month!*

Two schools on Broadway, both on the north side of the street, are of long standing. Early in June 1852, just after the Clark's Point district was formed, Mr. Ahira Holmes began teaching in a rented house at the northwest corner of Sansome and Broadway. In 1870 a lot was purchased a little to the west and the following year the Broadway Primary School moved into its new quarters on the site. Today it is known as the Washington Irving School.

Five blocks west, beyond Powell, is the Jean Parker School, dating back to 1861. Until 1868, when it became the Broadway Grammar School, it was the location of the "colored school," which was moved to a new location on Russian Hill that year. The name of the grammar school was changed about 1903 to honor the former principal.

The Broadway German Methodist Episcopal Church was organized on February 28, 1859. The building was located on the north side of Broadway between Stockton and Powell. Around 1879 it became the St. Paul German Methodist Church and, after the conflagration of 1906, moved to Folsom Street.

Before and after the fire, the five blocks of Broadway between Sansome and Powell were fronted with groceries, restaurants, lodging houses, hotels and a few saloons. Around 1917 there were 35 hotels and lodging houses along here but less than half that number ten years later. While both transient and semipermanent guests are accommodated in the ten hotels still remaining, only one current name — Marconi Hotel — was there in 1927.

Until the fire, the famed Barbary Coast flourished along Pacific Avenue, generally between Kearny and Grant, and provided the liberal entertainment so well described in Herbert Ashbury's classic *The Barbary Coast*. Of course, there were the usual reactionary characters who felt their sole purpose in life was to defend one and all from the vices that offered diversion to a small group of people. The fire, sweeping the area, broke the spirit of the Barbary Coast and, public opinion swinging with them, the reformers finally succeeded in closing the cabarets in 1915. The Barbary Coast and, soon thereafter, the legal alcoholic drink became only fond memories.

Night life continued in the North Beach area through Prohibition but on a different scale. There were speak-easies and the inevitable police raids until Repeal became effective late in 1933 and started the slow revival of night club entertainment and dancing to big bands. During World War II the block of Pacific Avenue between Montgomery and Kearny was known as the International Settlement, with a big archway at Kearny Street beckoning servicemen and others to a row of night clubs. Along Broadway there were such restaurants as New Joe's and Vanessi's (owned by Silvio Zorzi) or places of entertainment such as the Bocce Ball, featuring budding opera soloists, and Finocchio's, famed for its female impersonators.

When the night clubs departed for the Tenderloin District (Mason Street near Market), the International Settlement became a ghost street. No longer were barkers drawing crowds — some were the best part of the show — and padlocked doors greeted fun seekers; eventually the unlighted sign on the archway was removed. After a respectable period, interior decorators, spilling over from Jackson Square, moved into the vacant buildings.

The beginnings of the 1960s witnessed a general migration of night entertainment to Broadway. The well-established restaurants found they had new neighbors such as Barnaby Conrad's El Matador and the indoor-outdoor Enrico's Coffeehouse. At 494 Broadway was the art gallery where Walter and Margaret Keane displayed hundreds of pictures of sad-eyed moppets. It was about this time that the Off Broadway (on Kearny Street) and The Condor were featuring go-go dancers, usually

The Condor's sign at Broadway and Columbus Avenue exceeded height restrictions so it had to be lowered in October 1971. A concession to modesty was made at the same time.

(Right) The Condor is not without a sense of history.

Something different in the way of entertainment, the hungry i offers "college coeds."

attired in something little more than a bikini. And then in June 1964 Carol Doda made news heard 'round the world when she appeared on The Condor's stage and performed without her bra. Within minutes the dancer at the Off Broadway made a similar adjustment in her costume and from that time on the word topless took on a new meaning.

The story of this phase of night club entertainment is much too involved to attempt even a summary here. However, with the change in public attitudes and the liberality of the U. S. Supreme Court, there was little that the guardians of public morals could do. One night in April 1965, almost a year after the first topless event, 18 police officers stormed into several establishments — Big Al's, Chi Chi, The Condor — to arrest the star performers, among them Carol Doda, whose silicone-enlarged bosom was the subject of many conversations and newspaper articles. Other clubs including the Off Broadway, where Yvonne D'Angers performed regularly, were raided the next day. In all, 14 clubs were raided and 35 people were arrested. A speedy trial followed — after the selection of the jury, a ticklish matter which required two days in itself — and defense attorneys Melvin Belli and Patrick Hallinan by their presentation of the case convinced the jury to return a "not guilty" verdict.

With that the show went on. In the summer of 1966 Varni's Roaring Twenties presented a nude girl on a swing to a packed house that included two policemen, who hustled the performer down to the Hall of Justice and booked her on charges of indecent exposure. But the tide was turning and three years later the "bottomless" look was introduced. While perhaps they would have shocked the patrons of the old Bella Union a century ago, today's shows continue to draw heavily, particularly attracting visitors from still unliberated communities across the land.

Well known to tourists are the names appearing on these signs on Broadway, looking west from Kearny Street.

The Vallejo Street wharf extended some distance into the Bay from Front Street, which passed by the doorstep of Daniel Gibb's imposing warehouse building. Hotel runners with their liveries are waiting to pounce on disembarking passengers to solicit their trade. The old signal station is on the top of Telegraph Hill, which in 1866 already bears scars of early quarrying. (—*Library of Congress*)

The twin warehouses of Daniel Gibb & Co. have changed little since this lithograph was prepared by Kuchel & Dresel of San Francisco, probably in the late 1850s. Although the firm name was taken down long ago, the street signs on the buildings remained until only recently. Vallejo Street runs between the two; behind them is the Fremont Hotel, rising above the new level of Battery Street. (—*California Historical Society*)

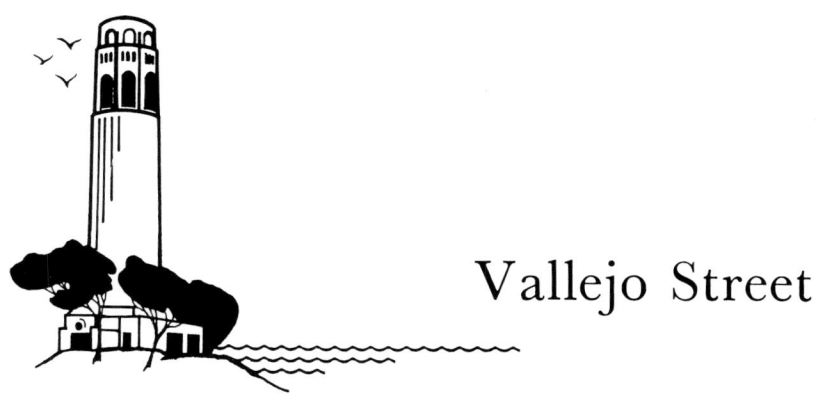

Vallejo Street

Vallejo Street provides the only automobile approach to Telegraph Hill from the east side, although the labyrinth of sharp turns and one-way streets makes this course difficult for the uninitiated. Vallejo also leads the way to certain singular features.

The steep ascent begins at Sansome by the multilevel garage, which was built in 1954. Above this location the night quiet of Vallejo Street near Prescott Court was shattered on July 3, 1901, by the shouting of the frightened residents of several buildings as they hurriedly escaped from a three-alarm fire. In the excitement and confusion, panic-stricken women attempted to rescue missing relatives and only the combined efforts of the police and firemen restrained them. Some exaggerated reports developed, although once the confusion had subsided the actual death toll was only one instead of five persons. The casualty was Mrs. Antonia Taratini, an aged paralytic. After her son-in-law had taken his wife and child out of the house, he went back to carry Mrs. Taratini from the flaming building, but she was so badly burned that she died in the hospital later that day.

Outside stairways had provided access to the different levels of these three and four-level clapboard structures, which were largely occupied by Italian fishermen and their families. Five buildings were destroyed (three on Vallejo and two on Prescott Court), four others were damaged and nearly eighty people were homeless. The flats were rebuilt or repaired as necessary — only to be completely leveled by the big fire five years later.

The last of several groceries on this part of Vallejo was at the northeast corner of Montgomery. Looking westward from this point up Vallejo, a first glance indicates that auto passage might be possible but, on closer inspection, two concrete barriers are apparent, dissuading venturesome motorists. Furthermore, in recent years trees have been planted in the street, which have softened the monotonous gray concrete.

After surmounting the steps, one is rewarded with sweeping views. Even more spectacular are the vistas to be enjoyed from the multistoried apartments on the north side. Extensive remodeling has been carried on in this sector; not surprisingly one of the most attractive transformations is the apartment of George T. Rockrise, a well-known contemporary architect.

Across the street was a sequestered compound sheltered by a wall consisting of several houses and a "higgledy-piggledy Italian garden," to use the words of the wife of James O. Wilhite, who lived there for 25 years, finally selling the property to John Bentzen of the Pacific Ship Repair Co. in 1965. The fifty-vara lot is one of the largest single pieces of property on Telegraph Hill. On it are a building of two flats, a three-bedroom house and four one-bedroom cottages. In addition to the main garden with wonderful camellias, each tenant had a little plat of land for his own horticultural meanderings. When the Whilhites owned the property, a fine community spirit prevailed in the compound; around the barbecue pit the tenants joined together for outdoor suppers on warm evenings. Animals were given free reign; at one time there were eight dogs and three cats in the compound, which was large enough to provide a play area for the young Wilhite boy as well as for the children from the neighboring Italian and Spanish families.

Wood sidewalks (above) spared pedestrians' shoes from the dust in summer and mud in winter along unpaved Vallejo Street down from Kearny to the church in the early days. (—Bancroft Library)

Concrete steps (left) were already in place on the rise west of Montgomery in 1934. Later the center portion was paved and still later trees were planted in this part of the street. (—Dept. of Public Works)

This eastside view from Telegraph Hill on a stormy November morning in 1970 shows the lights of Oakland still shining.

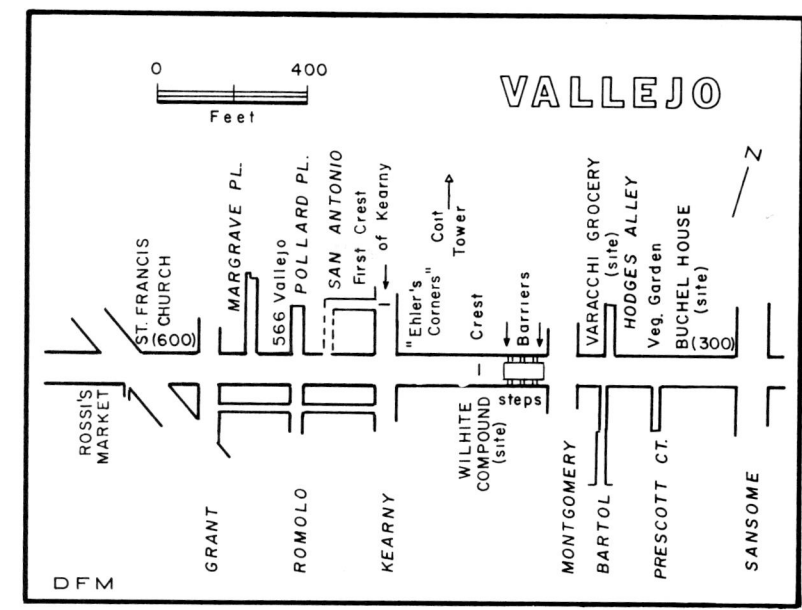

Two views of Vallejo Street from just east of Grant Avenue cover a century. Though the strong brick walls are the same, St. Francis Church is now painted white, some window patterns have been altered and spires have been added.

(—*Top, California Historical Society*)

The balconies of this apartment house overlook the private swimming pool.

From Kearny Street, Vallejo Street rises to the crest. The Wilhite compound was on the south (right) side of the summit.

Dropping down the western slope, Vallejo crosses Kearny at Ehlers' Corners, and in the next block is Pollard Place, one of the first short streets on Telegraph Hill. West of Pollard was a large, gently sloping lot; its interior location, surrounded by full-grown buildings, denied it the sweeping views generally associated with the Hill. When the three-story apartment house was built here in 1955, several innovations were employed: garages are easily approachable from Pollard Place, while pedestrians enter at 566 Vallejo Street; but the greatest drawing card and most unique feature is the private, outdoor swimming pool just below the balconied apartments.

At Columbus Avenue is St. Francis of Assisi, the first Roman Catholic parish church in San Francisco. Using an existing building, the first mass was said here on June 17, 1849. However, the small building was overtaxed and replaced in 1859-60 by the present, brick-walled, Gothic structure. Though the 1906 fire gutted the church, the walls remained standing; until a temporary building was erected next to the ruins in 1907, services were held in the Cooney residence at 291 Union Street. Rebuilding was slow, but Christmas services were held in the restored church in 1913. The twin towers, 95 feet high, are a prominent landmark, and the adjoining gymnasium was completed in 1948 through the generosity of Frank Marini of North Beach.

After Beniamino Bufano created his 16-foot statue of St. Francis in Paris in 1927, it was relegated to a near-by warehouse for 23 years and almost forgotten. Finally a local subscription for the freight charges brought the statue to San Francisco. Placed near the entrance of the parish house of the St. Francis Church, it was dedicated on October 4, 1955, on the Feast of St. Francis.

Then late in 1960 the new priest felt that the large statue with its heavy, outstretched arms interfered with wedding ceremonies and funeral processions. Besides, its 12 tons were cracking the front steps. It would have to go. And so it went to Oakland in March 1961; nervously watching its removal was Benny Bufano, who remarked, "To carve it, two and a half years; to wreck it, two and a half seconds." But the statue not only made the journey to Oakland, it also traveled back to San Francisco and is now by the I.L.W.U. Memorial Hall near Fisherman's Wharf.

"Ehlers' Corners" was about half-way up the Hill at Kearny Street.

Noontime at Green, just above Kearny. Green Street drops down to Columbus, then climbs up Russian Hill.

The escarpment of Green, a reminder of the quarrymen, is well demonstrated in the photograph at right, the eucalyptus trees notwithstanding. The white building on the near right occupies the site of the old fort before the Hill was carved away.

Green Street ends abruptly at the top of the precipice. The home of James Ross, before he moved to Marin County, was at the right edge of the picture below.

ing the barrel staves. Mr. Effisimo was rescued in time but at a terrible price — the entire tank was in ruins and every drop of wine was lost!

Garibaldi Street was friendly; on warm evenings families sat on their front steps until 9:30 or so, sipping wine and singing songs of their native Italy. The older people, not beneficiaries of formal education, loved to while away their time by telling stories of the past, often repeating the same stories many times.

Returning to Green Street and descending the west slope, the visitor passes Windsor (Green) Place. Here Maria Cereghino, a widow, lived in a Mediterranean villa before the fire. According to her nephew, Sil Cantella, this lady built the first apartment house on Telegraph Hill. In doing so she created an unusual building: owning the lot on the east side of Reno (Reed) Place and using her charm and persuasion, she secured approval of the Board of Supervisors to enlarge her structure by building over Reno Place.

At 466-478 Green, just before Grant, was the three-story plant of the Italian-American Paste Co. For over forty years here the firm manufactured semolina and flour pastes, Vegeroni (vegetable macaroni) and spaghetti. Early in the morning of January 15, 1954, workers were surprised when a passer-by pointed to smoke drifting from the windows of the macaroni drying room on the top floor. The fire department responded quickly, and by the time 31 units were on hand hoses had been spread all over the street, twisting and turning like giant strands of spaghetti. In spite of dense smoke, firemen brought the blaze under control in 45 minutes. The inside of the building was gutted and August Cervelli and Michael Maffei, owners of the business, estimated that 47,000 pounds of macaroni had been lost.

Following the usual period of indecision, the paste factory became a restaurant. Fred Kuh renovated the building and opened the Old Spaghetti Factory Cafe and Excelsior Coffee House in 1956. The extended menu had but one restriction: no spaghetti, but this rule soon gave way. Usually referred to as just "the Old Spaghetti Factory," the restaurant has also been used for local gatherings, parties and an intimate theater.

At the northeast corner of Green and Stockton during the pre-Christmas rush of 1962 by-

One of the narrowest streets on Telegraph Hill frames Coit Tower at noon. Measuring 9′ 6″ in width, Windsor Place ranks second to School Alley, which is only 8′ 5″ wide.

standers watched the swinging iron ball wreck the old building of the newspaper, *L'Italia,* said to be the largest Italian-language journal this side of New York. In its place rose the Columbus Savings and Loan Association building. Across Green Street is the famed Italian Village market.

Diagonally across the intersection, at 613 Green, was one of the early Protestant churches. Organized in February 1865, the Fourth (or Green Street) Congregational Church soon boasted of a wood structure "neatly finished and tastefully furnished." In the last century, fireworks celebrating Independence Day were responsible for forty or fifty fires in San Francisco each year, and in 1881 this church and the house next door were victims. Damage to the church was confined to the roof, but later the entire building was lost in the 1906 inferno. Rebuilt, it had become the Green Street Italian Church by 1917; however, with only a small number of parishioners, services ended and the structure was converted to the Nuevo Teatro Italiano de Varieta in 1924. Three years later it

The same location at the end of Green Street in 1927 and some 40 years later. In the older picture at left the houses in the background are on Union Street. The later photograph shows Hoeffler's apartments at the right descending from Calhoun Terraces. (—*Left, Dept. of Public Works; below, Bancroft Library*)

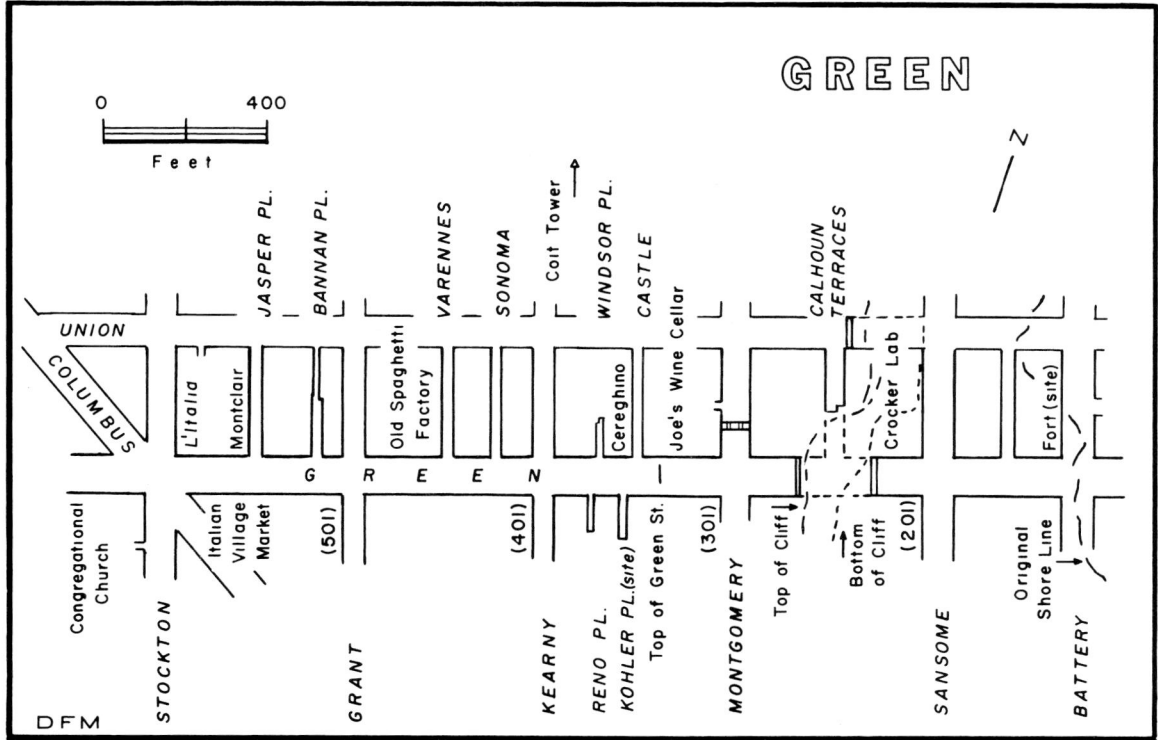

"Joe" Massucco. In back of the house was "Joe's Wine Cellar," a highly valued oasis patronized by a steady clientele during Prohibition. Drinking wine, laughing with the girls who repeatedly sang "Chug-a-Lug" or playing a game called Cardinal Puff filled many happy hours for those seeking relief from legislated drought. There were raids, of course. One took place shortly after Green Street had been graded and paved with glistening white cement; Prohibition agents vigorously attacked the wine barrels with axes, and red wine flooded Green Street to stain the cement and serve as a reminder of the sad event.

A favorite of newspapermen, Joe's Wine Cellar is still mentioned when columnists turn nostalgic. During its popularity, some poet scribbled a few lines which Massucco had printed. In part the verse reads:

> I go to this place that nobody knows,
> That only goes by the name of Joe's.
> It's only a cellar at the foot of some stairs,
> One long table and a few odd chairs,
> A red oil cloth for a table spread,
> And great huge barrels of Dago red.

Further up the Hill there was another "rescue station" of the Prohibition era. Situated behind a neatly trimmed hedge and garden at the end of Kohler Place was a businessmen's club which was particularly popular during lunch time when men taxied up the Hill for refreshments.

Castle Street, linking Green and Union, had three other names in times past: Garibaldi, Vincent and St. Vincent. On Castle Street, the housewives raised herbs in old pots and boxes in their roof gardens, while the men made wine. Nearly every Italian family enjoyed its own homemade wine, a pleasant avocation followed all over Telegraph Hill. During grape season the men sauntered down to the refrigerator cars on the side tracks in the produce district to select the grapes; boxes of them lining Garibaldi Street announced the season for wine making. Grape presses and storage and wine-aging barrels could be found in almost every basement. Friends and neighbors participated in the crushing and, when the work was done, enjoyed a spread of cheeses and cold meats.

Wine making presented problems and, in some cases, serious hazards. For example, Mr. Effisimo, a man of rotund proportions living on Garibaldi Street, had the misfortune of falling into the opening at the top of a large wine tank. Soon it was agonizingly apparent that the wine maker was stuck and was approaching suffocation as there was little oxygen in the top of the tank. Fortunately his four sons came home from school about that time and, seeing their father's legs thrashing about wildly, quickly tried to pull him from the trap. When these efforts were of no use the boys sadly took axes to the iron bands hold-

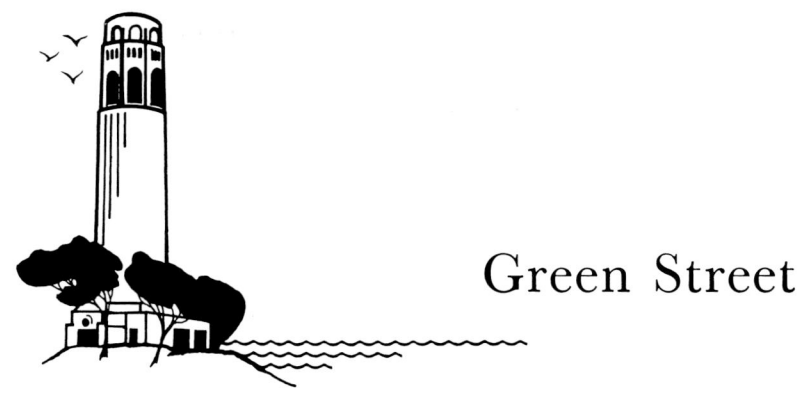

Green Street

Standing on the corner of Green and Sansome, watching the cars dash by, one looks upward at the high cliff which makes westward passage impossible. Now industrial buildings fill the large cavity left by the quarrymen. The two-story building on the northwest corner is not without historic significance; momentous events taking place here some forty years ago constituted a decisive step in the development of television.

An inventor since childhood, Philo T. Farnsworth grew up in Idaho and Utah. When he was twenty, his ideas for the transmission of pictures through the air came to the attention of George Everson and Leslie Gorrell of San Francisco. Impressed, they persuaded him to undertake his research in their city, and for this purpose the Crocker Research Laboratory was established in October 1926 with the financial backing of banker W. W. Crocker, Roy N. Bishop (Sperry Flour Co.) and others.

The laboratory was in the loft of the Giusti Building (202 Green Street). Downstairs was S. A. Giusti's cabinet shop and the garage of the Sperry Flour Co. This particular site was not without its hazards; on Washington's Birthday in 1927 rock and earth plunged from Calhoun Terrace, carrying along small sheds, chicken houses and fences. Children playing near the slide were frightened by the initial noise and ran to safety just in time. Rocks and debris piled up against the back wall of the Giusti Building but, except for a few broken windows and a general shaking of the structure, it escaped undamaged.

With Farnsworth working night and day, the time arrived for the first test on September 7, 1927. The lab was bristling with apprehension, and when the test failed the mood of the day changed to gloom and disappointment. Undaunted, Farnsworth reasoned that it was only a matter of technical adjustments, and the success of the next test a few hours later confirmed his opinion. Farnsworth moved his laboratory to Philadelphia in 1931, and further research made public demonstrations possible within a few years. When he died early in 1971, the "Green Street Lad" left over 300 patents in the television and radar fields.

The end of Green Street at the top of the bluff is an enclave of Italians where the Briano and Bini families own several apartments. The families' ties are strengthened by the fact that two brothers married two sisters. In this area, perched at the top of the precipice at 260 Green Street, are the house and colorful garden of Mrs. Frieda Klussman, famed as the Cable Car Lady in recognition of her work to preserve the lines. At the northeast corner of Montgomery and Green in the last century was a grocery store which was never successful; in 1899 the two-story building was described as "old and vacant."

Between Montgomery and Kearny, Green Street surmounts one of the shoulders of Telegraph Hill. The Ross house and the homes of the theatrical people here were swept away in the 1906 fire, as were all the other structures along the west side of Montgomery and south side of Green. The many apartment buildings lining Green Street today were rebuilt after the fire and subsequently renovated.

Some decades ago one of the best-known addresses was 310 Green Street (near the crest, and not at the foot of Green Street as sometimes reported), which was the home of Giuseppe

Entrance to Reno Place is made through the gated arch (second from the right behind the van) beneath the bay windows of Mrs. Cereghino's building.

was renamed the Green Street Theater and Sidney Goldtree became the manager. With stage productions considered risqué for those days and a speak-easy below, lively times were the rule, causing the law to step in frequently for one reason or another. And then the actors themselves made news: a leading man was put out of the way one evening when two men stopped in his apartment and were so ungracious as to drop their host out of his sixth-story window.

Changes were subsequently made in both the theater and entertainment. During the 1930s, the San Francisco Theater Union offered regular programs, the most notable being the world première of John Steinbeck's *Of Mice and Men* in 1937. A five-year run of *The Drunkard* entertained audiences during and after World War II, and later the theater featured art films. But time was running out; by the end of the summer of 1955 the old Green Street Theater was abandoned and empty save for old stage props and dust-covered furniture. It had lost all its friends and, as an easy victim of wrecking crews, it vanished quietly without protest. All that remains to identify the location today is the macadam parking lot next to the bank.

Morning shadows form patterns on the signs at the Old Spaghetti Factory.

Little boys lined up across Union Street for this 1890 stereopticon view of the harbor. Down below, the sugar refinery boilers would incur the wrath of environmentalists of today but there would be cheers for the wind-driven sailing vessels.

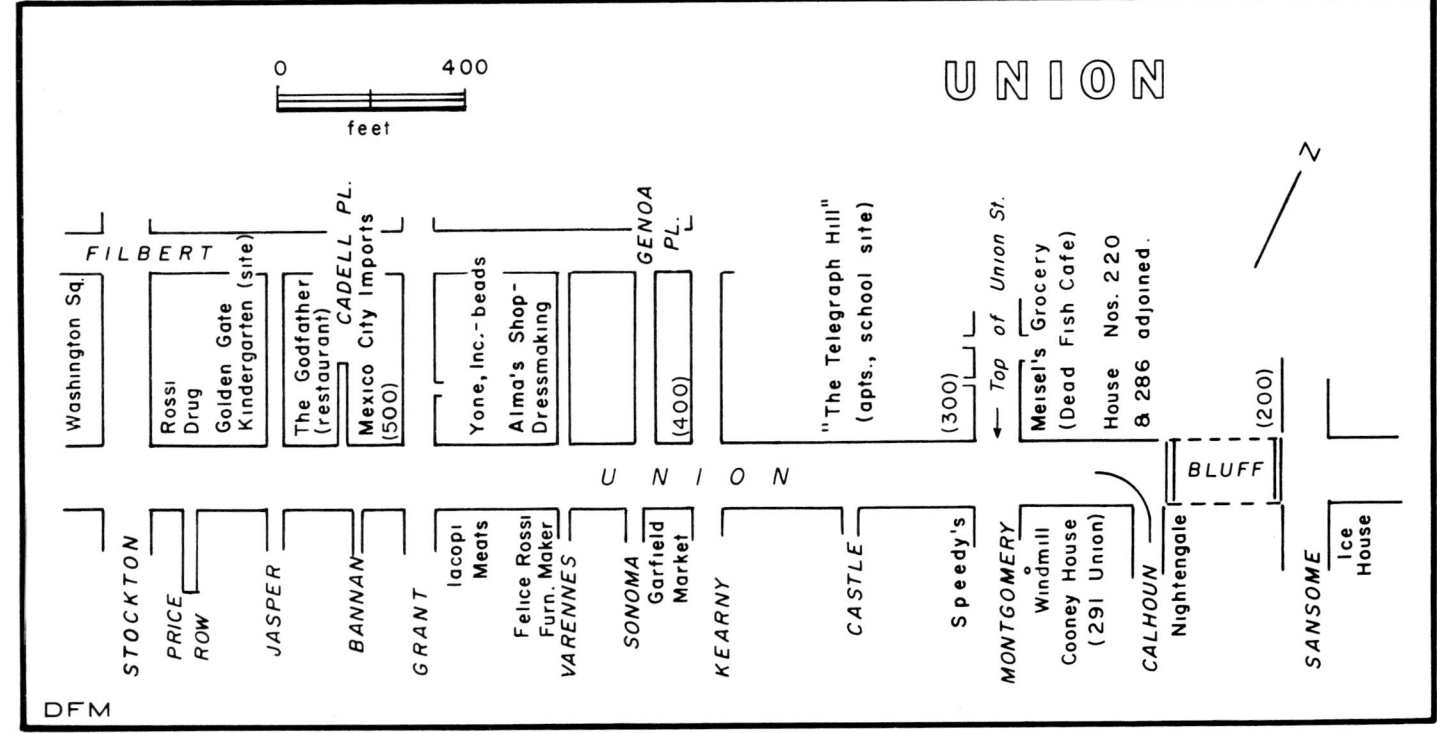

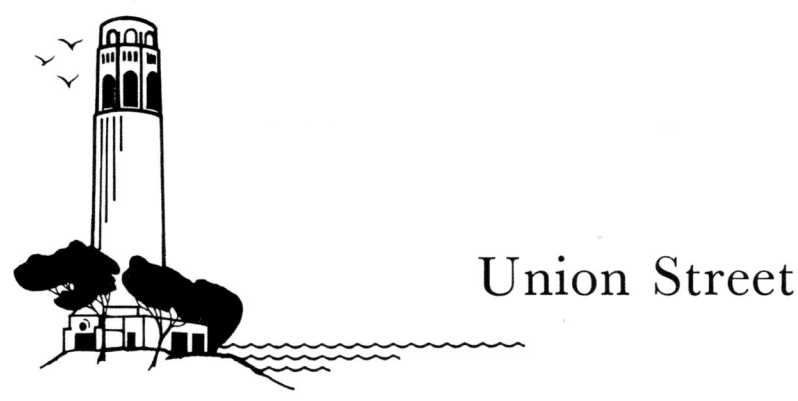

Union Street

On Telegraph Hill, Union Street is divided into two parts. West of Montgomery it is the automobile access to this part of the Hill. To the east, Union extends for only half a block to terminate by the escarpment at Calhoun Terraces. At the bottom of the cliff (at Sansome), Union resumes its course to the water front, passing old warehouses now largely converted to studios for artists, dancers and decorators.

Most of the structures between Calhoun and Montgomery are respectable antiques. Before 1880, when Sansome Street was at the top of the Hill, houses and shacks lined Union and Sansome, and beyond there were a half-dozen dwellings on the south side of the street where the Ice House is today. The Irish dominated this part of Union, with exceptions such as a butcher from Bavaria, a laborer from Portugal, a cooper from Wales and an English sailor, George Nightengale, who lived with his wife and children in one of the two flats at 211 Union.

By 1899 all but two of the houses on the south side of Union and east of Calhoun were gone because of the quarries. Nightengale had then moved to the adjoining house, but the constant blasting made him sell out to the Gray Bros. and move away. On the north side of Union east of Calhoun, where there had been eight houses in 1880, there were only four in 1899 and now there is but one. This house, at 212 Union, was the home of "Tubby" Smith, who gained some recognition as a heavyweight prize fighter.

The extensive remodeling at 290 Union belies the small-town charm that this house had before it was changed. In 1880 it was the domicile of James McEvoy, a rigger and stevedore by trade, but about 1900 an engineer, John Roberts, and his family began their long period of residence in this house.

Meisel's Grocery and The Dead Fish Cafe

At the northeast corner of Montgomery and Union stands a two-story building. Its address has varied from 298 Union to 1300 Montgomery, though the building has quietly rested in one place. The structure's varied uses well qualify it as one of the Hill's historic buildings.

Here in 1876 Henry Toetge operated a grocery; five years later a German immigrant, Herman A. Meisel, began his long tenure at this corner. Meisel sold everything from shoelaces to groceries to whisky. When he opened his store at five in the morning he was greeted by a line of housewives waiting to buy ten cents' worth of whisky for the small flask in their husbands' lunch pails.

Remembered as a grand fellow, neat in appearance and sporting a trim mustache, Meisel was indeed a community leader. Reflecting the personal habits of its proprietor, the store was a tidy place, which pleased the ladies and enhanced its stature as a neighborhood meeting place. To adults Meisel was a friend in need, acting as the local banker when necessary. Appropriate decorations lined the windows at Christmas, and at all times purchases made by children were rewarded with a handful of jelly beans. As the boys and girls approached maturity, the store became a place for the boys to meet the girls and vice versa.

With Meisel's advancing years his son Arthur assumed the operation of the store. The senior Meisel died in 1915 at the age of 65, and Arthur's

(Above) By 1926 square false fronts had replaced bargeboards on the Union Street houses shown on page 164. The sailing ships have made their last voyages and the sugar factory has departed. Tattered ruins of kites hang on the wires.

A family group (right) posed along a dilapidated fence near Calhoun. Union Street is in the background.

(—Both, Ted Wurm collection)

Now a quiet apartment house, the building below was once the flamboyant Dead Fish Cafe and, before that, Meisel's grocery.

proprietorship was cut short by the war with Germany. While he was in the U.S. Army, the store was managed by a man named, coincidentally, Kaiser. Lacking the fine touch of the Meisels, the store fell upon hard times, and when Arthur returned the store was struggling for its survival.

In July 1921 Arthur Meisel sold the property to Juan and Pilar Rodriguez, who had come to San Francisco in 1908 from Granada, Spain, via Hawaii. The store was closed and the building was leased to Juan Ortega of the Filbert Steps for a billiard room. After several years the games ceased, and in 1929 the Rodriguez family tried its hand with the grocery business but shut down after four years.

Next came the almost legendary part of the building's story, when a lively and flamboyant blonde felt she was destined to create a great restaurant at this corner. Her background has never been fully documented, but it is known she had been married several times and there is the impression that she was a refugee from English nobility. The simple listing of her name in the 1934 city directory — Mrs. Honore Gledhill — gives no clue that her full name was as long as a string of freight cars: Honore Cecilia Paget Salvin Bowlby Gledhill. Mrs. Gledhill and her husband lived in one of Clyde Robinett's apartments on Montgomery Street. Perhaps by chance or perhaps by choice, Mr. Gledhill ran a tennis shop several miles away from the restaurant.

Mrs. Gledhill selected the name, The Dead Fish Cafe — really no worse than The Fly Trap restaurant in the financial district. Neighbors were hired to paint the interior a deep red and black. The menu reflected the personality of the colorful proprietress, and at the entrance on Union Street was a large doorman dressed as a Cossack, ready to welcome guests or maintain order as required.

Fun and frivolity ruled the roost but did not bring enough cash customers, and The Dead Fish Cafe lasted less than two years. While the Rodriguez family missed the $50 monthly rent, it was now possible to sleep at night in their upstairs apartment. The first floor was subsequently converted into apartments (as it is today), but to do so the black walls had to be *plastered* as all available white paint was inadequate for the job.

But Lady Bowlby earned her place in history and will always be a heroine in the eyes and hearts of the artist colony on Telegraph Hill, even though she was upstaged by her attorney. One night she stepped out of the front door of her restaurant, offered her verbal opinion of Coit Tower, then pulled out a pistol and fired a shot at the tower. This form of protest found little sympathy from the local constable; Honore was arrested but released on bail pending her trial. At that time her lawyer made news by severely chastising Lady Bowlby before the bench. It was his opinion that, instead of discharging a pistol at the tower, she should have used a howitzer and used it often. If a vote had been taken among the local residents, there is no question that the jury would have returned a verdict of "Not guilty."

The Cooney House and Store

Silhouetted high in the sky at 291 Union Street is a three-story house which is not only one of the oldest houses on Telegraph Hill and in San Francisco but also the first and for a while the only store at the top of the Hill. Even more remarkable, considering the migratory nature of the Hill's population, the ownership remained in the same family for nearly ninety years.

Born in Ireland about 1816, John Joseph Cooney went to England in his youth where he met and married Hannah Woods. Ann and Ellen, the first of six children, were born before the family sailed to Australia. Although they were settled and owned property in Sydney, the gold excitement drew them to California; by that time William and John Joseph Cooney, Jr., were born. Arriving in San Francisco, the family bought a small lot on Telegraph Hill from Benjamin R. Buckelew with the deed dated August 2, 1850. This lot was part of a larger city lot, No. 186, granted by the alcalde of San Francisco to Buckelew on March 28, 1848.

Besides the usual household items, the Cooneys brought a generous supply of wood from Australia with which to build a house. Before construction began, they lived in a tent on their lot to keep an eye on the precious lumber. The following year the two-story house was completed and the grocery store opened. John Cooney was engaged in pargeting, the skilled trade of forming figures from moulds which he purchased from England by catalog. Eventually the figures decorated downtown buildings or some of the grander homes. Each morning Cooney put on his top hat and went to work, leaving his wife Hannah in charge of the store.

John, Jr., became a painting contractor and moved into his own home after he was married. Ellen taught at the near-by Union Grammar School or at one of the two schools down on Broadway. Ann did all the housekeeping and helped her mother with the store. "Hannah never got her hands in dishwater," is one family recollection. The Christmas of 1879 was a sad time for the family, as John J. Cooney had passed away a few weeks before.

But Hannah carried on, and capably too. Merchandise in the store wavered from groceries to "Yankee Notions" — ribbons, laces, widow's weeds and various drugs housed in little glass cases — usually imported from England in spite of the generic term.

Back in the early 1860s a kitchen and dining room were added to the rear of the house, and sometime before 1880 the house rose to the present three stories. The family now owned two pianos; the larger one was upstairs, and the smaller, square piano was purposely placed in the dining room adjacent to the store. In this way Mrs. Cooney could follow the children's practicing while she was tending the business. This piano, a "Parlour Gem" manufactured about 1865 by Marshall & Traver of Albany, New York, is still in the family.

From time to time Hannah Cooney was confronted with problems, but she was not easily intimidated and was quick to consult her lawyer, Michael Cooney (no relation). When the dining room and kitchen were added to the house, a part of them inadvertently extended into the adjoining property as much as 14 inches. This lot, held by a Mr. Bovee in 1852, had by 1860 come into the possession of attorney E. B. Mastick, who built a barn and a high fence along the back of his property. Pleasant, neighborly relations deteriorated when Thomas and Ellen Furlong bought the house and lot in May 1876. Furlong, a city policeman and a former stevedore, promptly arranged for a survey and learned of the transgression of the kitchen. The matter remain unresolved for several years and finally went to litigation.

At the trial, Mrs. Cooney described the general harassment she suffered from Mrs. Furlong, which not surprisingly the latter generally denied. Mrs. Cooney explained that it was necessary to put a fence on the roof of the kitchen to prevent Mrs. Furlong's yelling at the Cooney children playing in their own back yard. Mrs. Furlong made life even more difficult when she discovered that by placing a pole under the fence she could shake the Cooney kitchen. Things were thrown into the Cooney's back yard; one time it was a dead cat. Of course, the Furlongs had their story, principally supported by the fact that Mrs. Cooney's building was on a part of their property. The jury recognized this point and found for the Furlongs; though not awarding the alleged $5000 damages the plaintiffs had requested, the jury did award them $600. Mrs. Cooney came out all right in the end, however: she appealed the case and in 1887 the California Supreme Court reversed the decision of the lower court.

Mrs. Cooney was involved in still another legal battle with the Furlongs, but in spite of the lawsuits, or maybe because of them, the Cooney family enjoyed prosperity, as evidenced by the ownership of various parcels of property. Besides the home at 291 Union, they owned five other pieces of real estate in San Francisco, including the lot and two houses at 287-289 Union, which lot at one time had been the property of E. B. Mastick.

Around 1890 the family concluded that it was time to move to another location. Plans were made, possessions were packed, and then like a foreboding omen Ellen suddenly became ill and died. This tragedy caused the family to reconsider, and they decided to remain in the old home. Hannah died about 1895, but Ann continued the store until about the time of the earthquake.

After the store was closed and as various members of the family moved away or died, the vacant

Tall and stately stands the former Cooney home at 291 Union Street. The two buildings on the left were also owned by the Cooney family, and Mrs. Furlong lived on the right side. The modern apartment is on the site of the Hoeffler Compound.

rooms were converted into small apartments and rented to outsiders. Some of the apartments had great views, but from one the only view to be had of the outside world was through the garbage chute. For some period of time, the former store was used by the Catholic sisters as a place to teach the catechism to neighborhood children.

When Nellie (Ellen Martha Kelly Cooney), the widow of William, sold the building to Marjorie Slate in July 1937, the long record of Cooney family ownership came to an end. The daughter of a Berkeley professor, the new owner taught weaving and was part of the artist colony then living on the Hill. A charming woman with long hair, she enjoyed walking around the Hill with a parrot on her shoulder.

In 1955 the property was sold to manufacturer's agent Allen Lathrop and his wife Dorothy, who continued for a while to live on Genoa Place. They soon moved to 291 Union and made many improvements before selling this property early in 1972. During one renovation a plumber, climbing through a ceiling opening to work under the eaves, found an old, handmade bootjack and a venerable black top hat. From the name and address of the hatmaker, the time of purchase was established, and it is believed that this was the same hat Mr. John Cooney donned every morning as he went to work, nearly a century ago!

The last of the street grading and paving on this part of the Hill took place in 1939-40, when Calhoun and the quiet section of Union underwent major transformations. Only by slashing the second (lower) peak of Telegraph Hill at the corner of Montgomery and Union was a reasonably graded approach to Calhoun Terraces made possible. Due caution was taken not to undermine existing buildings, and the 12-foot concrete wall there not only stabilizes the foundation of the building at the corner of Montgomery and Union but also demonstrates the depth of the cut. For years afterwards, the old garage under the house at 291 Union was perched helplessly above the new grade, until the Lathrops lowered it so that once again it could serve its intended purpose.

Speedy's

Not long ago a New Yorker was lucky to find an apartment on the Hill, but he hesitated, remembering the last words of advice before he left the East: "Don't do anything about an apartment on Telegraph Hill until you see Pete at Speedy's." When he explained this to his prospective landlady, Mrs. Lena Massucco, she laughed and told him that Pete was her brother. Once assured, the New Yorker moved in.

The New Union Grocery, at the southwest corner of Montgomery and Union (301 Union),

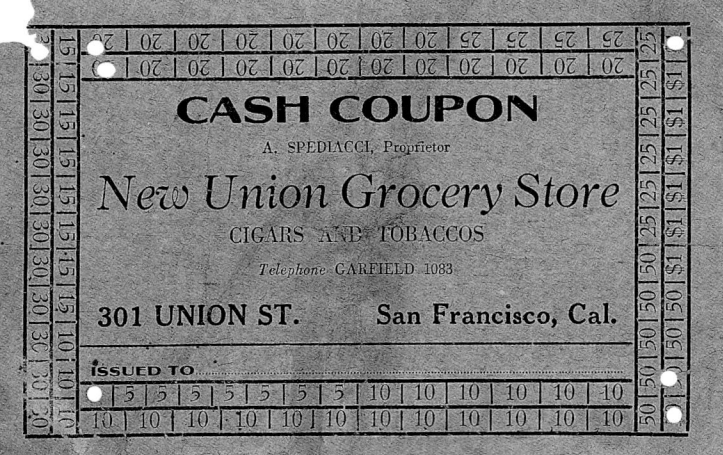

For some years, until the store was remodeled, the entrance to Speedy's was at the corner.

Emma Spediacci and her married daughter Mary S. Panattoni (right) are behind the counter in this 1926 photograph. Mops, sausages, brooms, washtubs and pails hang from the ceiling. On the top shelf in the rear are cans of imported olive oil and at the far right are various kinds of macaroni.

When the punched card indicated cash purchases totaling $25, the holder was suitably rewarded.

(—Center and left, Mary S. Panattoni)

is known across the country as Speedy's. Sharing the fame is the Spediacci family, the proprietors for nearly thirty years. More than just a commissary of groceries, meats, liquor and other household needs, Speedy's is the local meeting place. Here the newcomer inquires about apartments — there are occasional vacancies — and patrons meet during the day or after work when stepping off the No. 39 bus. News, opinions and greetings are exchanged as shopping goes on. The front window is the community bulletin board, with notices of apartments wanted or offered, furniture or cars for sale or baby-sitting services.

Back in 1860 Martin Lammers operated a grocery at this corner, and about 1880 Henry Eggert ran a butcher shop in the same location, complementing Meisel's grocery across the street. For a while Eggert had his meat market on Kearny but by 1903 was back at his old stand, this time with a line of groceries. Eggert moved off the Hill shortly before the fire devastated the block and for some years there was no market at that location.

In the late 1890s Pietro Spediacci left Bigliolo, Massa Carrara province, Italy, to work for his brother-in-law, Angelo Pedrini,* who was lumbering near Lagunitas in Marin County. After three days' work, Spediacci was killed by a falling tree. About a year later his son, Achille Spediacci, came to San Francisco where he met and married Emma Frediani, who had immigrated from Marlia (near Lucca), Italy, in 1903. The combination of personal thrift and low prices enabled Achille to buy a house at 25 Alta, not far from the Bay City Wood Co. down on Front Street, where he worked as a laborer.

Their life on Alta Street was a happy one as the children were born: Mary, Annie, Bruna, Lena and the only son, Peter. When more Spediacci cousins arrived from Italy, they found temporary quarters here until settling in houses of their own; at one time there were nine cousins boarding with the family.

With household funds limited, many nights Achille trudged up the Filbert Steps with a load of firewood strapped on his back. Still, there were pleasures to be had within the modest budget.

*The same Pedrini family formerly operated the Roma Macaroni Factory on Francisco Street.

Every Saturday morning a gang of children would converge on the Standard Biscuit Co. on Sansome or the American Biscuit Co. along Battery to buy a large bag of broken cookies for 25 cents. Sunday excursions to the picnic grounds were the highlights of the warm summer months for the Spediacci family. Everyone carried something. Father led the procession with a gallon jug of homemade wine under each arm; the others brought lunch baskets while the smallest carried a loaf of bread. At the foot of Market Street, they took the ferry connecting with the train to California Park, near San Rafael, or Lagunitas. Or they crossed the Bay to Oakland to go to Idora Park or Neptune Beach in Alameda.

In January 1915 the Spediaccis bought the present building on the southwest corner of Montgomery and Union while it was being constructed. While the other flats in this building were equipped with illuminating gas, the Spediacci flat was wired for electricity as well and was one of the pioneer places on Telegraph Hill so equipped.

Downstairs, accommodations were made for a corner grocery which Joseph and Remedia Garban opened in 1915. After Joseph's death, Mrs. Garban carried on for about a year, but this was too much for her; around 1920 a dozen Spanish families in the neighborhood took it over and ran it as a cooperative. Financial difficulties ensued, so Mrs. Spediacci bought out the Spanish Cooperative in 1923 and, using the $2400 realized from the sale of the Alta Street house in August 1920, she began operations.

Although Emma had worked in a small store in Italy, she was handicapped because she could scarcely speak English. However, with the assistance of her family, much hard work, a natural warmheartedness and a genuine interest in her customers, the language barrier was lowered. Some of her children worked in the store while others delivered.

Emma Spediacci catered to the Spanish people, whose culinary tastes were quite different from today's patrons. Many items, such as *morcelia* (Spanish blood sausage with onions) and *chorizo* (Spanish pork sausage), were made by the Spediaccis. These same customers wanted freshly killed chickens, so live birds were kept in the garage.

Fisherman's Wharf was at the foot of Union Street for many years, until moved to its present location around Christmas of 1900. A sharp eye can distinguish the Cooney home on Union Street (upper center) and other structures remaining today. (—Bancroft Library)

Monterey cheese was treated with salt, pepper and olive oil, after which it was aged in pigeonholes until it had dried to the proper grating stage. For the Italians, they made *salsiccé* (pork sausage with wine and nutmeg). In those days, sausages were hung from the rafters along with the push brooms and washtubs. The Spanish people, with all of their earnings concentrated within a few months, settled their bills at the end of the canning season. (A few did not settle at all.)

Naturally the Spediaccis made wine in the basement. A family affair, grape crushing was a reunion for all the relatives living in the Mission District and on Telegraph Hill. Crushing was done with bare feet — after two preliminaries: first the big stems were removed to prevent foot injuries and, before jumping in the bin, all feet were washed with a hose. Salami, cheese and wine were spread on the tables for one and all. Some of the family wine was sold to a restricted clientele; much of it was given away by the glass to friends. At Christmas regular customers received a package containing homemade ravioli, a jar of gravy and half a gallon of wine. In the 1940s and '50s, Speedy's carried "Telegraph Hill Pale Dry Sherry," bottled by C. Schilling of Madrone, California.

The corner grocery required hard work and long hours. Lorenzo Lombardi, who operated a bakery and grocery down at the corner of Sonoma Street, delivered his wonderful coffeecake and doughnuts at 4:30 every morning. An hour later customers began arriving at Speedy's, and by 9 a.m. all these delectable pastries were gone. In the first few years, Achille remained on the woodyard payroll, but on his way to work he left orders at the produce market on the site now occupied by the Golden Gateway.

As the original store was small, 100-pound sacks of sugar had to be stored on the third floor. Emma's daughters learned to thrust the sugar sack around the hip to carry the weight as they climbed the stairs. Wholesale deliveries were left at Kearny, as cobblestones prevented draft horses from pulling loads up the last block of Union. So members of the family walked to Kearny to carry goods up the steepest block of Union. No wonder the staff was exhausted at the end of the day when the store finally closed, sometimes as late as eleven.

In lieu of jelly beans as a premium, Speedy's offered a card which was punched with the amount of each cash purchase. According to the conditions written in Italian, the customer received a dollar in merchandise when the punches totaled 25 dollars.

The hard work paid off. Within a few years, the store had a Model T Ford truck instead of a horse and wagon. In October 1928, Ernest Chiodo bought the store and ran it until about June 1932, when he sold it back to the Spediaccis because of his wife's health. For the next twenty years ownership switched among the Spediacci siblings. During the Depression years starving artists bought food on credit when both the buyer and seller knew the bill would never be paid — it wasn't. During World War II there were shortages and ration stamps, yet the Spediaccis never lost their touch of kindness. Servicemen, anticipating a brief leave, telegraphed Speedy's to turn on the heat in their apartments and stock the refrigerators. Entrusted with the keys, the Spediaccis graciously obliged. And so the story goes. The success of the store is a tribute to the cumulative effort expended over the years and the warm, friendly spirit of the proprietors.

Known to his friends as "Gatto," Achille Spediacci had a wonderful sense of humor and was the informal mayor of Telegraph Hill. The store sponsored baseball teams and underwrote parties at The Compound on Calhoun. Down in the wine cellar of the store, the Marchi Club held its meetings; now this Italian social club meets on Grant Avenue. A year before Achille's death, four generations met on January 27, 1952, to celebrate his eighty-first birthday, an event that found its way into the press.

Early in 1954 when the Spediaccis sold the business, the protests that arose were placated when Pete (Gino) Spediacci stayed on as a "consultant" to bridge the changing ownership. Pete greeted customers and assisted the new owners, Leon and Irene Wiatrak, while Ray Freeman continued trimming meat on the cutting block. In January 1964 George Atashkarian became the present owner.

When Pete finally decided to retire at the end of 1971, it was discovered that Ernie Thompson, another Telegraph Hill favorite, had the same idea. A former cable car gripman, Ernie had completed 14 years as the morning driver of the No. 39 bus. Always obliging and ready with a friendly greeting to brighten the morning, Ernie knew the names of his riders, particularly the pretty girls. A dinner was held at the Montclair Restaurant to honor these two men, and the tickets disappeared like water in the desert sand. Their friends, 108 in attendance, undoubtedly agreed with John Harmon, the master of ceremonies, who said that Telegraph Hill "brings to each person something more than just a place to live."

Down Union Street to Stockton

In days gone by, schools interspersed the line of dwellings in the three blocks to Stockton; now shops and studios provide the interruption.

The large, shingled apartment building opposite Castle Street is on the site of the Union Grammar School, which dated back to 1854. Increasing enrollment was met by leasing four rooms at the crest of Union Street during 1855-56. By 1862 nearly 1000 students were registered at the school, but truancy and illness halved the average attendance. The city's first high school classes were held here briefly.

Enlarged in 1867, the two-story brick structure became the Garfield School after the death of the president in 1886. As it was destroyed in the 1906 catastrophe, temporary arrangements for classrooms were made, among them being the old store now occupied by The Shadows. The name Garfield School was transferred to the school on Filbert Street, and a modest single-story wood building was erected on Union Street. Called the Ungraded Primary School, it was an annex for the new Garfield School. In 1950, the Rudolph Schaeffer School of Design (founded in 1926) took over the building, where it remained until February 1960 when it moved to Potrero Hill.

About the site of The Godfather restaurant (formerly the Paper Doll and later Rolando's) was the Union Street Experimental School. Organized in June 1881, it became part of the Golden Gate Kindergarten Association in 1887. The association, which began in 1879, operated the Hearst Free

---

Castle Street became one-way in December 1954. Since 1966, Angelo Sangiacomo's apartment building, The Telegraph Hill, stands on the site of this school on Union Street.

The faithful No. 39 bus pauses at the Garfield Market before crossing Kearny to begin its assault on the steep part of Union Street.

Over on Russian Hill, side-entrance cars were used on the E (Presidio) Line. Parking spaces were plentiful on this segment of Union Street in the late 1930s. (—W. C. Whittaker photo)

The morning sun brightens these buildings on Union east of Montgomery. With the exception of the first and last buildings with metalwork balconies, all others here date back into the previous century, admittedly some not without extensive remodeling. Goat Island and the Berkeley hills are in the background.

Kindergarten and the Helping Hand Kindergarten, both located at 512 Union since they were formed, in 1883 and 1887 respectively. A strong voice in the world-wide kindergarten movement, the association had the support of such people as Mrs. Leland Stanford and Mrs. Phoebe Hearst, the wife of Senator George Hearst.

Mrs. Hearst financed the three-story brick building at 560 Union, but four years after its completion the 1906 disaster rendered the $40,000 kindergarten a dismal loss, and only $500 was received in the insurance settlement. A temporary building was replaced by a larger structure in 1911, again thanks to Mrs. Hearst. This building, at 570 Union, was the headquarters of the Golden Gate Kindergarten Association until 1965, when it moved to 1315 Ellis Street and the property was sold for an apartment house.

Fifty years ago there were eight groceries in these three blocks of Union; now only the Garfield Market remains. At the southwest corner of Kearny, it dates back almost a century to when Austin O'Rourke was dispensing wet and dry groceries at this location. Continuing the walk down the street, people pass such diversified enterprises as a cabinet shop, a metal shop, a boutique, a Mexican import house and the unusual bead shop of Yone, Inc., on their way to the Iacopi Meat Market or the Rossi Drug Co., both neighborhood establishments of long standing.

Appearing prominently in the above 1870 photograph is the house at 31 Alta Street. At the Broadway wharf are the river steamers *Capital* and the smaller *Julia*. The latter came to an untimely end when it blew up at Vallejo in 1888. (—*San Francisco Maritime Museum*)

(Right) Looking west along Alta and across Montgomery in the 1920s. The house on the left is No. 31 Alta. (—*Society of California Pioneers*)

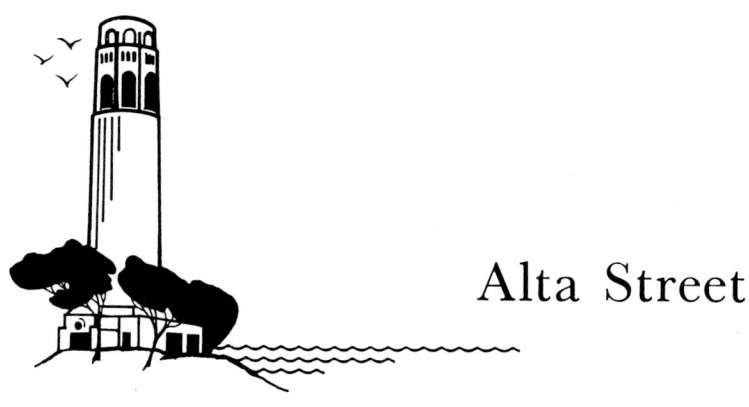

Alta Street

How Alta Street gained its name is not known; certainly there are other streets on Telegraph Hill rising to a higher elevation. But though it is narrow and not very long, Alta is surprisingly well known.

Unless further defined in conversation, "Alta Street" usually means that part east of Montgomery Street with house numbers of two digits. Sometimes this portion is referred to as Lower Alta. West of Montgomery, where addresses begin with No. 100, is the part often called Upper Alta, although in years gone by it was referred to as Alta Place.

Turning the calendar back a century or so, old photographs portray Alta Street with houses on the south side and almost none along the steep slope of the north side, a situation which provided residents with an unchallenged view of the Bay and the water front. For seamen, longshoremen and others whose employment depended on maritime activity, this was a distinct asset. Up to World War I, every member of a longshoreman's family watched for ships making their way to the docks, then largely concentrated along the east side of Telegraph Hill and southward to Market Street.

In more recent years the geranium-covered hillside has been taken over by apartments, beginning with Fred McNear's building (22-30 Alta) erected in 1936. Prior to that time the north slope was crisscrossed with footpaths leading down to the stairs to Sansome Street. At various times there were houses on the north side of Alta; around the 1880s the Moran family lived in a Victorian house at 32 Alta and, in the two decades prior to the First World War, George Morton lived in a small house with a quiet Indian girl. A former English sailor and somewhat mysterious, Morton settled in this honeysuckle-covered cottage and worked as a stevedore. One day the Indian girl was taken to the hospital, never to return, which added to the intrigue.

Eventually Morton went to the great beyond and the shack was abandoned. When inquiries failed to reveal an owner or heir, the neighbors demolished the shack in 1918. The basement, supposed to contain "treasures," was disappointing; the only thing of possible use was an old grindstone.

Alta Street residents at the beginning of this century were mostly of German and Irish extraction with a few families from other lands. Among the German families was that of John S. Miller (Müller) who came to the States in 1880 as a 16-year-old adolescent to help on his cousin's farm in Nebraska. Ten years later Miller was a "black powder" man in a railroad construction gang, a job which involved inserting blasting powder into drill holes while suspended over a cliff in a sling. After several years he tired of cliff hanging and came to San Francisco to find other work. Here at St. Boniface's Church he met his future bride, who had come from Ireland only a few years before. About 1900 the Millers moved to 27 Alta Street, which remained the family home for over fifty years. Now a stevedore, Miller's trained ear was ready for the whistle of the ships of the Pacific Coast Steamship Company as they approached their usual docks (Piers 9 and 11 at the foot of Broadway), for this meant that work would be available for him.

Of necessity, economy was the watchword among most of the Telegraph Hill families and the

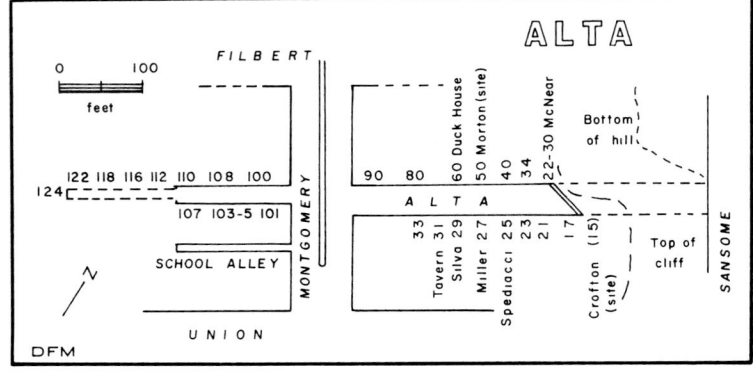

Millers were no exception. Oil lamps provided illumination until the three sons were in a position to finance the installation of electricity about 1923. The only source of heat was from the wood stove in the kitchen; hot water was at a premium. At the docks the boys picked up tree bark, the residue of lumber unloading, and when a building was dismantled all neighbors quickly gathered the scrap wood to feed their hungry stoves. Another scavenger operation involved clay pipes; John Miller dispatched his sons to the Embarcadero near Filbert Street where years before a large load of clay pipes had been dumped. In the course of time these had been covered by soil, but after some digging the boys could return with a handful for their father.

The Millers gained new neighbors when the Spediacci family moved into the house at 25 Alta several years before the fire. While the children played together, the housewives exchanged dinner entrées. In this way the Millers often enjoyed Italian food while the Spediaccis were treated to Irish or German dishes. Miller also made wine in his basement, selling it for 35 cents a gallon, but his ideas differed from the Italians: he changed his wine from one barrel to another on clear days to get a clear wine, while Italians changed theirs according to the phases of the moon.

On the Bay side of the Spediaccis was the Hefferman house (later occupied by the Caranzis, a Spanish family), and next was the home of a German family named Reubold. After an empty lot came the dwellings of William R. Noonan, employed in the produce business, and the Croftons, who were printers by trade (one later joined the police force). Between these two houses an alley extended to Union Street and served a small dwelling in the back. The Crofton house (15 Alta) was torn down about 1920 because of its precarious position at the edge of the bluff. The last of the Millers moved from Alta during World War II and the property was subsequently sold. In 1959 the new owners dimantled the old house and built a modern apartment with a generous amount of parking space.

To the west of the Millers was a Portuguese family named Silva (this house, No. 29, was remodeled in 1955); then came the larger structure at 31 Alta which adjoins the dwelling at No. 33. The latter address was the home of the Parottis, an old Spanish family from South America whose three sons died of tuberculosis as they reached maturity. Later Mrs. Monte lived there and, after World War II, the Landreths and then the Browns followed. On both sides of their family, the Landreths had ancestors who were well-known railroad builders, while the David Browns for many

After a retaining wall was constructed, Alta Street was graded in 1931 as part of the Montgomery Street improvement project. (—Dept. of Public Works)

Upper Alta is narrower than its counterpart below Montgomery. A new building on the near right has revised the scene since this photograph was taken in 1971.

years operated the India House, one of San Francisco's better-known restaurants.

The handsome three-story building at 31 Alta probably commands most attention on the street, partly because of its two balconies and also because of its antiquity. Built by a Captain Andrews about 1853, its occupants included the family of Johan H. Maas, sailmaker, in the 1880s; subsequently it was the residence of three bachelor brothers who worked as watchmen on the docks. In the late 1920s this address gained considerable notoriety when the quietude was shattered by a woman who went by the name of Myrtokleia. The wife of a master mariner, Charles F. Sawvelle, Myrtle sought excitement by converting the bottom of their home into a "night club."

Cards were sent to a prospective clientele announcing her Telegraph Hill Tavern as having "all the atmosphere of the Montmarte with a Marine View." Tea was served at two in the afternoon, followed by dinner at six and supper after ten; a Sunday morning breakfast was offered from eleven to two. The card included directions to the place, the two telephone numbers and the advice that the tavern was open every day. Mrs. Sawvelle, in spite of her reputed background of Russian nobility, worked to build up a good business. With considerable skill in the culinary arts, Myrtokleia enjoyed a moderate patronage, but the neighbors found the "after ten crowd" objectionable. One night in February 1927 the noise was too much and too late; so the police arrived at two in the morning to transfer the party in the Black Maria to the city jail for the rest of the night. Of those arrested, only Mrs. Sawvelle had to appear in court.

The press headlined the story "Wild 'Tea Party' Raided" but carried Myrtokleia's account of the event. It seemed that Elwood Decker, the artist who had painted clothing over the nude figures on the walls of Alex Bigin's cafe on the order of the police commission, had just completed another work described as "an esoteric blue damsel charging through a red fog," which was then privately exhibited at 31 Alta. Mystified by the complaint,

Again with No. 31 Alta as a landmark, the changes between the top photograph of 1950 and the contemporary scene are apparent. A sampling of the "Duck House" frescoes is on the left in both photographs.

repetition of what they said the night before, followed by declarations of what they were determined to accomplish the next day. Chances were, they would be back on the "soapbox" the next night without having disturbed the brushes during the day.

But, known as the Montparnasse of the West, Telegraph Hill and particularly this area continued to attract Bohemians and their girl friends, often starry-eyed little females from the East who wanted to learn about the romance of art and life in general. And that they did; the instructors were happy to recite and philosophize, offering sure cures for the problems of the world. The shacks and small flats then available at unbelievably low rents served as classrooms; teaching aids were *vin ordinaire* in gallon jugs and romantic candlelight.

Napier Lane (formerly Napier Alley) was a part of the artistic scene. From the Filbert Steps, the wood-planked lane is only 137½ feet (50 varas) long, but rotating tenants, perhaps living there only a few months, spread the name of this lane far and wide. A half-dozen houses line this way; at the end is a house reputedly used for shanghaiing sailors in the early days.

At the northwest corner of Filbert and Napier are two little houses quickly noticed by visitors because of their diminutive charm. In more recent times they were owned by a Mr. Kern, a former ship's waiter, who inherited the property from his brother. Mr. Kern is remembered for his two dogs, Brownie and Husky (the latter found when he was abandoned as a puppy near Coit Tower on a cold night), as well as for his old, badly disheveled hat, thick glasses and long cigarette holder. Climbing the steps was not easy for him: "My legs ache when I go up dee stairs. I am 82 years old," was his oft-repeated apology in a heavy German accent.

A top contender for the most outstanding house on the Hill of the older period is the one at 228 Filbert, built by Phillip Brown. Its present owners, Marvin and Joan Levin, have dedicated themselves to the restoration and maintenance of this house and surrounding gardens.

Leaving his home in Jersey, England, Phillip Brown went to sea but soon settled down in San Francisco and entered the stevedoring business; for a while he furnished coal to the U. S. Navy under contract. Attracted to Telegraph Hill by its proximity to the water front, Brown temporarily moved into a house at the northwest corner of Montgomery and Filbert and bought the property at 228 Filbert for his home. Tearing down the little shack thereon, he completed his carpenter Gothic house in 1882. The form of the house suggests that there was a store in the basement, but Phillip Brown had decreed that his wife was not to be a shopkeeper, a policy which was upheld even after his death in 1901; instead, the basement became the family dining room.

Brown's offspring included Ida Mae Brown and George C. Brown. Ida had been a mezzo-soprano. Dressed in beautiful clothes (one, still in the family, was a striking yellow dress trimmed with black velvet), she gave concerts in the Association Auditorium in 1898, and contemporary newspaper clippings indicated that her voice was superb. Her brother George was state assemblyman from this district in 1901, but his life and her career were cut short when the family carriage stopped on a railroad crossing on Mount Tamalpais and the horse refused to budge. Hearing a train approaching around a blind curve, Ida ran up the track screaming at the engineer to stop his train. While the family left the carriage, George stayed with the reins hoping to persuade the horse to move out of the way in time. When the train crashed into the carriage, George was injured and died as a result. Though her beautiful voice was destroyed by the screaming, Ida continued to wear beautiful clothes, and all the neighborhood children looked at her with admiration. She died in December 1965 at the age of 95.

Sometimes 228 Filbert is referred to as The Captain's House, because Captain Laughton was a frequent visitor and for a while lived there. The front porch was his favorite place, and he spent so much time there observing and being observed that people incorrectly assumed it was indeed his home. Aunt Ida lived in the house with the other members of the Brown family until 1959, when they sold both this house and the smaller one at the corner of Darrell Place and moved down the Peninsula. Intervening tenants before the present owners of 228 Filbert included the family of John Grossman, whose landscapes are receiving merited

Darrell Place is a narrow walk amid abundant foliage.

recognition. The smaller house, by the way, is now owned by the Flood family of Comstock fame. Since purchasing the house, they have made many changes, including the addition of the gazebo in the rear; that it closely resembles the design of an interior gazebo in a house on Chestnut Street can be understood, as the same architect worked on both projects.

Darrell Place, running north almost to Greenwich, is also a narrow path for pedestrians. With the exception of one basement apartment, all of the living arrangements are on the east side of Darrell, most of them of recent construction. In 1899, when it was still called Norton Place, two houses separated by a saloon were the only structures, and even in the 1920s there were only two apartment houses on this street.

Among the more recent artists and writers who have lived along Darrell Place was Barnaby Conrad, who maintained a studio in the basement at 20 Darrell. A bullfighting aficionado, Conrad painted and wrote about the subject and also found time to establish a restaurant, El Matador, on Broadway. It was his pet snake, a boa constrictor, that made his neighbors a little uneasy and finally, first the snake and then Mr. Conrad found quarters elsewhere.

Mr. Kern of Filbert Street owned a four-unit apartment here, and almost daily he inspected his several properties. The top apartment, 30 Darrell Place, sported a small, low-hanging, wrought-iron chandelier of indifferent design in the living room; its sharp edges contrived to lacerate the foreheads of tall people. After his painful encounter with the swinging lamp, one young husband neatly removed the lethal obstacle, carefully storing it. Mr. Kern, being a short man, had no such difficulties and when he saw that the chandelier had been removed, he almost went into a state of shock. Recovering slightly and gesturing with his cane, he declared, his eyes piercing, "That is a genuine imitation antique." He then told the new tenants to move out at once and he would refund their rent in full. A timely display of tears on the part of the pretty wife and some smooth talking by the husband about this being his bride's first home saved the day, and the mollified Mr. Kern allowed the couple to remain, even without the lamp.

Today the south side of the 200 block of Filbert has four buildings, usually with three flats each. A small house set back from the street bears the last of the old numbers (221) on this side of the street. Revised numbering became necessary as the present buildings contained more dwelling units. The red apartment house at 273 Filbert (at one time it was 257 and long ago an earlier structure was 229 Filbert) was the home of the Juan Ortega family in the 1920s. From Malaga, Spain, the family went to Hawaii in 1906, where the father worked in the sugar mill on the Pepeeko Plantation. Letters from other expatriates persuaded them to come to San Francisco and settle on Telegraph Hill. At first the family lived over Meisel's store, but as the size of the family — five boys, six girls plus the parents — dictated larger quarters, Ortega bought the building on Filbert Street. While the family lived on the top floor, the two lower floors were rented as before. Subsequently

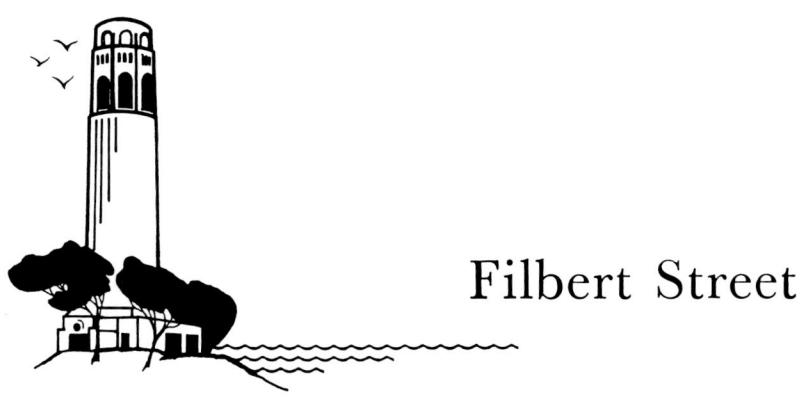

Filbert Street

Perhaps one of the most colorful streets in all of San Francisco is the section of Filbert Street on the east side of Telegraph Hill. The soft walk along the wooden steps, through the gardens of flowers and shrubs punctuating the ground cover of baby tears *(Helxine soleirolii)*, is a memorable experience.

Not too many years ago the first two blocks of Filbert near the docks passed through a series of brick and stone warehouses. Fires have taken their toll and now there is only one major warehouse left. The parking lot at the southeast corner of Sansome and Filbert is the site of one of the Gibraltar Warehouses which was gutted in a spectacular fire that began late in the afternoon of March 22, 1962, and burned most of the night. Diagonally opposite the parking lot is the H. G. Walters Warehouse of four stories. On the roof are a house and a small guesthouse separated by a garden. The railroad spur serving this warehouse is unusual because it is the only spur track in San Francisco partly owned by a hospital.

Well known are the Filbert Street steps which, taking the place of a graded street, begin at Sansome and rise to the summit at Telegraph Hill Boulevard before dropping down to Kearny Street, where Filbert resumes its course as a normal, paved street. These stairs are the only access to homes along the way, except at the crossing of Montgomery Street. The climb is not to be treated lightly, yet it is not as formidable as suggested by the legendary name, "The Street of a Thousand Steps," which prevailed half a century ago. At that time the Spanish residents referred to Filbert as "The Street of Vision" because during dark nights the fearful winds made it easy to hear howling and mighty music around the Hill top.

But even the multitude of steps was an improvement over the situation prevailing in 1888. Miss Florence Finch-Kelly wrote a long article about the difficulties of finding a particular resident of Telegraph Hill.

> It requires some physical exertion to mount a Telegraph Hill stairway, but that is nothing in comparison with the mental effort necessary in finding one's way after reaching the top. We jump a ditch that serves as an open channel for sewage, make a detour around a pile of tomato cans, bring up in a blind alley that purports to be a street leading directly to the house we seek, try a path that ends abruptly on the edge of the cliff, and narrowly escape a landslide that goes careening down the bluff, and which has lost its precarious hold just a moment too soon to give us a free toboggan ride. . . .

Instead of a thousand steps, there are actually only 248 from Sansome to Montgomery; admittedly, a climb all the way to the summit will bring the total to 365 steps, give or take a few (depending on whether or not you count the curbs when crossing Montgomery Street). The most interminable climb is the first lap of 83 steps from Sansome Street, where the wooden stairs on a skeleton framework were replaced by cliff-clinging concrete steps in 1972. The change in no way relieved the tedium of the long and lonely flight of stairs along the precipice of the former quarry; although milkweed, red valerian and yellow and orange nasturtium flowers have taken root in the crags and blossom bravely each year.

At the top of the concrete steps is 216 Filbert, where a brick walk leads to a small apartment house clinging to the edge of the bluff. Its landlady

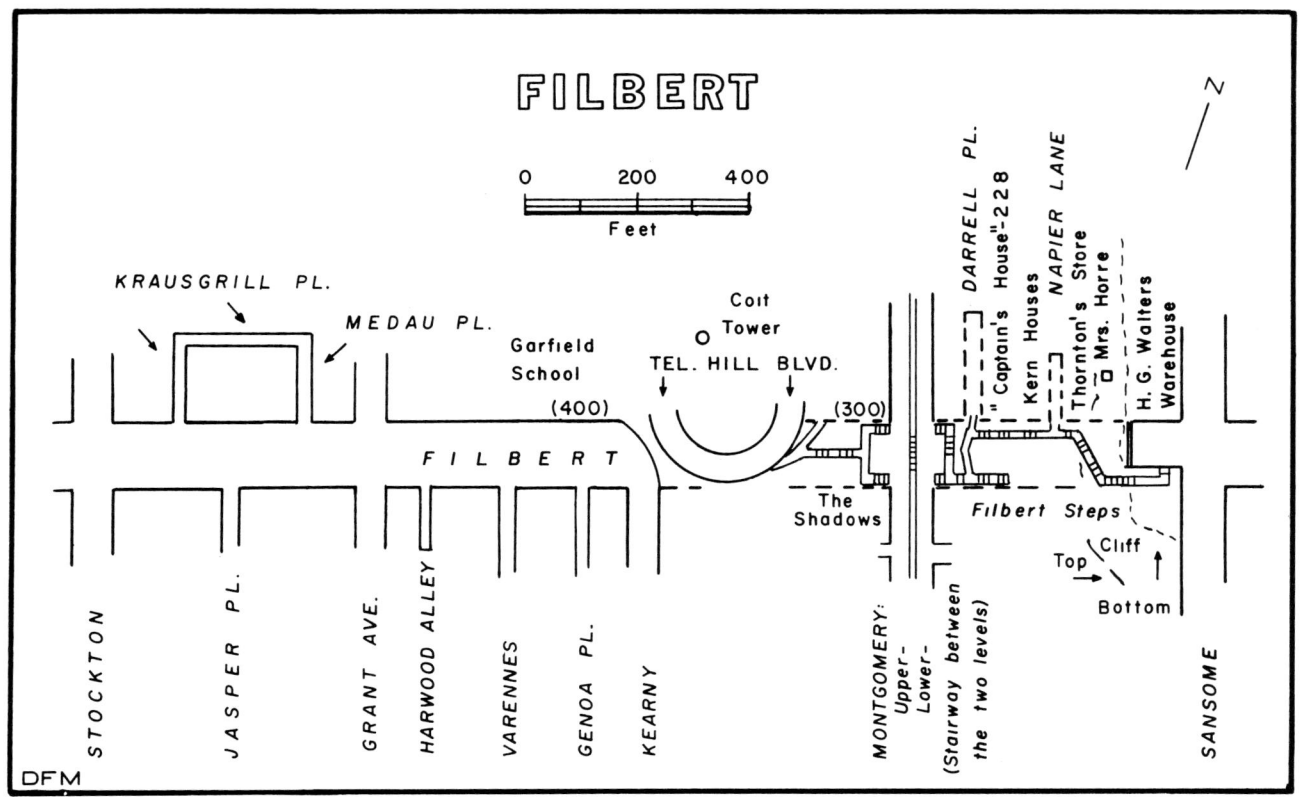

from about 1936 to 1945 had a penchant for cats, and prospective tenants were warned that the felines had the run of the place. Of course, witty newspapermen, who often constituted the bulk of her tenants, made something of that rule; one wrote a poem about the house with all the cats and the landlady who, of all things, was named Mrs. Alex Horre.

A delightful person, Mrs. Horre would sit in a bosun's chair to transform the cliff into a garden. Most people found her suspended in mid-air when they inquired about a vacancy. Not wishing to be dislocated from her perch, she would tell them to look at a particular room, and to those who demurred after their inspection, she would yell cheerfully, "Think about it and give me a call. I'm the only Horre in the book." And there was the famous time she told a new clerk at Speedy's to charge some groceries to her account. "What's the name?" he asked. "Horre," was the reply. Still puzzled, he rejoined with, "I know, but which one?" At that moment a senior clerk stepped up to smooth ruffled feathers.

Continuing upward on wooden stairs, the climber is rewarded by the sight of a wonderful garden of trees, shrubs and flowers generally surrounded by older houses sustained with tender care. Numerous visitors, photographers and artists pause to admire this garden which, as stated on the recently installed plaque, reflects the devoted interest of Mrs. Grace Marchant, who came to the Hill from Southern California some 35 years ago. For a long time she made pottery and jewelry, but now the enlarged garden takes all of her time except that necessary to continue her real estate activities.

The duplex at 222 Filbert Street (at the corner of Napier Lane) was the home and grocery store of Michael Thornton, who operated the shop for about forty years, almost until he passed away in 1918 at the age of eighty. In the early days, there may have been a saloon here; old-timers say that Thornton ran a "blind pig" (selling booze without a license). Born and raised in Ireland, he was a short man, never without his shillelagh, which was possibly a carry-over from his days as a laborer.

From about 1920 until World War II a good portion of the population on the east side of Telegraph Hill was composed of people interested in art, although the accomplished artists on the Hill during that time were a minority. In larger numbers were the Bohemians, the occasional painters and students who devoted too much time to expounding their sophomoric philosophy, often a

Morning sunlight on the Browns' house at 228 Filbert Street with the docks below. Master of the Filbert Steps was Fugi (below), the Shiba dog which was brought from Japan to the Brown house when still a puppy.

Sansome Street (below) was still closed to traffic the morning after the big fire at the Gibraltar Warehouse. The site is now a parking lot.

Mrs. Sawvelle explained, "We were sitting around admiring Elwood Decker's new painting. We weren't even drinking anything but tea and I was making a panful of biscuits for a little supper when the police came and made us all get in that black wagon." She reflected for a moment, then admitted, "Some of the guests who arrived late were making quite a bit of noise but we didn't realize that this was disturbing anybody." Not discouraged, she declared, "We are going to start all over again with a tea room and this time there will be no nights in jail."

But it did not work out quite that way. Her food was exotic, her liquor was good — but her timing was poor because these activities took place during Prohibition. The homemade brew got Mrs. Sawvelle in trouble again. When she was incarcerated for ninety days and was appointed jail cook, she was not disturbed in the slightest; she tackled the new job with gusto. Her fellow prisoners never ate so well, in or out of jail, and it was a sad day when she was liberated. Those remaining behind presented her with such gifts as they could find, along with testimonials of appreciation. However, the Telegraph Hill Tavern lasted only a year or so, and then Mrs. Sawvelle moved to Carmel.

Some years later one of the apartments at 31 Alta was inhabited by Silvio Cantela, who was actively interested in the neighborhood and its colorful traditions. Beginning in 1956, he staged an annual Peach Blossom Festival for several years in his diminutive back yard. Some years, when nature failed to keep her appointment with springtime, special arrangements were made to procure blossoms for the bare branches.

The "Duck House" at 60 Alta Street is so named because of the mallard ducks painted on a yellow background encircling the stucco-walled building. Helen Forbes, the artist and owner of this building, had collaborated with Mrs. Dorothy Puccinelli (Cravath) to paint frescoes at the Mothers' House in the San Francisco Zoo, depicting animals entering and then disembarking from Noah's ark. Later these two ladies painted the prize-winning frescoes in the Merced post office.

As the outside walls of the building at 60 Alta were being plastered during its construction in 1936, Miss Forbes and Mrs. Puccinelli painted the frescoes of wild ducks, which they nicknamed "Sweese." The permanency of this work was something of a challenge, as some artists felt that rain, fog and smoke from the steamships would soon destroy the frescoes. Helen Forbes, after careful investigation, settled on a traditional Italian formula, and these frescoes are in fine condition 35 years later without a covering of varnish or a preservative.

Fronting on the Filbert Street steps and almost below her apartment were two vacant lots each 25 feet wide. Buying the lots and calling on the services of Gardner Dailey, Miss Forbes planned three apartment buildings each with three units. The first building (261-65 Filbert) was completed only a few weeks before Pearl Harbor; construction of the others was necessarily postponed, and with the death of Helen Forbes near the war's end all further plans for construction were terminated.

Alta continues westward for a short distance beyond Montgomery Street. The corner apartment house (100 Alta) was built during 1951. The next building to the west (102-104 Alta) contained several small apartments, in one of which the floor sloped eight different ways, according to its tenant. Residents here came from varied backgrounds; one young teacher carried the same name and was distantly related to Ed Schieffelin, the discoverer of the mine in Arizona that resulted in the founding of the city of Tombstone and the activities of the famous lawman, Wyatt Earp.

Around World War I this building was the home of the Ingrazzia family as well as the workshop of the father, who manufactured ovens. (His son, well known for the restaurant bearing his first name, has operated New Joe's on Broadway for many years.) The old building was replaced by a larger structure in 1972.

At the most western end of Alta, where no cars can trespass, are these houses. Behind them are apartments on Telegraph Hill Boulevard with views in almost every direction.

Probably unique in San Francisco is the H. G. Walters Warehouse. On its roof are a residence, garden and even a guesthouse.

A summer day brought out sailboats to maneuver in the tidal currents between Alcatraz (left) and Angel Island. The apartments on the left have Montgomery Street addresses while those in the center are on Darrell Place.

Lower in the picture are houses reached from the Filbert Steps. The tall redwood tree on the right was planted hopefully to ensure continuation of an idyllic tryst (page 13).

Different street levels are reflected in the rows of buildings along the east side of Telegraph Hill. The top line represents Montgomery, the next group extends along Darrell Place (partly hidden by the "idyllic tryst" redwood) and below that Napier Lane. Completing the picture are the houses along Filbert and the H. G. Walters Warehouse (right).

Juan Ortega bought the adjoining property on the west side and in 1949 replaced the Castro house with a building of three flats.

Gold has been found at several places on Telegraph Hill including Filbert Street. In the early days of San Francisco, the daughter of Governor John McDougal found some gold quartz while playing at the base of the Hill. She rushed a sample to her father and he confirmed the fact that it was gold, but confusion set in when she attempted to identify the site. Although many joined in the search, her vein was never found. Then there was some excitement at Broadway and Dupont (Grant) Street in 1851, but after a fifty-foot tunnel was dug the search was abandoned. Later, on September 29, 1851, another gold-quartz vein was discovered while a street was being graded above Clark's Point, but it too had little to offer except a few days of hopes and expectations. The next year gold was found near the top of the Hill, and on October 22, 1853, a well digger working on Green Street below Grant found seven nuggets at a depth of thirty feet.

It was about 1878 that a heavy rainstorm of several days' duration revealed placer gold near the present Filbert Street steps, and for a short time all the neighbors were busy panning gold. In 1936, it was at this spot that a house was torn down and the refuse burned. Raking through the rubbish was rewarding, as about twenty dollars in silver coins had been carefully hidden and long forgotten. Another mineral, lignite, was reported found on Telegraph Hill in 1884, but no record remains of the location.

Above Montgomery Street, Filbert Street continues to Telegraph Hill Boulevard as concrete steps lead through well-manicured gardens. On the way is the studio model of *Creation* executed by Haig Patigian, from which the large-scale version was made for the Treasure Island Exposition in 1939-40, where it stood opposite Ralph Stackpole's *Pacifica*. Elios Anderlini, a family friend, was given this model following the death of Patigian, and after taking the necessary steps to preserve it he placed it in the garden about 1950. The statue's nude figures upset some people at first, but things

Dating back to 1882, this house built by Phillip Brown at 228 Filbert is one of the architectural gems of the Hill.

quieted down when its part in the exposition was explained. Several years later the model was missing one autumn morning. The papers picked up the story and the statue was located on the Berkeley campus, the victim of students caught up in the spirit of the Big Game with Stanford.

Several houses above The Shadows, turtle racing was a popular sport in the 1920s, with much betting on the outcome, but then the police stepped in and ended this form of diversion.

Farther up the street at 312 Filbert, was a lot which had been vacant for several years following the burning of its house at about the time of the turtle racing. There in 1932 Ralph Stackpole, artist and sculptor, built his split-level home (of which the dominant feature was the living room) set back from the street. In former days admittance could be gained only by ringing a bell, at which time someone would open the ordinarily locked gate. Stackpole's work is varied; in San Francisco the pylons at the Pacific Coast Stock Exchange Building are his most frequently observed work. Contrary to the posthumous recognition usually accorded artists, Stackpole's completed pylons were honored with a grand celebration including the usual movie-première searchlight display!

Concrete steps lead down Filbert Street on the west side of the Hill. The absence of flowers is noticeable but is redeemed by the fine views of the Golden Gate and the hidden gardens of houses built on short streets such as Genoa Place and Harwood Alley. The latter place was the scene of a lovers' quarrel in the fall of 1959 when Bimgo, a beatnik poet, threw his clothing and furniture out of the window into the alley. His departing girl friend, not particularly impressed with this show, kept walking away, at which point Bimgo took the dramatic step and threw himself out of the window, 18 feet above the pavement. The girl vanished and the poet ended in the hospital in a paralyzed condition.

At the northwest corner of Kearny and Filbert stands the Garfield School, with over a century of history though under different names. The fifty-vara lot was acquired by the city in 1859, and the two-story, wooden Union Primary School was completed eight years later. In the early 1890s its name was changed to the Lafayette Primary School, and when rebuilt after the fire it became the Garfield School, taking the name from the school on Union Street.

Concrete steps on Filbert carry over to the west side of the Hill by the Garfield School. SS. Peter and Paul's Church was located at the left before moving to its present location.

Looking west from Grant (above), Greenwich Street descends to Columbus Avenue and rises again on Russian Hill. The noontime sunlight marks the opening of Kramer Place.

From the same location at Grant (below), Greenwich climbs east toward Pioneer Park but is suspended at a convenient turnabout. For too brief a period in the last century, cable cars traversed this street.

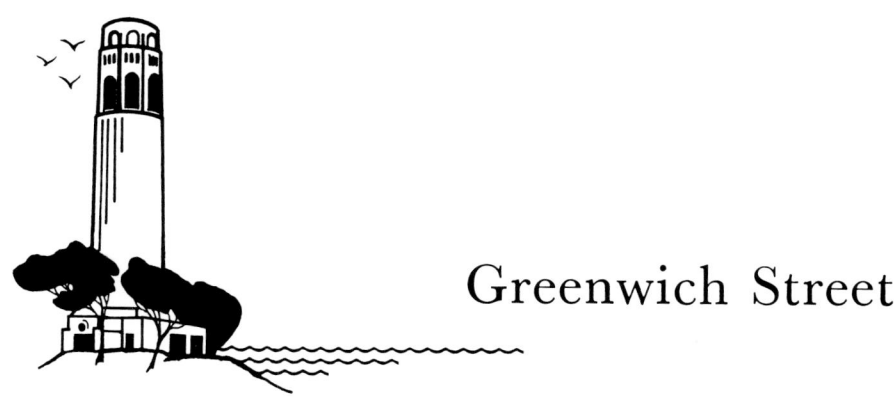

Greenwich Street

From Sansome the Greenwich Street steps rise with the terrain to Montgomery and on up to Coit Tower, passing through gardens and by dwellings both old and new. Apartments and cottages in the first segment above Sansome were served by comfortable wooden steps until 1968, when they were changed to concrete. An earlier change is responsible for the absence of buildings on the north side of the steps, which as late as 1904 was lined with frame houses in a pastoral setting. Additionally, there was a little lane, Pringle Court, running north for 50 varas (137½ feet) and providing access to several houses. Coleman O'Toole, a ship rigger, lived at 4 Pringle Court for over twenty years, until the quarrymen whittled away this part of the Hill. Mr. O'Toole then found quieter living arrangements on Potrero Hill, a safe distance away.

A little farther up the Hill, again on the north side at 240 Greenwich, lived John Runge and his wife. While he worked as a laborer at the American Sugar Refinery down on Battery Street, his wife, Frederica, ran a grocery shop in their home. Opened in 1888 amid considerable neighborhood competition, the operation suffered a disadvantage as everything had to be carried up the stairs from Sansome, and the store was short-lived.

Along the south side of the stairs, where the topography has not been rearranged, there are a number of buildings, some dating back to the last century. The apartments at the northeast edge of the bluff, however, were constructed in 1957 by Al Merrill, who presently owns considerable rental property in this neighborhood. Years ago some of the Brown family of Filbert Street lived in a house at this location.

Above these apartments a cluster of small houses forms another Telegraph Hill compound. Many decades ago this particular compound was inhabited by Mexican girls who, if the stories are true, worked together in the world's oldest profession. In recent times the cottages have been rented to people engaged in more mundane occupations.

Stories of cats on Telegraph Hill are legion and the best-known feline tale of the Greenwich Steps concerns Cass, a large, white animal with light brown spots. Cass and his idolizing owner, an admirable young man, were residents of this compound. A temporary financial stringency caused the tenant to plead for a deferment of his rent, to which the landlord obligingly acquiesced after being assured that the money would be soon forthcoming. At the end of the first month, the tenant charmed his landlord into accepting more promises in lieu of an immediate cash payment. This performance worked so well that it was repeated again and again. Finally, when the back rent totaled about $1000, our delinquent tenant decided to move away, but, although feeling frightfully remorseful he was unable to make any payment. Morally he felt compelled to make amends in some way by leaving something significant; making the supreme sacrifice, he presented his cat to the landlord, who promised tender loving care. The valuable feline, usually seen sleeping serenely on the Greenwich Steps until the late 1950s, became the legend of "Cass, the Thousand-Dollar Cat."

This part of Greenwich Street has undergone many changes. For example, the San Francisco City Water Works maintained an 87,000-gallon reservoir here for a few years after 1858, until it

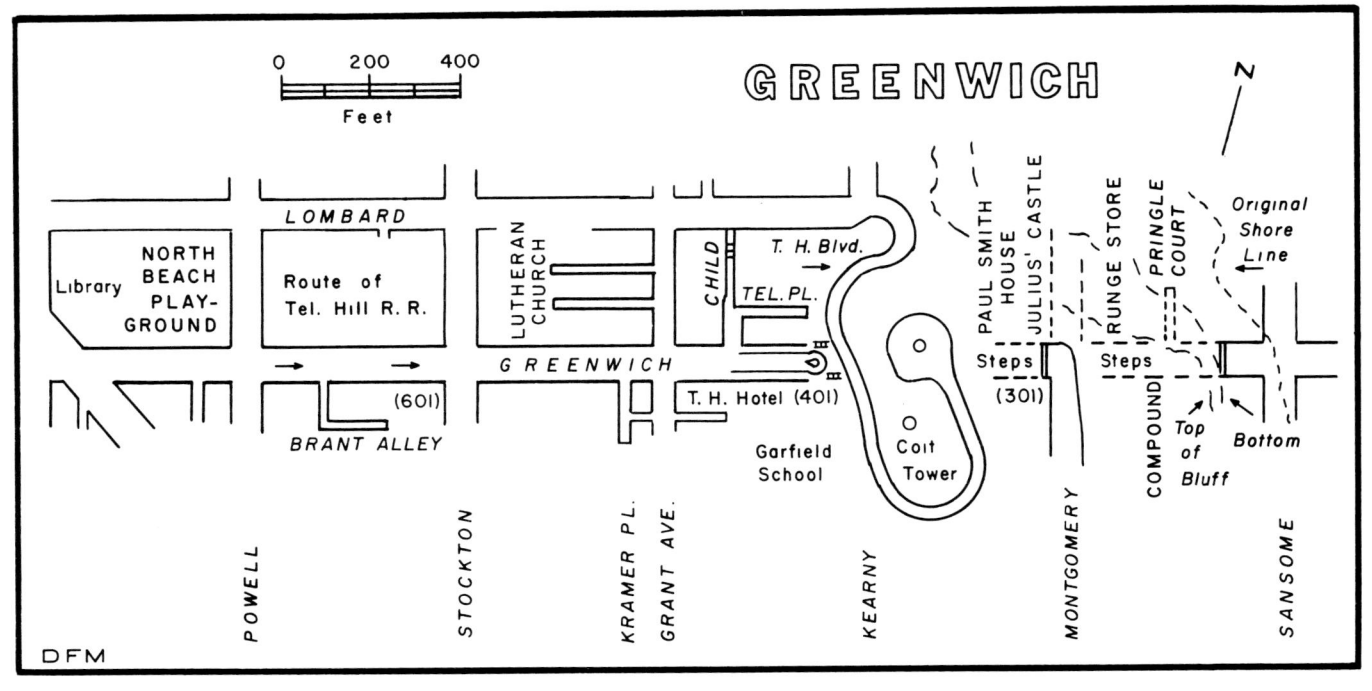

Engraved and published in 1873 by D. Appleton & Co., this scene shows Greenwich Street, the north slopes of Russian Hill and the Golden Gate. (—*Southern Pacific*)

From Montgomery, wooden steps down to Sansome led people to their homes. The time is around 1910. (—*Society of California Pioneers*)

With the exception of the false-front store at the top of the picture (now the site of Julius' Castle) virtually all these buildings in this 1904 photograph vanished within a few years, along with the ground beneath them as the Wetmore quarries expanded their operations. (—*Wells Fargo Bank History Room*)

This early photograph of Greenwich Street has the same identifying row of stepped houses (right) as the engraving opposite. (—*Bancroft Library*)

At the top of Greenwich, this huge sign with letters fifty feet high was built in 1908 to welcome home the Great White Fleet. (—*J. B. Monaco photo*)

was replaced by a larger facility on Russian Hill. The little cottage at 285 Greenwich was formerly at 1422 Montgomery Street but was moved in 1940 to make way for another building; subsequently the cottage was enlarged.

Julius' Castle, at Montgomery, is discussed with that street, although its address is 302 Greenwich. Steps made of used brick wind up the Hill through trees and shrubs past the restaurant to Coit Tower. Built in 1940, these stairs materialized largely because of the work of John J. Lerman, a park commissioner who was particularly interested in Telegraph Hill. Just above Julius' Castle is a shingled house which one might expect to find in Berkeley. Above that is the "Paul Smith House," named for its most famous tenant; three doorways, each on a different level, provide entrances to the several apartments in this structure.

It was Mrs. Mabel Farrington Gifford, a teacher of elocution and later the chief of the State Bureau of Speech Correction, who built what has become one of the showplaces on the Hill. Mrs. Gifford bought the property in 1921 and lived there in one of the small houses made with lumber from the "Welcome" sign until she completed the present stucco building in 1937. During the 1930s, bankers could not envisage adequate security in Telegraph Hill real estate, notwithstanding the great views, as neighboring lots were covered by shanties. Consequently Mrs. Gifford was obliged to finance the building on a shoestring, but it was finally put up and quietly impressed all who saw it. One impressed individual was Paul C. Smith, who liked it not only enough to rent the middle level in 1939 but also to put a lot of money in the top two apartments when he moved upstairs ten years later.

Born in Seattle, Paul Smith came to California to finish high school at Pescadero. For the next ten years he roamed the country, working in lumber camps, coal mines and on farms before going into investment banking and then becoming a foreign correspondent. His association with the *San Francisco Chronicle* began in 1933, and four years later he was editor-in-chief and general manager. During World War II, Paul Smith served in the U. S. Navy and Marine Corps; many secret military meetings were held in this house, with important people slipping quietly down the shrub-lined stairs

From Sansome, the Greenwich Steps lead to Montgomery and Julius' Castle and on to Coit Tower, passing the "Paul Smith House."

from the top or climbing up from the bottom, either way without being observed. After the war newspapermen and others considered themselves fortunate when included in the various parties or gatherings at the "Paul Smith House." His special way of entertaining was providing Sunday breakfasts, from which lively conversations flowed. Leaving Telegraph Hill in 1952, Paul Smith went to New York, but failing health has since relegated him to a life of inactivity in a hospital.

The top of Greenwich Street (389 steps from Sansome) joins the circle of Telegraph Hill Boulevard, which is on the site of the German castle and the end of the cable car line. From here down to the next crossing of the boulevard, Greenwich loses its identity, though there are pedestrian ways linking the two parts of the street. The most direct route is a sketchy trail while the more sedate passage is by a longer but paved pathway. Just below the lower segment of Telegraph Hill Boulevard, Greenwich comes back to life at a loop bordered with flowers and continues west. On the north side of this juncture lived Harold Gilliam, a contemporary author and newspaper columnist. Mike's Grocery is at the corner of Grant, and in the same building during the early 1930s was a lodging house, more grandly listed in the directory as the Telegraph Hill Hotel, with the entrance at 485 Greenwich Street. Child Street and its byways, Telegraph Place, join Greenwich on the north.

Telegraph Hill played a part in the fragmentary history of several churches. On August 20, 1853, the Reverend W. C. Pond conducted the opening services of the Second Congregational Church, which was on the north side of Greenwich just above Stockton. Among the church's trustees was William A. Pfeiffer, for whom the short street is named. About six years later this edifice was shared with the German Evangelical Lutheran Church, with the Reverend F. Mooshake officiating on Sunday afternoons; Mooshake was something of a nomad, preaching to his flock from various borrowed pulpits. Apparently the Lutherans bought this former Congregational church about 1862, when the Reverend J. M. Buehler sermonized under the banner of the First German Evangelical Lutheran Church.

However, serious problems arose in November 1862 when property owners along Dupont (Grant) sought to lower the grade of this street at its crest near the Greenwich intersection. When this was done, it also involved a similar adjustment of Greenwich all the way down to Stockton; some lots were then well above the new grade. The Lutheran church was so remote that its members began to complain; "Men will not worship in a temple reached only by ladders or balloons," was one observation. The difficulty was overcome by purchasing a lot on Geary Street by Union Square and erecting a new church.

The old building on Greenwich was vacant until 1886, when the parishioners of St. John's German Evangelical Church (organized 1879) climbed up the many stairs to move in and remain for nine years; then the church changed its name to St. John's Evangelical Lutheran Church and moved to Mason Street on Russian Hill. The old church building was destroyed in the fire of 1906. The two-story apartment house presently perched on this lot at 568-70 Greenwich is still high above the street, but in early times Church Place, now Edith Street, provided an easier approach from the east.

Farther down Greenwich, past long rows of post-fire apartment buildings, is the North Beach Playground, a part of the Recreation and Park Department financed by a bond issue approved by the voters in September 1903. Five years elapsed before the 14 pieces of property were purchased and Greenwich Alley was closed. For many years a branch library for North Beach had been advocated, but when it was finally approved, two more years were necessary to fix its location, as everyone had a different idea. Finally, in 1957 Mayor George Christopher recommended that one corner of the playground be used for this purpose, a recommendation which was approved by the supervisors, and the library was built.

In the late 1930s, No. 8, a Baldwin steamer, stands by the engine house (right). The same picture taken today would show many more housing units in the background than at this time. (—Roy D. Graves photo)

Kearny crosses Lombard in the lower center of the picture above. To the right, with the canopy, was Lange's grocery, which is the site of the present seven-story apartment building. (—*Roy D. Graves collection, Bancroft Library*)

Some years later the sea wall had reached the old Meiggs' Wharf. Later the intervening area was filled. The long house in the foreground was the home of H. T. Graves and behind it, facing Chestnut, is the Gundlach house. (—*Wells Fargo collection, San Francisco Maritime Museum*)

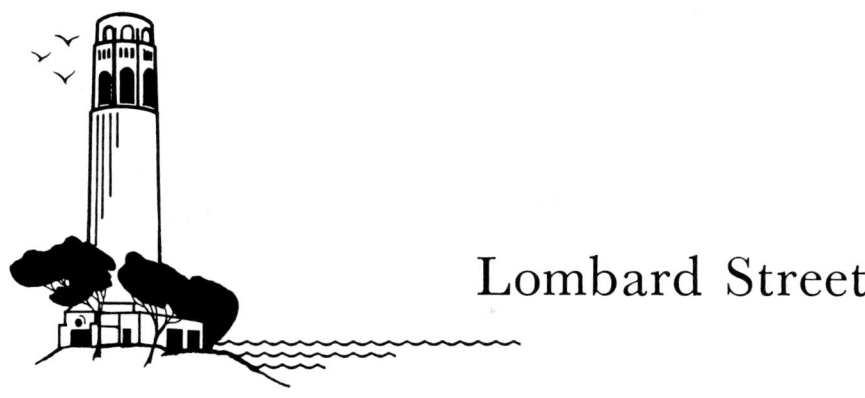

Lombard Street

As photographs of aristocratic homes will attest, Lombard and Chestnut streets* around Grant and Kearny were the stylish addresses on Telegraph Hill before the fire, a tradition that still continues but is now shared with other parts of the Hill. However, some sections of Lombard were occupied by commercial ventures.

For example, in 1898 the narrow-gauge tracks and freight sheds of the North Pacific Coast R.R. were located at the water front, on the north side of the first block west of Battery Street. Opposite the railroad yard were a woodyard and the City Warehouse, which was used by the Gulf Bag Co. (Bemis Bag) at that time. In the next block was the famed Sea Wall (North Point) Warehouse, fronting on Sansome. Dating back to 1853, this warehouse was constructed by Adams & Co., early California bankers; its destruction in 1969 brought forth many protests and discredited those responsible.

On the southwest corner of the latter intersection was the Lombard Warehouse, and behind it was a row of six dwellings. There a fire on October 30, 1891, attributed to young miscreants, swept through the buildings, scarcely allowing the occupants enough time to escape with their clothes. Later this property was quarried by the Wetmore brothers.

Reverberations of the quarrying, dormant for over fifty years, still occur in the form of rock slides. A major slide on February 2, 1971, followed by another five weeks later, prompted the temporary evacuation of the four-level apartment house at 266-68 Lombard. Recognizing that future slides could endanger 15 other buildings, the city authorized an emergency expenditure of $392,000 in an effort to stabilize the ground. A 120-foot retaining wall was built and a series of holes 200 feet deep were drilled to pump out the accumulation of underground water. Regrettably the miniature park at the end of Lombard was a casualty, and the park's plaque honoring Guglielmo Marconi, developer of wireless telegraphy, was removed and is now in storage.

At present there are only two structures on Lombard between Kearny and the bluff, both on the north side. Back in 1899 there were three dwellings on the south side of Lombard east of Kearny, all belonging to John Kleinhans, an officer of the Schammel Packing (vinegar) Co., which was located at the southwest corner of Powell and Chestnut streets. On the north side of Lombard were five buildings, including the corner grocery and two houses belonging to F. W. Lange. Master Mariner Thomas Collett lived next door, while another house stood between his home and the cliff.

The seven-story apartment house at 290 Lombard on the site of Lange's grocery marks the beginning of Telegraph Hill Boulevard, which winds up to Coit Tower. Before this building was erected in 1940, most of that property had been vacant since the fire. This large structure, in addition to the usual foundation, is supported by 16 piles go-

---

*House numbers on these two streets, as well as on Francisco and Vallejo, were changed during the 1880s and 1890s as the water front moved eastward into the Bay. Thus 201 Lombard became 301 Lombard, etc. All references herein reflect the present numbering, unless otherwise noted.

Following the major slide at Lombard near Kearny in 1971, an extensive program was undertaken to prevent further slippage.

ing down 40 to 190 feet. The top two floors constitute one apartment; there are two apartments on each of the middle three floors, three apartments on the second floor, a lobby and two garages on the first floor and a larger garage in the basement. Though often considered the property of Louis Ghirardelli, the building was owned by Mrs. Ghirardelli and her son by a previous marriage, James C. McCandless of the Hawaiian family of artesian well drillers. Louis Ghirardelli died in June 1948, but Mrs. Ghirardelli continued to live in the top apartment until her death in December 1961. The building was then sold to Marriner Eccles, a Utah banker and one-time chairman of the Board of Governors of the Federal Reserve System.

Though the building was considerably higher than any other in the neighborhood, there were no objections raised during its construction. But once it was completed, the howls began. At one meeting, a number of aroused Italians shouted out all the dire consequences they had in mind for Mr. Ghirardelli when they got their hands on him. Never once did they look around to see this gentleman sitting quietly in the back of the room taking it all in. While nothing immediate came of this meeting, architect Gardner Dailey was disturbed by the loss of the view from his residence; so one day in 1941 he went to see Morse Erskine, a lawyer who had just settled with his family on Chestnut Street. Dailey inquired if there were any legal way

Looking down from Coit Tower after the slide but before the preventive work was undertaken. The drill rigs in the top photo are working about where the autos are here rounding the curve. Kearny Street is at the left of the picture.

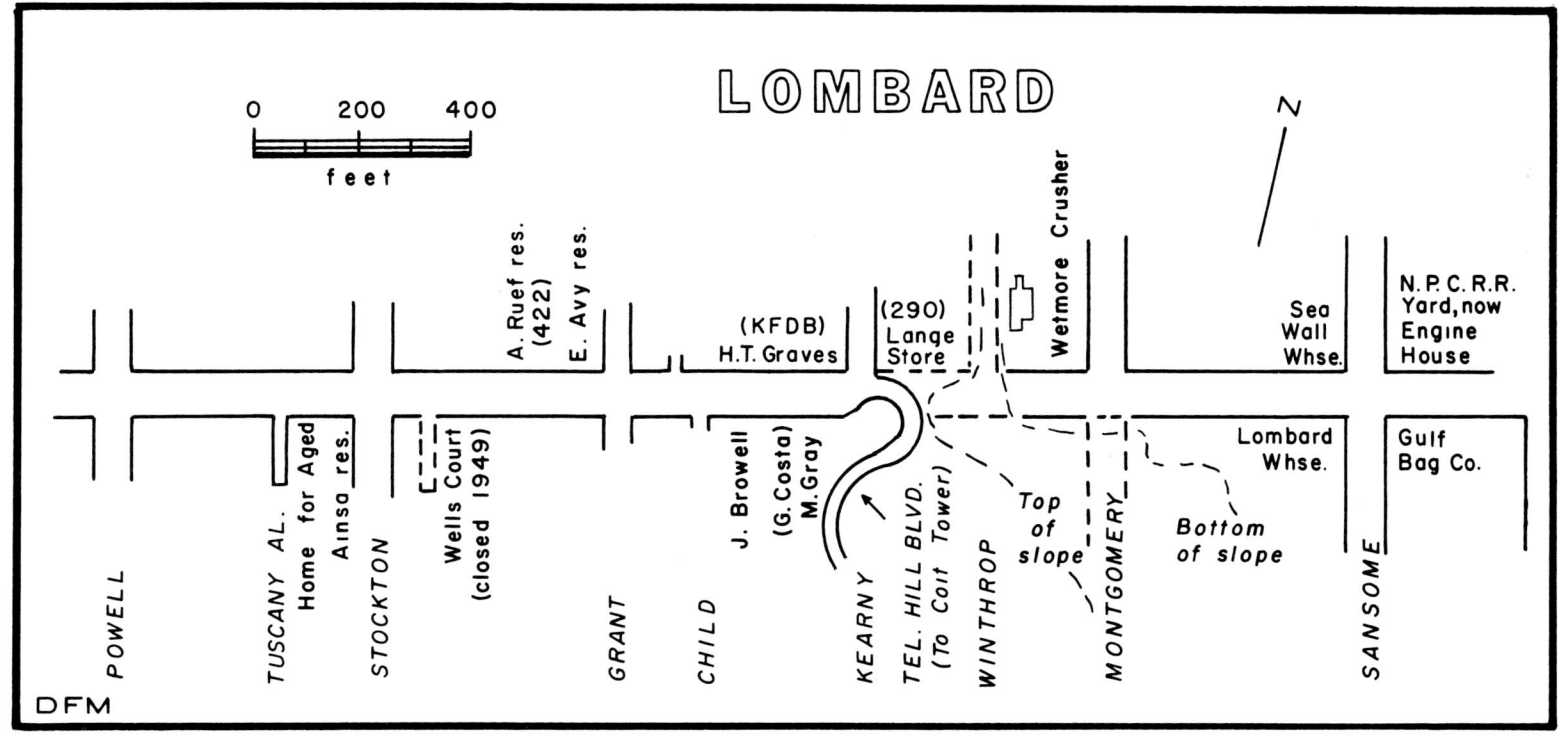

to keep further tall structures from being built. Mr. Erskine searched the law and concluded that there was indeed a way. His wife, Dorothy Erskine, sent out letters to neighbors seeking support of a forty-foot height limitation on that part of the Hill, enclosing post cards for replies. When some 400 affirmative cards had been returned, these were presented to the supervisors, and with the personal support of the residents, by now including Mr. Ghirardelli, the measure became law.

The spectacular view of the Bay made the apartments at 290 Lombard particularly desirable. Among the tenants were William L. Hughson, the world's first Ford automobile dealer; Herb Caen, San Francisco columnist and author; and Marguerite Higgins, war correspondent.

During the 1870s the Hiram Throop Graves family lived in a long, single-story house at the northwest corner of Lombard and Kearny. Graves, proprietor of the California Wire Works (subsequently merged with the firm of A. S. Hallidie), was later associated with the Masonic Savings Bank. His grandson, the late "Uncle Roy" D. Graves, was a knowledgeable western historian with a fine photo collection (now in the Bancroft Library) and was always generous with his information and pictures.

Two 100-foot wooden towers and several small buildings appeared on this same corner in 1922. One building contained electronic gear, the other a well-padded studio, and all were for the radio broadcasting station built by Ralph M. Heintz for the Mercantile Trust Co. (now the Wells Fargo Bank). With its permit dated August 23, 1922, in hand, KFDB began broadcasting from its 1500-watt transmitter (then considered the most powerful on the Pacific Coast) and under favorable conditions could be heard as far away as Honolulu or Atlanta. Broadcasting time was brief: only one hour each morning, afternoon and evening during weekdays, while on Sunday the station was silent. The life of KFDB was short; by August 18, 1923, it was off the air. The towers and buildings were removed, and in their place six flats were completed in the summer of 1925.

At the southwest corner of Kearny and Lombard was one of the finest houses on Telegraph Hill. Before the early 1890s, it was the home of Matthias Gray, both wholesaler and retailer in all things relating to music. After that the large house

A sweeping view of Telegraph Hill and the Bay as an afternoon storm is ending. Immediately to the left of Coit Tower is Greenwich Street. The next left is Lombard Street. (—*Gabriel Moulin Studios*)

Substantial apartments line Lombard Street as it rises toward Kearny Street.

Each year thousands of tourists drive to Russian Hill to descend the crooked part of Lombard Street. Then they cross Columbus Avenue (foreground) and continue on Lombard to Coit Tower at the top of Telegraph Hill.

and spacious garden passed into the hands of Giacomo Costa, a real estate investor sometimes in partnership with Joseph Cuneo. Proud of his home, Costa fought to save it from the fire following the earthquake. With the aid of his son Enrico and Bendetto Pagano, a neighboring carpenter, and a basement full of wine, he covered the exterior of the house with wine-soaked rugs and the building was saved.

Next to the Costa home was the house of Jeremiah Browell, also on a large fifty-vara lot, this one terminating at Child Street. Born in England in 1828, Browell came to California in the early days, working as a carpenter and later as a building contractor. He also manufactured sewer and water pipe and "patent chimneys" in his plant at 442 Jackson Street. His daughter, Josephine, married Charles Graves, who grew up across Lombard Street.

In the next block, beyond Grant, was the residence of Eugene Avy, a wool commission merchant and sole agent for "Gold Leaf" Tobacco Sheep Dip. Two houses farther west lived Abraham Ruef, a lawyer whose political activities in the early 1900s gained him a lasting place in the tawdry political history of San Francisco.

Across Stockton Street at 405 Lombard was the home of the Manuel Ainsa family. Ainsa, so the story goes, was a Spanish merchant prince who sailed into San Francisco harbor in one of his ships with a cargo that included $500,000 in gold. Finding a home he considered suitable for his family was not an easy task. Finally he leased an "inferior dwelling" on Lombard near Dupont (Grant) at a whopping rental of $500 per month. In 1860 he paid a fancy price for a prefabricated house just imported from Australia; he had it set up on his Lombard Street lot and lived there for another seven years or so. In the same general location some years later was the Hebrew Home for the Aged and Disabled.

In the 1890s, when the quarries were active, there was considerable blasting on Lombard, usually according to a fixed schedule. At such times Martha Washington, "the stout colored lady of Lombard Street," would rush her flock of goats out of harm's way.

James Kitterman, proprietor of a furniture store on Stockton Street near Vallejo, lived at 532 Lombard in a house on a large lot and owned several parcels of real estate near his home.

The scene has changed since 1904 when this photograph was taken. Gone are the house above, the Pennington Steel Works (left) and the Globe Mills. The lower building, last used by a wine distributor, remains. (—*Society of California Pioneers*)

The Gundlach double house was one of the grandest on Telegraph Hill. When Jacob Gundlach's daughter married Charles Bundschu it became known as the Gundlach-Bundschu house.
(—*Richard Sims collection*)

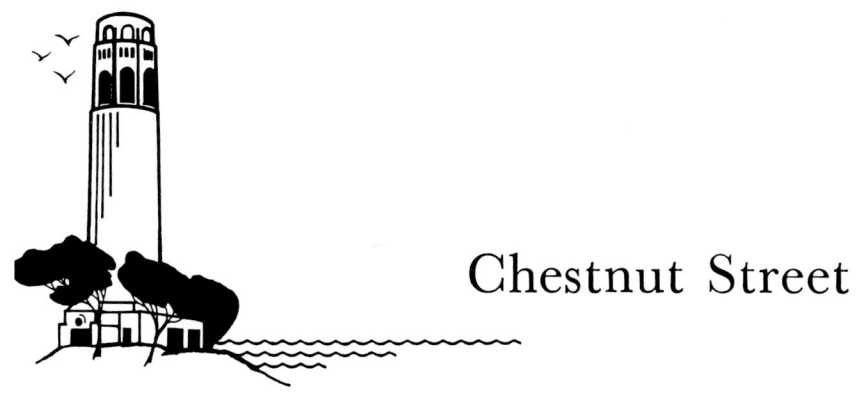

Chestnut Street

Chestnut Street, on the north side of the Hill, forms a cul-de-sac, and for those seeking a quiet area it is a most satisfactory location. But this is not to say that nothing ever happens on Chestnut Street — even in recent times occupants of the full-balconied apartments, placidly enjoying the wide views of the Golden Gate and Marin County, learned some surprising news about a neighbor in their morning papers. During the spring of 1956 a federal narcotics agent moved into an apartment in the 200 block to gather evidence for use in the prosecution of an alleged narcotics conspiracy. Part of the plan was to lure suspected members of the ring with all-night parties and girls, but before the first invitation was issued the agent carefully bugged every room. The subsequent trial was complicated by the usual legal appeals and added charges, but the press had a delightful time making the most of the story concerning the Telegraph Hill apartment.

Though the area is relatively quiet now, it was quite different when the quarrymen were approaching from the north to threaten the very existence of Chestnut Street. After their work was finally halted, Chestnut Street was left for many years in a primitive condition. It was the kind of an area where a man called Puck, known as the Sage of Telegraph Hill, lived in a small, one-room cabin by a decaying willow tree. When he was interviewed in 1916, the absence of a street made it difficult for the reporter to identify the location precisely; he let it go with a general reference to the intersection of Kearny and Chestnut streets. A small stove, an oil lamp, a cot, stacks of magazines and two windows looking out on the Bay constituted the interior of the cabin. Living in the area for forty years in one shack or another, Johann Heinrich Puck was now an old man with a neatly trimmed beard that framed his face. After rolling his own cigarette and smoking it in a long holder, he quoted various philosophers, always in the finest English. As he went on talking, volunteering that he had been a Socialist in his younger days, one could not help but wonder about the life story of this man.

Later, another man found privacy in this neighborhood. While walking around the base of Telegraph Hill in 1943, George Yeomans pushed aside a heavy growth of milkweed to find a little 10 x 15-foot cabin at the base of the cliff. Made of scrap lumber, the unoccupied house was surrounded by landslides, which gave it a snug feeling. Yeomans moved in, adding necessary improvements as time went by. A wood stove held off the winter chill and a bucket of water was obtained from a neighboring warehouse as needed. That his house had no address — it was described as "west of Winthrop and 120 feet south of Chestnut"— was unimportant. No one ever bothered this retired house painter until February 1956, when city officials held a formal hearing and ordered Yeomans to vacate the premises. To be certain that no one else would move in, the owner of the lot was ordered to dismantle the shack. And so the quiet little Shangri-La of one man came to an end.

In the last century the fashionable sections of Chestnut and Lombard streets ranged between Kearny and Powell, but within these three blocks shanties were mixed in with the homes of the wealthy, a factor said to have prevented this dis-

From Grant Avenue, Chestnut drops down the swale before climbing Russian Hill.

trict from enjoying a real estate boom. Several lots were a full fifty varas square, however, and on these were placed moderate-sized houses.

The home of Edward D. Heatley, at the southwest corner of Chestnut and Kearny, was considered the show place of the block. A commission merchant from England who arrived in San Francisco in 1850, Heatley moved to this location within his first few years in the city. While a relative handled the London office, Heatley guided his San Francisco operation, changing partners from time to time. Nearly every morning he was out riding his horse with a cluster of dogs in the tradition of his native English countryside.

After Heatley's demise, the property, then running across the eastern third of the block from Chestnut to Lombard, went to the Tallant Banking Co. Presumably the mansion was lost in the sweep of the 1906 fire, but previously, in August 1905, the city had for $11,000 bought half the property (southwest corner of Kearny and Chestnut) for possible enlargement of Pioneer Park. The next January the city bought an L-shaped piece of land across Chestnut Street for $3500, ostensibly for the same reason. Actually both pieces were acquired to limit the quarry operators.

For many years there were no buildings on these lots except in 1907, when the Outdoor Art League of California was granted authority to build a cabin for its temporary headquarters with the understanding that the league would take care of the plants and trees. In later years neighbors built a bocce ball court on the larger lot, which was then studded with poplar trees. Various civic groups petitioned to have a park developed here, but after John McLaren said the fifty-vara lot was unsuitable for park purposes, the Park Commission turned down the request in September 1937. A few years later the city sold this former Heatley property, and the new owners built several wide-view apartment houses. The L-shaped piece of land was turned over to the Recreation and Park Department in March 1941.

Jacob Gundlach's home was on the west side of the Heatley estate. Gundlach, until 1874 the proprietor of the Bavaria Brewery on Vallejo

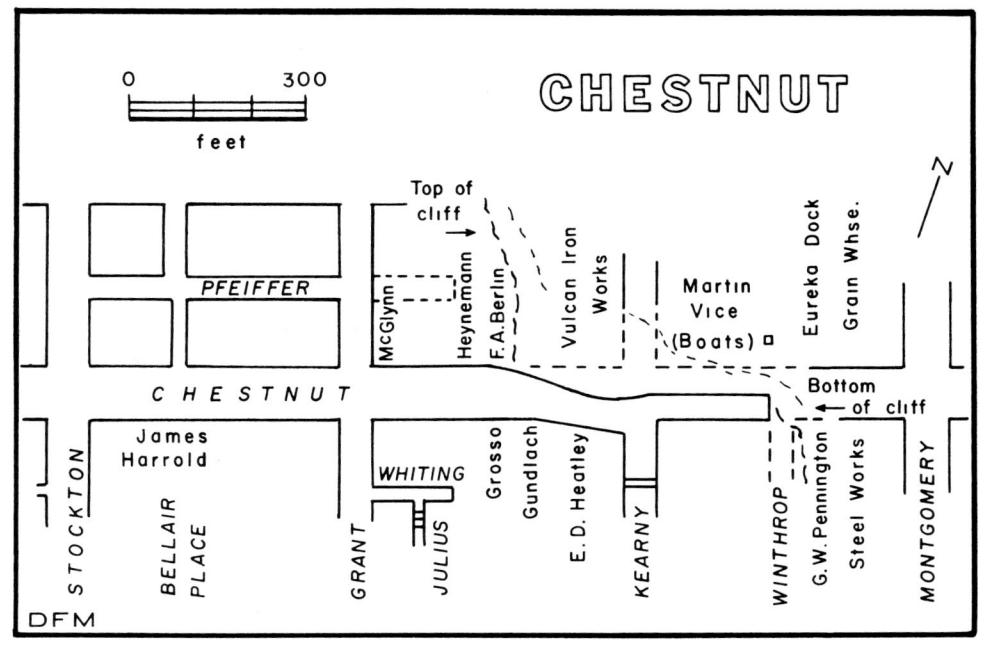

Street, had arrived in California on Christmas day of 1851, after a year-long journey from Germany that included a shipwreck on the Canary Islands and a long delay in Rio. Selling the brewery to Philip Frauenhalz, Gundlach went into the wine business at the Rhine Farm at Vineburg, near Sonoma, bottling his wines under the Bacchus label. Jacob Gundlach was also one of the founding directors of The German Savings and Loan Society, now part of the United California Bank. His large family of five girls and two boys required a double house when they moved to Chestnut Street, and when Francisca, the oldest daughter, married Charles Bundschu the new couple moved into the family home. The son-in-law became a partner in the wine firm and was active socially: in 1889 he was president of the German General Benevolent Society and also the Deutscher Verein, renowned for its costume parties.

Two houses away lived the Frauenhalz family, and even today the two daughters are remembered for their exceptional beauty. Across the street Thomas Magee, the well-known real estate man, offered for sale a one-story, five-room house with modern conveniences on a forty-foot lot with a very fine garden and a view of the Bay — "a perfect panorama." The price was $6000 and the property (now 258 Chestnut) was sold to Frederick A. Berlin, a lawyer who invested in Telegraph Hill properties. Of course, at that price the year was 1885! In 1904 Richard M. Sims married Louise Bundschu, and they lived in Mr. Berlin's house (by then on the brink of the bluff). At that time Sims was a young lawyer in the office of City At-

The tall building is 290 Lombard, at Kearny. Residents of these apartments look across Chestnut to see Angel Island and Marin County.

torney Franklin K. Lane and was assigned to battle the quarrymen. After the fire the Sims couple moved to Berkeley.

The fire of 1906 not only swept away the Gundlach-Bundschu house, it also destroyed the Bacchus Wine Vaults on Bryant Street which contained California vintages that had been carefully nurtured for two decades. All outstanding orders from customers had to be canceled and the German insurance company refused to settle the fire losses, but the wine company managed to survive. The vineyards near Sonoma are still owned by the family, although the grapes are sold to other wine makers.

After the fire Jacob Gundlach's property remained vacant until Dr. A. G. Grosso built the present house, about 1913. Now high above the sidewalk because the crest of Chestnut Street was lowered three feet when it was graded and paved in 1930, this house can only be reached from Whiting Street. Originally carriages entered the property from Whiting on a drive that looped around for an easy exit. The garden, cascading down the Hill, occupied what are now four separate lots east of the house. Pedestrians entered the premises through the wrought-iron gate at 235 Chestnut and walked up the path through the garden to the house, passing the aviary, fish pond, chicken house and various fruit trees.

Dr. Grosso, his wife and five children lived in the large, well-built house with the extensive garden, but their style of living did not always emulate the grandeur of their residence. Instead of utilizing the handsome kitchen, they cooked on a gas plate in the basement. The house, a mixture of ornate and primitive fixtures, boasted sculptured stone mantlepieces but lacked any semblance of closets. Dr. Grosso, both a pharmacist and an optometrist, made witch hazel in his basement, then sold it in his drugstore under the name Fernet-Branca. Enjoying the loyal patronage of his fellow Italian countrymen, he saw no reason to speak English and so never bothered to learn the language, though he was in business here for some twenty years.

Among the several major industries around Black Point (Fort Mason) was the Pioneer Woolen Factory. Its president, Herman Heynemann, lived

Goats and their herders took full advantage of the permissive attitude of most Telegraph Hill residents but were finally outlawed by a 1928 ordinance. Their banishment from the Hill evoked this newspaper sketch. (—*San Francisco Examiner*)

on the north side of Chestnut on a lot adjoining the Berlin property. About 1900 a baker named Gimbel and his wife bought the house, but Heynemann retained the larger portion of the lot, which extended down to Francisco Street.

The property at the northeast corner of Grant and Chestnut was filled by a two-story house set in a spacious garden and belonged to Frank McGlynn, a real estate man active fifty years ago. The present Mediteranean-style house, with its tile roof and its garden sculpture, was built in 1932, though it appears similar to a house pictured on the same spot in 1890.

Across this intersection, at the northwest corner where the grocery now stands, lived Joseph Capprice, a very active figure in San Francisco politics who also ran a liquor store on Clay Street in the 1860s. The first record of a grocery store at this corner was in 1869 with James Smith as proprietor.

Louis DeMartini completed the construction of this Mediterranean-style house at the corner of Grant Avenue in 1932. It had taken three years to build.

Next to the grocery on Chestnut Street was the residence of Mrs. Maria T. Tempany. Back in 1861 when her merchant husband died, Mrs. Tempany established a private school in her home at the northwest corner of Francisco and Grant, but in 1867 she moved to 226 (now 326) Chestnut, where she continued her school for a few more years. She spanked misbehaving children without hesitation, as many prominent people acknowledged later.

In the 1890s, James Harrold, a commission merchant, resided almost opposite Bellair Place. A few years later his property and the adjoining lot came into the ownership of Abe Ruef. In recent times, the author of foreboding doom for California, Curt Gentry, lived at 439 Chestnut.

Around the base of Telegraph Hill and in North Beach there were ten breweries in 1876, and of these, three were situated on Chestnut Street. The North Beach Brewery site is now occupied by the Francisco Junior High School, while across Powell Street and in the next block John Harrold and William H. Lyon operated the Empire and Lyon breweries. Before World War I, the Acme Brewery made beer on the east side of Sansome at Greenwich, and after Prohibition had ended, the Globe Brewery moved into a building across the street.

An important ingredient of beer or ale is malt. Not far from Francisco Street at 2108 Stockton, is the former Pioneer Malt House which dates back to the late 1850s, when it was operated by Francis Tilgner. For a time Philip Frauenhalz was associated with this firm before taking over the Bavaria Brewery. For over fifty years the Pioneer Malt House was owned by Charles Bach but in more recent times has been part of the Bauer-Schweitzer Malt Co. It is truly remarkable that this business has been at the same location in San Francisco for well over a century!

Deliveries of beer barrels to various establishments around Telegraph Hill took advantage of the terrain. Brewery wagons carried the loads to the top of Montgomery or Filbert streets, at which points the teamsters rolled the barrels to the saloons or houses. Rolling barrels was fun and added a touch of excitement if the barrels got away. The same methods were used to return the empties, for once delivered it was only a matter of time before the barrels appeared at the bottom of the Hill to await pickup. Guiding the empties over a safe course were the "Rock Rollers," young men of Telegraph Hill who were rewarded for their services by free beer at both the saloons and the breweries.

The water front around Telegraph Hill was bustling with sailing ships in the early days of San Francisco. In this classic drawing by C. B. Gifford, the view is to the north along Sansome Street with the Lombard and Greenwich docks at right angles and the North Point Dock on the left. (—*Society of California Pioneers*)

A contemporary late-afternoon scene from North Point and Kearny streets, looking beyond Bay Street to buildings fronting on Chestnut Street. The railroad tracks continue westward through the Fort Mason tunnel to the Presidio.

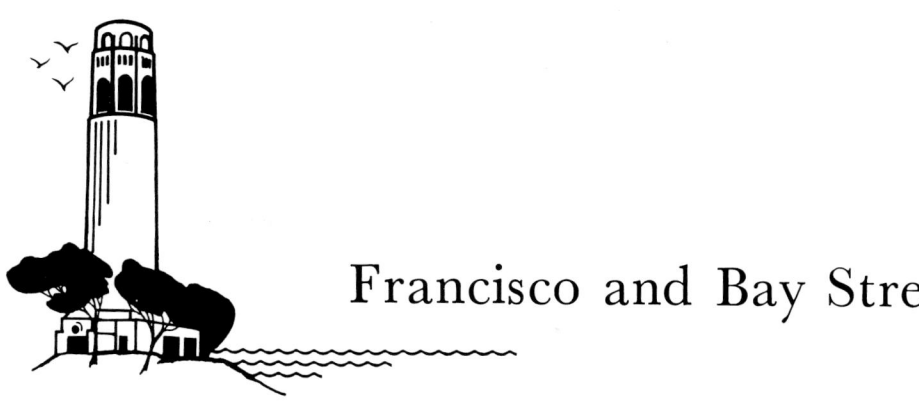

Francisco and Bay Streets

Francisco Street east of Kearny was almost 100 feet above sea level in the early days, or about twice the present height near the crossing of Grant Avenue. Bay Street, one block north and a major auto route to Marin County, passed over North Point, which like Tonquin Point disappeared from maps many years ago as the shore line reached out into the Bay. (Tonquin Point is near the foot of Leavenworth Street and took its name from a ship wrecked on a near-by shoal.) Much of the area north of Francisco Street between North Point and Tonquin Point is filled land; a great deal of the work was done in the fiscal year 1876-77, when $147,000 was spent filling and grading the five blocks of Francisco Street between Jones and Grant.

While there were some dwellings along Francisco and Bay in earlier days as now, much of the property bounded by these two streets was devoted to industry providing jobs for men on the Hill, a situation that continues today. At the southwest corner of Montgomery and Francisco, a seven-story building was erected in 1917 for the National Paper Products Company; since its renovation in 1970, the edifice has been the headquarters of the Fibreboard Corporation. Most of this block was formerly occupied by the Eureka Grain warehouses. The block west of Kearny between Francisco and Bay was given over to the Joshua Hendy Machine Works, which are now located in Sunnyvale, California. Across Francisco Street and along the west side of Kearny, where the Hill had been quarried almost all the way to Chestnut Street during the 1890s, the Vulcan Iron Works had its foundry.

Shortly west of the iron works site, the modest bluff is surmounted by a short flight of 74 wooden steps, which is the first east-side approach to the Hill north of the Greenwich Street steps. At the top of the stairs on the south side of Francisco Street stands the two-story building which housed the Roma Macaroni Factory, Inc., for over fifty years until it moved to South San Francisco in 1968.

Opposite the factory is a one-story stucco building with a considerable history. About 1935, Alex Stergois came from Tahiti to join local men in establishing a Tahitian-style cabaret at 2014 Grant Avenue, just north of Francisco Street. It was Stergois' famous Rainbow Cocktail, made from a secret formula based on a combination of rums, that drew crowds to the Tahiti Club. One of the waiters was Chester Christian, also from Tahiti and part of the Fletcher Christian family of Pitcairn Island.

After a disagreement among the partners, Stergois moved into the building at the northeast corner of Francisco and Grant which had housed the Old Wooden Shoe during Prohibition days. Here he operated as Alex Stergois' Tahiti Club. The former Tahiti Club continued and for a while a small orchestra played first in one club then the other, switching a number of times during the evening. In time the Tahiti Club on Grant became The House that Jack Built and remained there until about 1947 when it moved to 670 Broadway. After Stergois sold out about 1940, two other night clubs followed at this location — The Bistro and The Beachcomber. Later the building was used as an office by the Roma Macaroni Factory. More re-

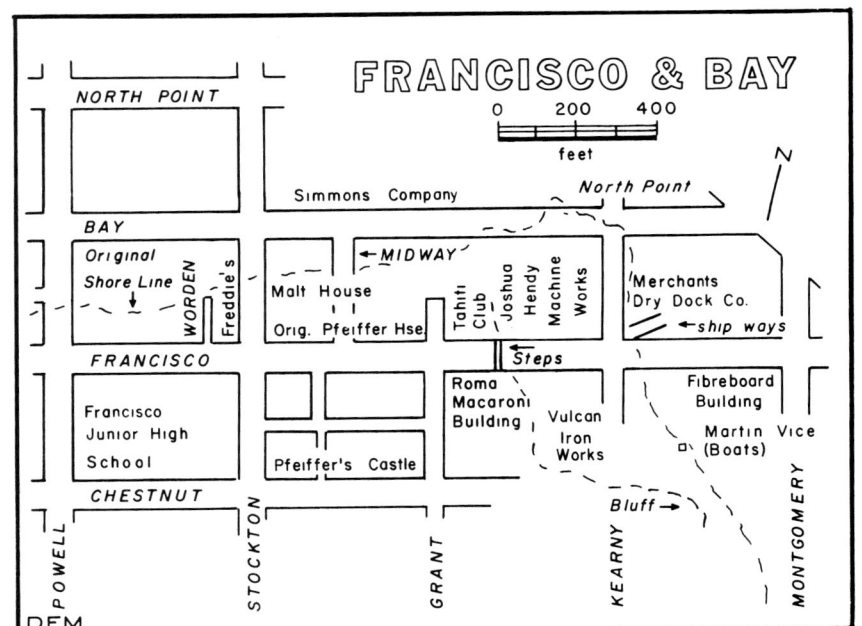

Looking west on Francisco from Grant Avenue. The slope of the streets is generally mild here.

The former Roma Macaroni Factory as seen from Bay Street on a summer afternoon. Sunlight on the handrails indicates the upper part of the Francisco Steps.

Situated along the north side of Francisco and east of Midway, these modern apartments form a geometric pattern.

cently it has become the office of architect John Campbell and others.

William A. Pfeiffer made his home at the northeast corner of Francisco and Stockton streets in 1859 when he came from Sacramento after his mercantile business had been burned a number of times. He built a flour mill at Francisco near Grant which was not a notable success, and after the great storm of 1863 ravaged the fins of his Dutch windmill, Pfeiffer abandoned this enterprise. Near by, on Stockton near Chestnut, Pfeiffer built an elaborate, three-story brick house so much more ornate than any in the neighborhood that it was called Pfeiffer's Castle or, by those less kindly inclined, Pfeiffer's Folly. In 1862 his home was purchased for the Home for the Care of Inebriates. Mr. Pfeiffer's name graces a street near his home.

The pioneer school of North Beach and Telegraph Hill was opened on November 17, 1851, at the northeast corner of Filbert and Powell streets. Shortly thereafter the school was transferred to a large brick building on the southeast corner of Francisco and Stockton. In 1857 this structure became a city hospital and the students were transferred to the Powell Street School, near Washington Street, and the Union Grammar School.

In 1869 John Joost operated a grocery at the corner of Stockton and Francisco streets. Today, at the same corner, there is considerable traffic at lunch time as people drive some distance to pick up French bread sandwiches at 300 Francisco Street. Locally known as Freddie's, the store's official name is the New Quality Market, an appellation seldom heard.

The San Francisco Stock Brewery, at the southeast corner of Powell and Francisco, became the St. Louis Brewery about 1900 and, like its neighbor on Chestnut Street, is now the site of the Francisco Junior High School. At the same street crossing were the Eureka Flour Mills, operated by Isaac Friedlander in the 1850s. In the last half of the Nineteenth Century, wheat was a major California export and he was an important figure in the trade.

Just before World War I, the Simmons Company, manufacturer of mattresses and iron and brass beds, moved from Mission Street to 198 Bay Street, where the plant eventually occupied six and a half acres. After a ravaging fire, the company moved in 1963 to a new plant in San Leandro. In its place in 1966-67 were built several hundred apartments, appropriately called Northpoint for the old landmark.

In 1869, when the Comstock Lode of Virginia City was in its beginnings, some silver ore was shipped by wagon to San Francisco for treatment. Selim Woodworth & Company's smelter at the southeast corner of Francisco and Taylor reduced ore from the Ophir, Chollar and Monte Cristo mines at that time. The Selby smelter was located further west at the foot of Hyde Street.

Columbus Avenue

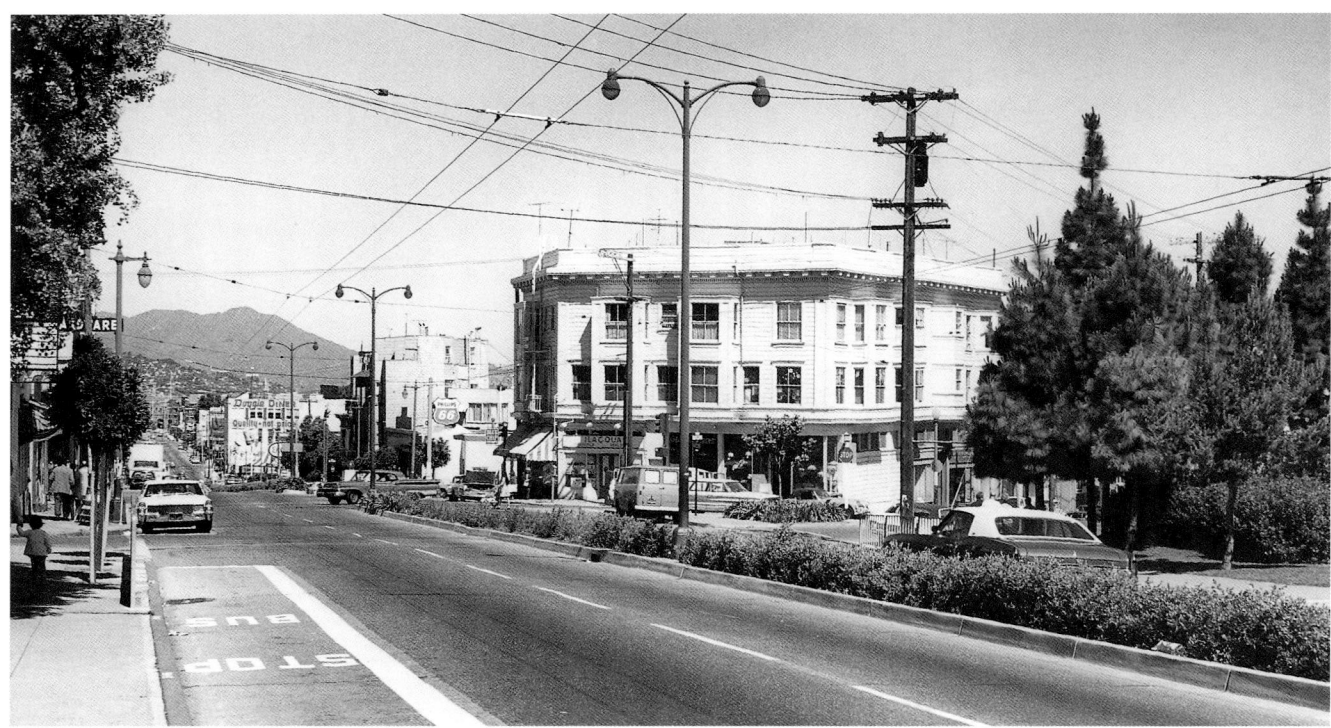

On a clear day Columbus Avenue from Washington Square appears to lead straight to Sausalito and Mount Tamalpais.

To finance the construction of Columbus (Montgomery) Avenue, an act of the California legislature was necessary to enable the City and County of San Francisco to issue bonds. Even with this precaution there was considerable litigation. *(—Wells Fargo Bank History Room)*

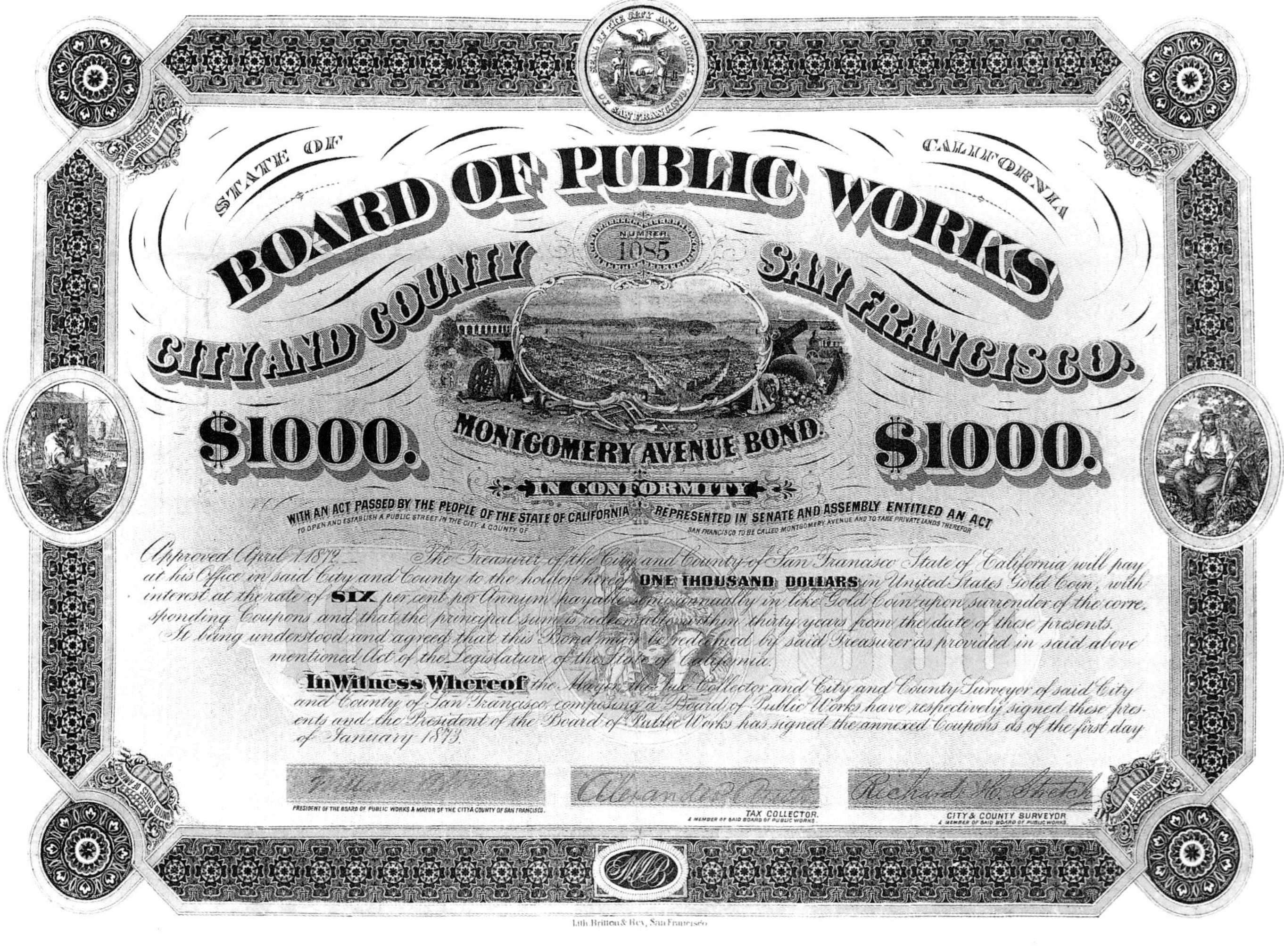

STATE OF CALIFORNIA

BOARD OF PUBLIC WORKS

NUMBER 1085

CITY AND COUNTY SAN FRANCISCO.

$1000. MONTGOMERY AVENUE BOND. $1000.

IN CONFORMITY

WITH AN ACT PASSED BY THE PEOPLE OF THE STATE OF CALIFORNIA REPRESENTED IN SENATE AND ASSEMBLY ENTITLED AN ACT TO OPEN AND ESTABLISH A PUBLIC STREET IN THE CITY & COUNTY OF SAN FRANCISCO TO BE CALLED MONTGOMERY AVENUE AND TO TAKE PRIVATE LANDS THEREFOR

Approved April 1 1872. The Treasurer of the City and County of San Francisco State of California will pay at his Office in said City and County to the holder hereof ONE THOUSAND DOLLARS in United States Gold Coin, with interest at the rate of SIX per cent per Annum payable semi-annually in like Gold Coin upon surrender of the corresponding Coupons and that the principal sum is redeemable within thirty years from the date of these presents. It being understood and agreed that this Bond may be redeemed by said Treasurer as provided in said above mentioned Act of the Legislature of the State of California.

In Witness Whereof the Mayor, the Tax Collector and City and County Surveyor of said City and County of San Francisco, composing a Board of Public Works have respectively signed these presents and the President of the Board of Public Works has signed the annexed Coupons as of the first day of January 1873.

PRESIDENT OF THE BOARD OF PUBLIC WORKS & MAYOR OF THE CITY & COUNTY OF SAN FRANCISCO.

TAX COLLECTOR. & MEMBER OF SAID BOARD OF PUBLIC WORKS.

CITY & COUNTY SURVEYOR & MEMBER OF SAID BOARD OF PUBLIC WORKS.

Lith. Britton & Rey, San Francisco

Clark's Point, at the southeast corner of Telegraph Hill, was chiseled away to accommodate an American Russian Commercial Company warehouse to store ice from Sitka. In 1856, the hillside leading up to the semaphore offered plenty of room for dwellings. (Society of California Pioneers)

View of North Point, around 1865.

A cluster of stairways and balconies climb Telegraph Hill beyond Gerke Alley, a short lane in the 1600 block of Grant Avenue.

Pfeiffer Street as seen from Grant Avenue. Russian Hill is in the background.

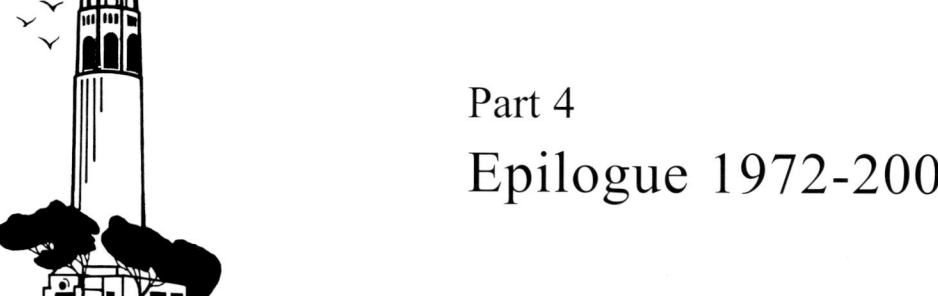

Part 4
Epilogue 1972-2000

Telegraph Hill has weathered with the years since the first edition of this book first appeared in October 1972. Yes, there have been significant changes, yet many of the Hill's special qualities have demonstrated their stability. The older houses on the east side are tangible evidence of the past with some now entering their third century. Even with the new habitations rising on or around the Hill, the special ambience and affection in caring for the community continues as strongly as before. The invasion of office buildings and large apartment structures along Sansome and Battery Streets created concern and rightfully so. The encroaching financial institutions usurping neighborhood shops in North Beach brought higher rents and caused small entrepreneurs to move elsewhere or simply retire from business.

Though parking of residents' cars remains just as frustrating as ever, some success has come in efforts to mitigate the handicap and preserve the sanity of the motorists. On the more positive side, a proliferation of flower gardens tended by local volunteers continues to brighten the scene.

The preservation of the Hill and its special features reflects the vigilance and work of its citizens. Some names will be found in this supplement but limited space excludes many worthy names. Telegraph Hill Dwellers, a neighborhood residents' organization founded in 1954 to preserve the No. 39 bus, has gained increasing recognition with the passing years. Membership, a healthy 500 just a few years ago, now stands at over 800 names. Though the Dwellers do not always win every battle, its actions and compromises serve to preserve much of the special way of life characteristic of Telegraph Hill. Blending forces with other civic groups in San Francisco, particularly North Beach Neighbors, Russian Hill Neighbors, and the NBCC, has resulted in all citizens' groups commanding more respect at City Hall. One example of blending is the Grant Avenue Fair, which began in 1954 and, after a hiatus in 1985, reappeared as the North Beach Fair in 1987 and is now the North Beach Festival.

Broadway, an active entertainment area for several decades, quieted down to a less exuberant style only to rebound in recent years. Unfortunately, Vanessi's, a popular restaurant of long standing among San Franciscans generally, closed its doors in 1989. Other restaurants marched in the passing parade until the time came for their departure, and other entrepreneurs filled their places. Though reflecting general revisions in lifestyles, the special ambience of Telegraph Hill happily prevails through the years.

The Rossi Drug Co. (above) occupied the building at the corner of Union and Stockton Streets for many years before the present occupant Caffe Malvina moved here. The North Beach branch of the Post Office and the Dante Building are in the middle of the block.

Italian names dominated this location of Broadway at Columbus Avenue in the 1890s (below). Behind the horses, the Broadway served as a temporary home for many. (*Roy D. Graves collection*)

Vanessi's Restaurant, on Broadway at Kearny (below), sported a new facade in this 1972 photo. It closed in 1989.

New Scenes on Old Streets

New scenes appear every day in our lives, and Telegraph Hill is no exception. People move away to new areas and some travel to their final destination. Local shops, after serving neighbors for decades, are succeeded by new businesses; and houses and apartments reflect the attitudes of occupants. Even churches undergo transition. In November 1993, plans to close thirteen Catholic churches in San Francisco were announced. St. Francis of Assisi on Vallejo Street closed in June 1994, but has since become the National Shrine of St. Francis. Our Lady of Guadalupe Church on Broadway was converted into a school.

North Beach attracted so many financial institutions in the 1980s that a moratorium was put in place. The Italian Village Market, particularly known for its fresh vegetables, succumbed to a savings-and-loan institution. Rossi's Market nearby survived under new ownership.

Bruno Iacopi, the popular butcher at Grant and Union, who specialized in homemade Italian sausage, died in 1984. His business was taken over by the popular Prudentes (Iacopi's niece and her husband), but they had to move out in 2000 after their rent was tripled. A few steps down Union Street is 50A Bannam Place, where a combination art gallery and little theater prevailed for two years until the Fire Department ordered it shut down for safety reasons. Reopening the forty-seat Bannam Place Theater hinged on raising funds to install a sprinkler system and, after a long wait, the sprinklers became a reality.

In 1978, revised zoning laws brought the demise of the Garfield Market at Union and Kearny Streets, which had been operated by the same congenial proprietors for thirty-five years. Today a condominium occupies this location. After twenty-nine years operating Wing's Grocery, a block south on Kearny Street, Rose and Wing Chin sold out in 1992 to Simon Marina, whose family had a grocery on Russian Hill. In refurbished premises, The Fog Hill Market began serving customers later that year, and, since 1997, has flourished under the proprietorship of Hanna Chedyak.

At the top of Union Street, the New Union Grocery, better known as Speedy's, has passed through several owners. Leon and Irene Wiatrack, after acquiring the store from the Spediacci family in 1954, held it for ten years before selling it to George Atashkarian who retired at the end of 1977, after thirty-one years in the grocery trade. Art and Marshall Dong, who had worked in the store, became the next owners. Though having disposed of his interest years before, Peter Spediacci stayed on until 1978, when he officially retired to spend his last eight years in Sonoma. A well-liked man, no one ever challenged him when he insisted that his prices were the same as the Safeway.

Many established businesses vanished from Grant Avenue between 1970 and 2000, among them Freddy Kuh's Old Spaghetti Factory and the Toy Sun Cleaners. The venerable Figone Hardware store, dating back some eighty years to the original Figone owner, stood vacant in 2000. Some businesses changed locales: Dante Benedetti's New Pisa, one of the last Italian family-style restaurants, moved a few blocks north to Green Street; and City Lights Publishers' offices moved from Filbert and Grant to reopen on the second floor of the City Lights Bookstore. At the corner of Vallejo and Grant, Ben Friedman began selling old phonograph records in 1958, then swung into posters featuring old-time movie stars, political figures, and rock musicians of the psychedelic 1970s. He moved the Postermat to

Columbus at Vallejo and did business there for some years. Part of his merchandising policy called for an annual "Going Out of Business Sale." He retired in the 1990s, and really went out of business. However, some familiar old firms, like the Savoy Tivoli, Caffe Trieste, and La Bodega, with its live flamenco performances, are still thriving on Grant Avenue. Peter Macchiarini, the widely known jewelry designer, celebrated his fiftieth year there in 1998 and continues to lend prestige to that colorful street. Two years later, the Macchiarini Steps on Kearny between Vallejo and Broadway were dedicated with an appropriate ceremony on April 9.

There were some changes in dwellings as well. For example, the former store and later apartment building at the northeast corner of Montgomery and Union proved no match for a bulldozer and was replaced by a modern structure in the late 1970s.

Down at 32-34 Napier Lane off the Filbert Steps, a fire that started at dawn on December 5, 1979 severely damaged the historic two-story residence. Fortunately for this section of the Hill, there was no wind and the fire department controlled the blaze quickly and effectively. At 16 Napier Lane, a short distance away, an old frame house had been dismantled and the new lot owner secured permission to erect two condominiums.

Parking: A Continuing Problem

Parking continued to take the toll of even-tempered automobile owners. The lack of garages in the pre-auto-age dwellings, plus over 100 housing units located on the slope east of Montgomery Street without an access road contributed to the problem.

Commuters from Marin County and the South Bay found it just a little too convenient to park their cars on Telegraph Hill and then walk or take the bus to work. After considerable planning, an identification program was formulated through the use of bumper stickers on residents' cars. It became effective March 1, 1978 when residents could purchase "A" stickers for a modest fee; a similar program followed in other sections of the city. Mention should be made of an earlier windshield sticker (depicting Coit Tower) instituted in 1962 by Dennis Flynn, treasurer of the Telegraph Hill Dwellers. While identifying local cars, it did nothing to restrain parkers from outlying areas.

The popularity of the two restaurants on Montgomery Street, The Shadows and Julius' Castle (it achieved landmark status in May 1980), contributed to the problem. As a solution, valets from the restaurants parked patrons' cars in public garages, and used vans to get people back to their cars. But as time went on, some valet parkers could not resist the temptation to park on Montgomery Street. On one memorable evening, an unidentified man jumped in a van and sped off. The would-be thief did not get very far, for he crashed just around the corner on Union Street and wisely abandoned the damaged vehicle. To make the parking situation worse, Jeffrey Pollack, owner of Julius' Castle and subsequent owner of the Shadows (enlarged in 1986 and later renamed dalla Torre), cited the cost of insurance as justification to discontinue the shuttle vans altogether. This threat of more congestion stirred a protest, and the restaurants were ultimately ordered to provide three valets to park cars outside the area.

THD, spearheaded by Nancy Katz, took steps to alleviate the parking situation here and elsewhere on the Hill. Working with the Department of Parking and Traffic, a few more parking places were created on Montgomery Street late in 1992, while diagonal parking added a few more on Vallejo Street the following year.

Familiar Faces

Between 1970 and 2000, many dedicated people contributed to the survival of Telegraph Hill's special ambience. One of these, a resident since 1953, was Charles B. Shearer, whose lot reached from Darrell Place to Napier Lane. Much beloved, Chuck and his toy beagle, Little Boy, patrolled that section of the Hill and served as a fountain of important information; some called him the "town crier." Chuck died quietly in a movie theater in November 1983.

A few of the familiar writers and artists who were memorable presences on the Hill between 1970 and 2000 included the *Chronicle's* crusty columnist Charles McCabe, filmmaker Jordan Belsen, guitarist Jeffrey Chin, and poets Pete Winslow, Jack Hirschman, Tisa Walden, Howard Hart, Philip Lamantia, and Lawrence Ferlinghetti, San Francisco's first Poet Laureate. The city named Price Row, a small alley off Union between Stockton and Grant, "via Ferlinghetti" a year after his City Lights

Bookstore spearheaded the city's renaming of twelve city streets after poets and artists who had lived in San Francisco.

Excellent stories and reporting filled *The Semaphore,* which started as a mimeograph sheet or two in 1956, and was called the *Telegraph Hill Bulletin.* It became a handsome booklet in May 1976. With issue No. 57, it expanded from a dozen to as many as 44 pages that informed the membership of important happenings on the Hill. Many volunteer editors have been responsible for creating a useful and scintillating publication, which has recorded nearly a half century of Telegraph Hill history. In recent decades, editors included Lynne Burwell [Burbiola], Kathleen Cannon, Clyde Steiner, Margaret Gwathmey, Patricia Cady, and Cheryl Bentley.

While Nancy Katz worked to alleviate parking problems, her husband Bob, in 1980, began a battle to halt noisy tourist-bearing helicopters from disturbing the tranquility of the north side of the Hill. It was several years before this nuisance was abated.

Referred to as the "Mystery House" because the identity of the owner is unknown, this handsome structure was situated near Stockton and Francisco Streets. A windmill provided water. In the background are Meiggs Wharf (left) and Alcatraz Island (center).

Scars left by the Gray Brothers quarry on Green Street are prominently displayed; the houses in the 200 block of Union Street form a row at its right. Many structures pictured here were replaced by high-rise Embarcadero Center buildings. (Sacramento and Drumm Streets meet at lower left.)

Office Buildings Replace Warehouses

Nothing is more permanent than change, which can be beneficial or detrimental depending on a particular viewpoint. But perhaps the most dramatic alterations in recent decades occurred around the east and north bases of Telegraph Hill as developers coveted these sites.

The need for close proximity of shipping piers and warehouses, mandated by short hauls of horse-drawn wagons, vanished with the more flexible motor trucks. Cargo ships began docking at other locations. Consequently, the once active wharves and related warehouses along the base of the Hill were ripe for the picking. Developers focused their attention on this underutilized area for potential hotels, offices, and apartment buildings. One by one the old warehouses—some fortunate enough to have escaped the 1906 fire—succumbed to the wrecking ball.

Where one promoter failed to have his way, another stood waiting in the wings ready to come up with a grand project, supported by glossy brochures filled with glowing expectations. Once during the extended development struggle, the San Francisco Planning Commission, acting on instructions from the Supervisors, made a wide swing away from a waterfront development scheme in April 1968. Supervisor William Blake expressed a common opinion: "This plan is too far out. You social planners couldn't build an outhouse in San Francisco."

Property acquired by the North Waterfront Associates ran into trouble when it commenced destruction of the venerable Seawall Warehouse just after Christmas 1968. Dating back to 1853 and originally called the North Point Dock Warehouse, this Sansome Street structure once belonged to William T. Coleman of Vigilante fame, and subsequently was owned by the John Seille family for almost a century. When replacement with an updated structure was being considered, the public was assured that there would be a six-month advance notice of demolition.

This was not done, and, at first caught off guard, several Telegraph Hill women, including Toby Bloxam and Nancy Katz, quickly rallied and frustrated the wrecking crew by occupying "Fort Seawall" the following Monday. The "battle" made the front page of the *Chronicle* and ended with the developers agreeing to salvage the bricks and iron shutters of the warehouse during demolition when funds could not be raised to purchase the building.

Another example of controversial development was Phase III of the Golden Gateway—announced in 1972—which envisioned a massive structure with several towers that matched Telegraph Hill in height, and would add forty town houses to the area. Residents took fright at this coming apparition and, after the developers refused to modify their intrusion, THD engaged counsel to litigate the proposal under state and city environmental statutes. After the Dwellers filed its suit April 30, 1973, a city-wide group formed the Committee for Responsible City Development. The lawsuit was withdrawn for technical reasons but real estate prices and financial hurdles the next year caused the promoters to peddle their wares elsewhere.

Levi's Plaza, designed by Gerson Bakar and Associates for Levi Strauss (blue jeans), now occupying seven blocks along Sansome and Battery Streets, had its beginnings in the summer of 1977. Demolition of old buildings commenced early in 1979. Sometimes the swinging ball chose seven o'clock Sunday mornings as the proper time to start work. The mighty Gibraltar Warehouse was reduced to rubble on April 7 when the concrete wall succumbed to the wreckers with a "swoosh." Grading began four months later, work sometimes starting before seven in the morning and continuing till eleven at night. Pile driving got off to a noisy start on September 10. Already Filbert Street between Sansome and Battery had been fenced off, taking away precious parking spaces and further antagonizing residents on the east side of the Hill. It also ended use of the railroad spur serving the Walters Warehouse. (On June 14, 1979, a Western Pacific box car, No. 38111, proved to be the last car spotted on this siding.) Finally, Levi's Plaza was completed, in 1982, and became an attractive office-park.

The Sperry Flour tower, a long-existing landmark, vanished overnight on November 9, 1979. During excavations, surprised workers found remains of an old wooden ship about 105 feet long. The contractor, cooperating with archaeologists, allowed them to investigate the "mystery ship," but nothing more than speculation evolved and the ship, then

Two sailing ships are docked at Pier 39 just beyond the Harbor Warehouse, which occupied a full block bounded by North Point, Grant, Kearny, and Bay Streets. A white ferryboat from Marin glides between Alcatraz Island and Belvedere. (*Bancroft Library*)

From the east side of Telegraph Hill, this sunny day offered a varied scene. A diesel locomotive of the State Belt Railroad moves along Filbert Street to pick up a car to add to the train standing along the Embarcadero. After seeing the harbor, a boatload of tourists returns to the dock at Fisherman's Wharf. During 1979, the view changed, when the concrete Gibraltar Warehouse succumbed to the swinging ball to make room for Levi's Plaza.

The Embarcadero Freeway near the Broadway exit before it was demolished in 1991.

covered up again, will continue to be a mystery.

Across Sansome Street, at the southwest corner of Filbert, an office building rose during 1982-1983, replacing the single-story building occupied by King's Antiques, which had previously housed a stevedoring office. Residential neighbors sought a reduction in height from seven to five stories and also better parking arrangements, but under prevailing political realities, the promoters secured a permit for the full-size, seven-level structure to be known as the Filbert Landing building. One enraged neighbor, observing men suspended by ropes chipping away loose rocks on the cliff for this project, cut one of the ropes. Fortunately for all concerned, the worker was safely on a ledge at that moment.

Builders failed to be discouraged by the steep and sometimes crumbling stone hillside along Sansome Street, and still more projects surfaced in succeeding years in spite of cliff erosion that the earthquake of 1989 had accelerated.

Additional buildings continued to rise around the eastern and northern base of Telegraph Hill. Among them were the Telegraph Landing in 1976, the Parc Telegraph condominium building in 1992, and the adjoining Lombard Plaza, a 118-unit senior-citizen housing project. The Walters Warehouse with the rooftop apartment at Filbert and Sansome Street was converted to an office building in 1999.

The Embarcadero Freeway, which had threatened to encircle Telegraph Hill, was completed as far as Broadway in March 1959. Long maligned by those who wanted to reunite the city to its waterfront, the freeway was forcibly closed by the October 17, 1989 Loma Prieta earthquake. After standing idle for two years in ruins, it was demolished in 1991 and replaced by a wide boulevard lined with palm trees.

The State Belt Railroad, which had served the piers along The Embarcadero since the early 1900s, lost its usefulness as ship cargos were handled elsewhere. In place of the railroad tracks, the Muni F-Line, in March 2000, began offering passengers transportation on handsome vintage trolley cars from cities around the world. The old roundhouse on The Embarcadero survives as an historic landmark.

The wharf (above) at the foot of Broadway in 1867, with river steamers ready to take passengers to Sacramento, Marysville, and San Jose. (Bancroft Library)

The low white building (left) in front of the Walters Warehouse at Sansome and Filbert Streets once housed the offices of the San Francisco Stevedoring Company. Later, King's Antiques operated here. The tall Filbert Landing building now occupies this site.

Seawall Warehouse, after more than a century of service, succumbed to developers in 1969.

During the rebuilding of Montgomery Street in 1931, a reinforced concrete wall replaced the timbers that had supported the street. A Pacific Coast Aggregates' Mack truck is about to dump a load of gravel.

The Montgomery Street wall north of Green Street was completed in October, 1931.

Freddie McNear's modern apartment building at the end of Alta Street provided great views for its occupants. In this 1942 photo, the building appears well secured. Unfortunately, the damage inflicted on the hill by the quarry operators continued long after their departure, and portions of the hillside slipped away from time to time. A major slide in 1992 necessitated evacuation and subsequent demolition of the building. The little cottage to its right was a cause célèbre in 1986 when a proposed expansion threatened the Grace Marchant Garden. Part of the wooden Filbert Steps appears in the lower right.

At 31 Alta Street, a house in classic Telegraph Hill style.

A quiet little house on Napier Lane over a century old.

the corners. On the fifth try, the cables dislodged a storage basement, scattering phonograph records and papers over the hillside. Under a light drizzle at sunset, on the sixth try, the valiant structure stopped fighting and tumbled down the cliff. The battle had been won, and the demolition crew cheered. Broken walls and floors scattered onto the ground below, settling against the walls of the seven-story Filbert Landing office building, which had already been evacuated, but suffered little damage.

Stabilizing work on Alta Street began under a contract with a tab of just under $600,000. By November 1992, workers of the Soil Engineer Construction, Inc. had driven fifteen piers twenty to thirty feet into the ground to provide a foundation for the restoration of Alta Street, completion of which was scheduled for the following February. While waiting to learn the fate of the apartment house, the *San Francisco Examiner* anticipated the next episode when it published a cartoon of the troubled house that pictured vultures (identified as lawyers) circling overhead. Benjamin Chavez refused to pay for the city's work; instead he sued the city for its share of the responsibility for his loss. It was a field day for lawyers but that episode is another story.

The Grace Marchant Gardens, 2001. *(Larry Habegger)*

Gary Kray and Grace Marchant working together in the garden, 1980. *(Larry Habegger)*

Gardens and More Gardens

The absence of formal streets in some parts of Telegraph Hill—Filbert and Greenwich being the most prominent—prohibit auto access but offer the reward of colorful gardens. In more recent years, other streets with untraveled pavements have been transformed into landscaped delights.

Known across the land, the gardens in the 200-block of the Filbert Steps reflect the diligence of Grace Marchant, who spent decades patiently toiling in the garden. Before the garden project could begin, decades of debris had to be removed, a labor Grace accomplished by tossing the junk over the cliff, which displeased city officials. But Grace had her way, and in the next thirty years roses, fuchsias, angel-trumpets, purple-flowered princess trees, and a carpet of baby tears covered the area.

The daughter of a South Dakota farmer, she moved to Long Beach in 1912 for her health, and participated in the early movie industry, first as a bathing beauty, next as a stunt woman, and then an RKO wardrobe mistress. In 1936, she moved to Telegraph Hill to be near her daughter, Valetta, who had settled on the Greenwich Steps. She became a realtor and in 1948 sold the property at 222 Filbert to her friend Edith Hyler. The following year she rented the lower unit and took up the challenge of the garden. This remained her home until her death December 13, 1982. Larry Habegger and Gary Kray, both neighbors, subsequently purchased the two-apartment building.

In her later years, when arthritis slowed her down, her friend and neighbor, Gary Kray, stepped in to help her. In time he would become her successor in gardening, and two decades later the land on either side of the Filbert steps was transformed into a hillside Mediterranean garden. While Grace had no master plan and planted as she went along, Kray had a plan which took form after the hard freeze of 1990-1991 caused extensive damage.

On occasion, the garden has been threatened by encroaching dwellings. The first threat came in 1984 when the owner of a small cottage at 221 Filbert Street announced plans to replace it with a larger structure. Gary Kray and Larry Habegger went to work to halt this intrusion. After establishing Friends of the Garden (FOG), they enlisted the support of The Trust for Public Land, which arranged to purchase the property from the owner with donations from neighbors. This bought time but no guarantee. Under the plan, FOG needed to raise $160,000 in less than six months. If they succeeded, the Trust would temporarily use its own funds for the balance so that it could buy the house for $320,000. To recover its advance, it would sell the property with appropriate protective deed restrictions.

A race ensued. While the fund raising was in progress, the owner processed his permit applications for dismantling and rebuilding. Imagination played an important part in the success of FOG in buying the property. One clever method was to "sell" square inches in the garden for $10; another was to sell tee-shirts illustrated by artist Hilda Kidder. Besides the usual solicitations for donations, a February 23, 1986 party at the Washington Square Bar & Grill, attended by Mayor Dianne Feinstein, Supervisor Louise Renne and other notables, added to the treasury. The campaign received all kinds of publicity in the press as columnists took up the cause. Rob Morse of the *Examiner* repeatedly promoted the square-inch sale in his column and Jon Carroll of the *Chronicle* also lent support. Phil Frank featured the project in his comic strip "Farley" on several occasions.

The great day came April 9, 1986, when the Trust

purchased the property and promptly resold it. The garden was saved thanks to the diligence of Kray, Habegger, and many other Telegraph Hill residents and friends, including supervisor Bill Maher, attorney Lee Gotshall-Maxon, Anne Halsted, Jane Winslow, Michael Olexo and Jean Driscoll of The Trust for Public Land, and over 4,000 donors who contributed $210,000 to the cause.

Almost a decade passed before a new force rose to imperil the garden. After the multiple-story apartment building at the end of Alta Street succumbed to a combination of historic quarrying and heavy rains, the property came into the hands of a developer who contemplated a six-story condominium on the site. Concerned citizens organized the Alta-Filbert Preservation Association in 1995 to curb the massive structure, which violated the Historic District ordinance in several important ways. Additionally, its long shadows would impede the growth of plants in the Grace Marchant Garden below. The proposed

From Alta Street, one can observe the entire length of Napier Lane, largely unchanged but for a large condominium that now fills the empty lot on the east (right) side. The shingled two-story house in the lower right was the home of Edith Hyler (upstairs) and Grace Marchant (first floor). The little house across the lane has been remodeled since this 1971 photo.

The Great Slide on Alta Street

Long after the demise of the incredible quarrymen, Telegraph Hill still suffers from their physical abuse of the early 1900s. From time to time, heavy rains trigger rock slides, temporarily closing Sansome Street. The five-unit apartment building built in 1936 at the east end of Alta Street provided tenants with spectacular views of San Francisco Bay. Occasionally in subsequent years, rock slides threatened to undermine the building's foundations, at which point Freddie McNear would scurry about to find a contractor to add a protective cement covering and life would go on as before.

A series of California dry years ended in 1991-1992 when rains pummeled the state. During a week in February, three rainstorms brought the season's total almost up to the average annual precipitation. It also raised havoc with the 1930's-style apartment at 22-30 Alta Street.

Diana Gaynor knew something was not right when she climbed the outside stairs on Saturday, February 15, 1992, shortly after 1:00 p.m. Returning to her apartment she became concerned when she felt the structure shifting slightly. Stepping out on her deck, she witnessed a section of the hillside cracking and falling with a thunder-like roar, which was enough for her to grab her cat and get out immediately. Responding to her telephone call, the fire department arrived and decided to bar entrance to returning tenants.

Over the weekend erosion continued. A section of the outside stairway followed the falling rocks as they plunged 140 feet to the base of the hill, and some observers expected the whole building to tumble down the cliff. Benjamin Chavez, who had acquired the building twelve years before, received notification from the Department of Public Works to decide within 72 hours whether to stabilize or demolish the structure.

Ken Maley, a thoughtful neighbor, provided an "underground railroad" through his quarters in the adjoining building so that tenants could slip into their uncertain apartments, gather cherished personal possessions, such as family photographs, and hand them out to Maley. This was an ingenius solution to the problem of unsympathetic city personnel barricading the shifting structure.

A week after the first slide, the building, though moving only slightly, became the top show in San Francisco, as hundreds looked up from Sansome Street. "Will it or won't it fall?" Speculative thoughts filled the minds of the crowds. Even after the fate of the building had been determined, many people quietly rooted for its survival. When the concrete barrier at the end of Alta Street fell and left a large crack in the street, observers were moved away from Sansome Street.

The next day, February 24, Chavez was quoted as saying: "If they say the building must be torn down, I will concur—not agree—concur, because this is open to future litigation." As it appeared that there seemed to be no chance of saving the structure, demolition proceeded under the supervision of Lawrence Kornfield, the chief building inspector of San Francisco.

The fate of the apartments made good copy for the press around the world. Columnist Herb Caen mentioned the event three times. One story reflected the embarrassment of a police officer and his lady friend who was riding with him when his patrol car ran out of gas, blocking all traffic in the vicinity. With no gasoline stations in the immediate area, his friend unsuccessfully went from house to house seeking a spare can of gasoline. Probably a radio telephone call to headquarters brought the vital fluid.

The clamshell scoop on a very tall crane working from Sansome Street attacked the abandoned structure but accomplished little other than disturbing a family of red foxes living under the building. Meanwhile, neighbors living at 17, 19 and 21 across Alta Street and 34 Alta Street were temporarily evacuated until the major work had been done. To save the end of Alta Street, cables were attached to pylons some distance away.

The building stood defiant. A flat tire on the crane, along with some bureaucrats from Sacramento, served to hamper progress. Two days later, the demolition experts seized upon the idea of using chain saws to cut the underpinnings of the structure so as to make the clamshell more effective. Each chain-saw operator wore a harness attached to a safety rope to guard against falling.

The engineers, agreeing that they had to contend with an incredibly strong house sitting on a weakened foundation, turned to another solution. By wrapping steel cables around the building and tying them to a strong tractor below, they felt the building would slip easily off the hillside. Though a logical idea, the apartments were not about to give up without a struggle. On two occasions, the three-quarter-inch cables broke.

Almost a week of demolition effort passed and Kornfield and his 36-man crew stood between frustration and determination. With heavier cables, the pulling exercise was resumed on Saturday, March 1, 1992. Again the building stood obstinate: four attempts left it in place with only cables cutting into

Calhoun Terrace as seen from Sansome and Green Streets. Frieda Klussmann, the dedicated cable car advocate, lived in the house in the upper left corner while down below, in the Giusti Building, Philo Farnsworth successfully conducted television transmission experiments in 1927.

building was more than twice the size of the demolished predecessor, which the architect explained was necessary because of the high construction costs, a standard argument of developers.

Three thousand people signed petitions opposing the condominium as did three-quarters of the district's property owners. At the hearing before the Landmarks Board in May 1999, people carried signs reading "Save Grace's Garden." The Board voted seven to one to recommend to the City Planning Commission that it deny authority for this construction. The developers returned with plans for a 7,000-square foot single-family dwelling but the major issues of size and shadows remained, and the Landmarks Board unanimously voted against it. At last, in 2001, the developers worked out a compromise with neighbors, reducing the building to a mass and scale consistent with the requirements of the Historic District and sensitive to the needs of the garden. A conservation easement protecting the Grace Marchant Garden in perpetuity, and limiting the size and nature of any development that can occur on the upper portion of this site, was donated by the developers to the Northeast San Francisco Conservancy, a tax exempt nonprofit corporation.

Grace Marchant's daughter and son-in-law, Valetta and Desmond Heslett, had emigrated to Telegraph Hill in 1933. Not to be overshadowed by her mother, Valetta also led a colorful life. Dancing in the Fred Astaire movie "Flying Down to Rio" in 1934 proved quite a contrast to handling a blowtorch in the Marin Shipyards ten years later. Desmond devoted thirty-six years to working for the *San Francisco Examiner* as an artist. Settling on Greenwich Street, they subsequently purchased a collection of shacks, which they upgraded to rental units, now the Greenwich Steps Compound.

When time permitted, Valetta developed her own garden around the Greenwich Compound which, though expanded over the years, never reached the size of her mother's Filbert Steps garden. Valetta died in 1995 and Des followed her three years later.

Darrell Place, a secluded lane leading off the Filbert Steps, took on a fresh appearance in February 1981 under the sponsorship of "Easy Way," the name Fred McManus chose for his project. The general cleanup yielded the usual bottles and cans, but also a bathroom scales, a camera, and a mailbox.

On the western slope of the hill, which Jack Early jokingly called "Alcatraz Heights," stood a legal but unused portion of Pfeiffer Street east of Grant Avenue, which had been relegated to a weed patch. With a fertile imagination useful in his marketing profession, Early adopted a hands-on approach to the Pfeiffer Street extension. Commencing in 1962, he quietly cleaned out the weeds, planted a few trees and shrubs. After twenty years, his improvements gained recognition and invited further action. In July 1982, Maggie Baylis, Jack Early, Nancy Katz, Herb Kosovitz, Nan Roth, and later Rhoda Robinson—all stalwart supporters for the beautification of the Hill—met at the site with landscape architect Paul Latteri to formalize plans for converting the 30 x 140-foot parcel into Pfeiffer Park.

Faithful volunteers eased the proposal through the political process, and the project was approved by the Board of Supervisors April 23, 1984. Following Early's design, landscapers formed a path and stairway winding through the plantings to a viewing platform at the upper end of the lot. As a condition for approval of his adjoining Telegraph Terrace condominium project, A. Cal Rossi funded the park and promised that his condo would care for it.

By the time it was dedicated on June 27, 1987, its name appropriately had become "Jack Early Park." Happily, San Francisco Beautiful presented him with an award for his civic contribution in September 1991, and the Dwellers honored him as a Good Neighbor five years later. Jack Elwood Early's life closed as the year 1997 ended, but THD was pleasantly surprised to receive a handsome, thoughtful bequest from his estate. Jack's dedication to beautifying Telegraph Hill is found in other areas, for example, in the poplar trees that he had planted to shade the concrete wall on Montgomery near Green Street. This work was organized by Christopher Ward in 1988.

Flowers for the Streets

Other people, stimulated by the work of Grace Marchant and Jack Early, took steps to beautify idle land near their homes. The cul de sac of Greenwich above Grant Avenue proved to be a likely candidate for improvement. In November 1992, after PG&E replaced a utility pipeline, a remaining pile of cobblestones almost begged to be put to some use. Local residents, forming a bucket brigade, moved the stones up

These wonderful houses on the Filbert Steps contribute to the lore of Telegraph Hill. While the upper house at 228 Filbert preserves its majestic appearance, the lower house has been remodeled extensively.

The Filbert steps, between Napier Lane and Sansome Street (below). The metal and concrete stairs replaced a venerable wooden staircase.

Montgomery at Green after the city established a barricade at Montgomery Street in 1928. The double stairways form an interesting pattern.

The road to Julius' Castle.

the hillside to form terraces in the garden tended by Maria Pimentell.

A different kind of garden sprang up at the end of Lombard Street, just above Kearny, when a flat-bed truck arrived with a load of sculpture, much to the surprise of Bert and Mary Ann Tonkin. Tonkin had indicated an interest in Albert Guibera's sculpture, but he hardly expected such massive creations. When Guibera found that Tonkin lacked space in either the garden or the house for his works, his suggestion solved the problem: "Put them on the roof." So a crane lifted them one by one to their permanent location. The addition to one of them of a large whimsical pair of spectacles looking back at the staring tourists has brought many chuckles.

In other parts of Telegraph Hill, the gray monotone of concrete streets has been relieved by artistic revisions. For many years residents along the eastern slope of Vallejo Street where it ends at Montgomery put up with a concrete expanse that had a charm exceeded only by gray prison walls. And there was even more dull concrete in the barriers erected to prevent autos from attempting the extremely steep hillside street.

Pushed by the 400 Vallejo Block Committee, the city allowed in the summer of 1974 that some improvement was due. THD recalled that telephone wires had been scheduled to be put underground back in 1961-1966, an initiative that had been forgotten. So, new landscape design sketches were produced, and the city projected that work would begin the next year. It was not until June, 1975, that a committee headed by Rod Freebairn-Smith, an architect living on the street, developed a plan for short flights of steps interspersed by walkways, attractive shrubs, and adequate lighting.

March 1977 witnessed a major step forward when the Departments of Utilities and Public Works completed the removal of poles and wires, under the watchful eyes of Ken and Marion Evers. Noisy jackhammers in the late summer of 1978 confirmed that work on the beautification of Vallejo Street was actually in progress, under a contract awarded to Frank Mock.

Balloons and a crimson banner added color to the pot-luck picnic on Sunday, October 7, 1979. This was the culmination of a long, fourteen-year struggle from the time that Rod Freebairn-Smith had first suggested the landscaping project to Mayor Joe Alioto. When Rod opened the champagne for the christening, his neighbors gave him a special newspaper with the headline: "Rod's Green Dream Comes True."

Again, a local group initiated a program in 1975 for lifting the appearance of that part of Kearny Street where autos climbing the hill from Broadway found access to the Vallejo intersection blocked by another concrete barrier. A left turn on Fresno Street offered the only egress. That project stalled, and then was taken over by Enrico Banducci's committee two years later. A study and some site drawings were made, only to be set aside. With the availability of $50,000 in Open Space Funds for this purpose, the project enjoyed a revival in 1982 with the support of Jerry Lubenow, Bill Snow, and Anne Halsted. Roger Owen Boyer and Associates was engaged to formulate a master plan for the entire block. Lacking a consensus, the plan went into hibernation for four years until Gerry Hurtado, a Kearny Steps resident, took the initiative to gather neighbors for discussions. Together they modified the suggested plan with sufficient compromises to be acceptable to all, a plan that would not attract drunks or dogs and would minimize interference with precious parking spaces. When the proposal hit its own stone wall because the cost exceeded the budget, action came to a halt again. Eventually a mini-plaza took form at the top of the Kearny Street block, and it was a happy day on July 6, 1989 when a ribbon-cutting ceremony celebrated completion of the project.

Dorothy Erskine died September 22, 1982 at the age of 86. Besides her family, she left numerous admirers, who respected her many civic contributions. Among those on Telegraph Hill, the tree-planting program of 1956 stands among those most appreciated. Though some trees succumbed to errant autos or lack of water, those that survived added serenity to the community and softened the harsh effect of gray concrete paving.

The 1994 renaissance began when the San Francisco Friends of the Urban Forest, supported by a state grant, allotted 400 trees to Telegraph Hill streets with available space for trees. In coordination with the Friends, the Department of Public Works made necessary cuts in sidewalks while neighborhood volunteers planted the trees. Tree planting continued, though on a small scale, in such places as the vacant lots above the new Garfield School after it opened in the early 1980s.

Plans for a new garden at 212 Union Street began in 2000. Don and Susann Putnam, who acquired the last house at the east end of Union Street, purchased the adjoining lot on the west. Recognizing that their project would be disruptive during construction, they endeavored to keep the neighbors informed in a delightfully whimsical manner. Their first notice read: "This Fence is an eyesore, an intrusion, a grotesque reminder of unwelcome construction, but it is also Temporary (2000 only)—Stoutly constructed—Illuminated for safety—Whitewashed for graffiti."

A subsequent progress report began: "Monday June 5th [2000] marked the start of our project, with the arrival of the first of many tractor-drive machines—our daily wake-up for the last eight weeks. For two months, the dust and noise have been simply awful . . . "

The project is a structural engineer's dream as well as a challenge. Before work could begin, the foundation of the house on the west had to be rebuilt. Next, 22-foot piles, two-feet in diameter, were driven along the rear property line of Alta Street neighbors. In essence, a garage with access to Union Street will be sandwiched between two dwelling units, one below and one above. To the east, a garden will serve as the roof of the extension of the apartment under the garage. The east border of the garden is flanked by the existing historical house which will be raised three feet to conform to the level of the new garden.

Two houses (above) on the east side of Montgomery between Union and Alta, with interesting nineteenth century facades. (1929)

Houses on Union Street (right), December 1939. A modern stucco finish has just been added to the house on the right.

Washington Square offered this tranquil scene some time before the 1906 fire, which consumed all the structures around the park, including St. Peter's Episcopal Church at the corner of Filbert and Stockton Streets.

Women and children enjoying Washington Square. Later, Sts. Peter and Paul Catholic Church on Filbert Street would rise behind the park bench.

Washington Square and Pioneer Park

To honor one of the oldest landmarks in San Francisco, a celebration was staged at Washington Square on May 13, 2000 to mark its 150th anniversary, and to acknowledge its new status as an official San Francisco landmark. Many contributed to the successful gathering with Aaron Peskin leading the participation of the Telegraph Hill Dwellers.

In its earliest days, the square served as a dumping ground for unwanted trash, but civic pride corrected this misuse and a modest but uninspiring park took its place. For a while after the 1906 earthquake and fire, temporary housing covered the park.

Ten civic groups formed the Committee for Beautification of Washington Square, which envisioned a redesign of the park by Lawrence Halprin and Douglas Baylis in 1956. Their plans revised the character of the square, basically by substituting graceful curved pathways for the harsh diagonal paths that extended from corners to opposite corners. On completion, a larger children's play area was opened in the northwest corner. In 1986, Maggie Baylis donated six new poplar trees to be planted at the center of the park, around the Benjamin Franklin statue, in memory of her late husband.

The need for customer parking inspired North Beach merchants to promote an underground garage under the square, but this evoked major concern after seeing the way such garages had disrupted the parks of Union and Portsmouth Squares. Backed by negative economic findings—garage revenues could never support the bonds—Mayor John F. Shelley vetoed the project. Though the proposal surfaced from time to time, the last time in 1976, landmark status makes a garage less likely.

On April 23, 1979, in spite of steady rain, Washington Square drew a large umbrella crowd to witness the opening of the time capsule planted by eccentric dentist Dr. Henry Cogswell a century before. The contents proved generally unexciting except for a tooth, allegedly from the mouth of Robespierre, a French revolutionist. A new capsule, to be retrieved in 2079, was planted at this time.

In 1997, a monument was placed in the square to honor Juana Briones, who raised cattle and grew vegetables on her ranch here during the 1870s.

For about fourteen years, Ed and Mary Etta Moose operated the Washington Square Bar & Grill on Powell near Union Street. Locally known as "The Washbag," the popular place attracted a clientele of colorful personalities from the worlds of politics, high society, and the news media—and many others who appreciated the ambience of the grill. Adrian Wilson, an internationally known fine printer, maintained his home, family, and press on nearby Tuscany Alley. Playing his jazz clarinet, Wilson demonstrated a second talent and joined the musicians at the Washbag until his untimely death in February 1988. The special status of the Washbag spurred Ron Fimrite to tell its story in *The Square: The Story of a Saloon,* which appeared in 1990.

Moose sold the restaurant, intending to move to Sonoma until early in 1992, when he happened to notice a "for sale" sign on the show rooms of the former Figone Furniture store on Stockton Street next to the post office and across Washington Square from his old bar. The temptation proved overwhelming, and Ed Moose soon bought the building and was back in the restaurant trade again. This time, he gave his name to the place and Moose's became a popular spot with the same crowd he'd attracted across the square.

A few doors down Stockton Street at the corner of

Telegraph Hill holds many little streets and hidden pathways. This walk, running parallel and above Montgomery Street, can be entered from Filbert Street.

Union once stood the Rossi Pharmacy. In the 1950s it was one of four drug stores around the square. Because of the genial proprietor, Gus Camoriana, and the warm helpful spirit of Livia Chodrick, the store long enjoyed a loyal patronage. Also it delivered prescriptions; Ron Canini while still in high school filled that responsibility and, after he became a pharmacist, joined Gus as a partner. When Gus died suddenly in March 1974, Ron sold the business. Carl Rollandi and Al De Luca, its proprietors in October 1981, were shocked when they learned that their lease would not be renewed because a savings and loan company wanted the location.

The imminent loss of the drug store distressed the neighbors, led by John Dolan, who gathered 4,739 signatures protesting the closing of the old firm after 55 years. On the strength of the petition and resulting publicity, the druggists secured a renewal of their lease at a negotiated rate. However, the drugstore was not to survive, and Caffe Malvina has occupied the site in recent decades, after its move from two earlier locations further up Union Street.

The No. 39 bus, which sparked the formation of the Telegraph Hill Dwellers in 1954, continued to plod its way up Union Street to Coit Tower and Speedy's, and intermittently over the years to Fisherman's Wharf. Although sometimes ridiculed, the No. 39 provides tired workers a welcome relief from walking up the steep hills at the end of the day. A champagne christening was staged on July 6, 1990 when an entirely new kind of bus appeared on the route, a shorter one that made it easier for drivers to turn around at terminals. It also provided wheelchair access and, more important for residents along the line, it was substantially quieter.

Pioneer Park and Coit Tower

On October 8, 1983, San Francisco celebrated the 50th Anniversary of the dedication of Coit Tower. The cover of the pamphlet for the celebration cleverly duplicated the cover of the 1933 program. Later in the year, Masha Zakheim Jewett, a daughter of one of the muralists, published a handsome book about Coit Tower and the artists.

Mayor Dianne Feinstein was there to rededicate Coit Tower and give it city landmark status. Columnist Herb Caen revealed some of the colorful biography of Lillie Hitchcock Coit and, after the orations ended, the participants went home to resume their daily lives.

Coit Tower and surrounding Pioneer Park continued to draw crowds of visitors, jamming the access road, which invited all kinds of solutions that eventually failed to alleviate the fundamental problem of too many cars on a small road with no outlet. Walkers created their own problems by disdaining the long-established pathways and striking out on their own, trampling bushes and eroding the precious few remaining patches of grass.

Inside Coit Tower, the first restoration of the murals began in 1970, protecting them behind glass partitions but limiting their visibility. Changes during the summer of 1982 corrected some of these problems. Five years later, the City Recreation and Park Department took pity on the condition of the outside of the tower and, after sand-blasting, applied a new coat of cement stucco to the aging surface. About that time, another restoration of the murals proved necessary, so the exhibit area was closed for nearly two years until July 7, 1990, when a civic celebration marked the return of the murals to public view. Two of the original artists, John L. Howard and Edith Hamlin, joined the celebration.

While this restoration work progressed, the grounds of Pioneer Park continued to deteriorate. Finally in 1995, the Pioneer Park Project began moving forward as a joint public and privately financed effort to restore and upgrade the grounds with new planting and additional walkways. Fund raising got off to a good start when Dr. Louis Kearn, founder of Coit Services, presented a $25,000 check. Specializing in draperies and carpets, the company then under the name Coit Cleaners was located then at Union near Powell.

The private fundraising went well, with an opportunity to "Step Into History." As the new pathways would require over 500 steps, those donating $500 or more would have their names set in tile at one step. This program was launched at a reception on August 18, 1997, but for a number of reasons delays ensued and it was not until 2000 that the Recreation and Park Department drew up specifications, obtained bids, and began work in the early fall of that year.

Looking at Coit Tower from Washington Square (above), one observes Stockton Street with Figone's Furniture Store and the Garfield School before its 1980s renovation.

St. Peter and Paul takes on a sterling appearance (left) in a motion picture night scene.

The movie, *Dark Passage*, starring Humphrey Bogart and Lauren Bacall was filmed in San Francisco and released in 1947. In one scene, Bogart with his head bandaged after surgery, climbed the Filbert Steps on his way to Bacall's apartment at 1360 Montgomery Street.

The Historic District

The east side of Telegraph Hill is unique. A portion of it escaped the fury of the flames that followed the 1906 earthquake and swept across San Francisco as far west as Van Ness Avenue and Franklin Street and almost to the top of Telegraph Hill in the other direction. This good fortune left intact 27 houses built before 1870, which are treasured by the community and cared for by present owners, although each one stands as a potential target for a real estate developer with visions of replacing it with a larger structure.

THD recognized this special situation and, as the first step, organized a Landmarks Preservation Committee in September 1980, with Katherine Koelsch and David F. Myrick as initial chairs. Many local residents assisted the group, which subsequently Nan Roth headed. Gee Gee Bland Platt, well qualified by her past experience, was engaged to undertake a preliminary survey. She arranged to send out questionaires in two mailings to 700 residents and, of those who returned their postcards, a large majority favored the concept of an historic district.

Gee Gee Platt submitted her November 30, 1982 report to the THD, which charted the additional work needed for the district plan to receive serious attention. This work included a more detailed account of individual houses in the area. For the next year, interest in an historic district remained alive but moved slowly. One day in 1984, when Anne Halsted took Supervisor Bill Maher down the Filbert Steps to view the venerable structures that would justify the historic district, they spoke with Gary Kray who was doing his usual volunteer work in the Grace Marchant Garden. Responding to the suggestion of Supervisor Maher, Kray and neighbor Larry Habegger wrote him a letter seeking the formation of a Telegraph Hill Historic District.

The two men joined other residents, including Anne Halsted, Rhoda Parks, Nan Roth, Jane Winslow, and George Rockrise to work out boundaries and to secure signatures of property owners. By the end of the year, the group had developed a proposal which Supervisor Maher submitted to the Board of Supervisors. Thanks to his continued interest, the Board passed a resolution on January 21, 1985 initiating the designation of the historic district.

Now the real work began. Anne Bloomfield made a house-by-house survey of the area bounded by Alta Street, Montgomery Street to Greenwich and down to Sansome Street, which included the Filbert Steps. Almost immediately, THD sought an enlargement of the area to establish Green Street as the southern boundary.

As part of the process, the San Francisco Landmarks Advisory Board reviewed the proposals and accepted the original and supplemental proposals on July 3 and August 6, 1985, respectively. The 27 older houses held their interest. Anne Bloomfield also assisted in the preparation of an appropriate ordinance for review by the Landmarks Advisory Board. From there the proposal had to be shepherded through the City Planning Commission before reaching the Board of Supervisors, which sanctioned the formation of the larger Historic District on October 27, 1986. With the mayor's signature, the Telegraph Hill Historic District became an accomplished fact on December 13, 1986.

Meanwhile, surrounding neighborhoods recognized the need for similar protective legislation. The Northeast Waterfront Historic District came into being in 1983 and the North Beach Neighborhood Commercial District was formed four years later. In more recent times, the North Beach Historical Survey of 1982 has been updated. Together these three special districts provide a means to curb inappropriate demolition and construction.

Until 1931, Montgomery Street between Union and Greenwich Streets was a single dirt road until it almost reached Filbert Street. Here the road forked, the short road (at the left) leading to Julius' Castle. (1926)

This house, its round window hidden by the trees, stood at the crest on the east side of Montgomery Street between Union and Green. It miraculously escaped the big fire. The long stone wall supported the garden. Green Street is in the foreground. (Society of California Pioneers)

From the west side of Telegraph Hill, looking toward the Russian Hill and the Golden Gate. The roof of the house at lower right marks the corner of Lombard and Kearny streets. *(Society of California Pioneers)*

A general view of the same scene many years later. The Golden Gate Bridge now spans the entrance to the Bay, but the gas storage tank at the far right vanished some time ago.

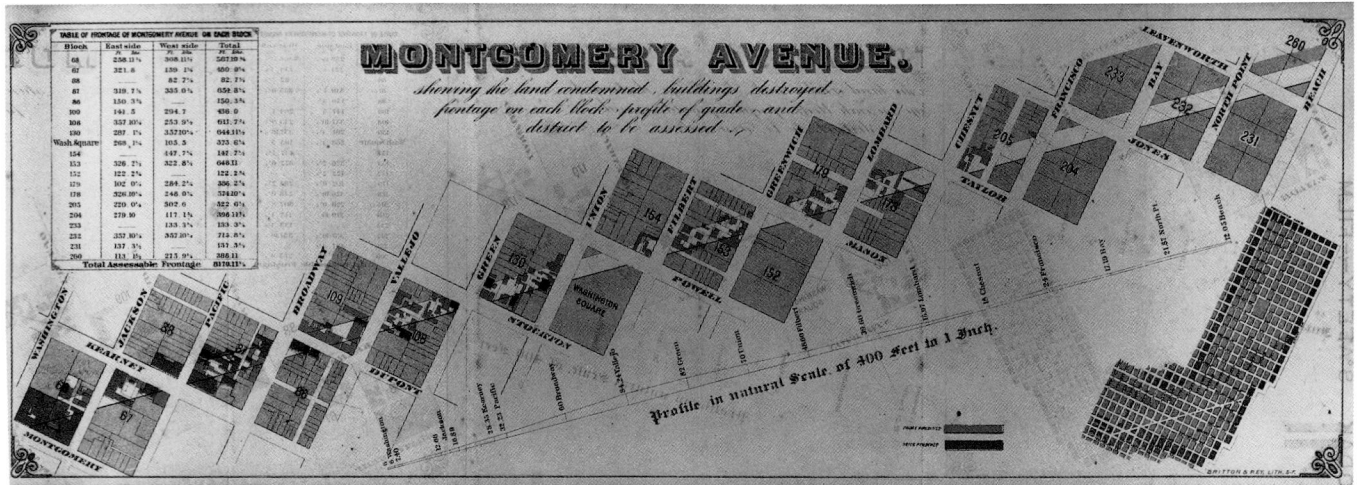

In 1872, the city planned a new street running from Washington to Beach Streets. This map, taken from the municipal Reports of 1872–1873, indicates the brick and wood structures to be removed in order to construct the street. Originally named Montgomery Avenue, it was renamed Columbus Avenue in 1909. *(Wells Fargo Bank History Room)*

Columbus Avenue in the 1970s, with a view of the St Francis and Saints Peter and Paul Churches.

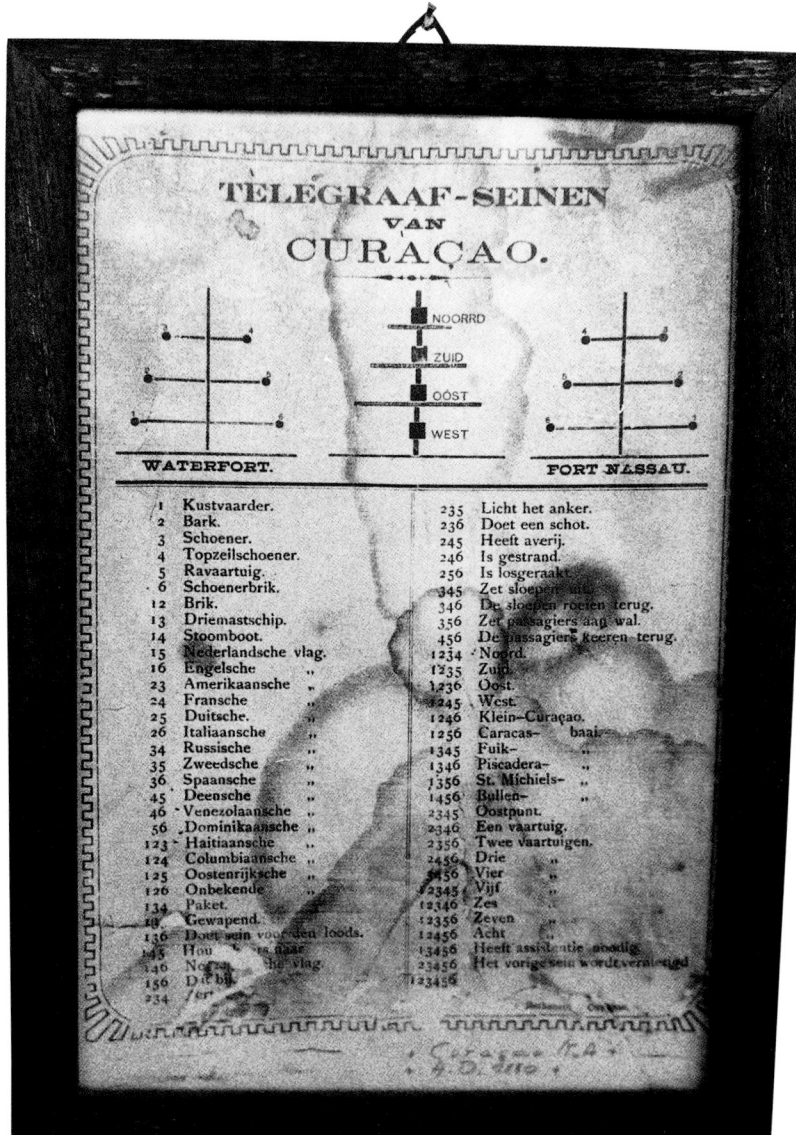

The method of announcing ships' arrivals at Curaçao's hidden harbor was the inspiration for a similar system of semaphores on San Francisco's Telegraph Hill. A copy of an 1880 announcement, Telegraaf-Seinen, is displayed in the Willemstad Museum in Curaçao.

An early view of Piers 21, 23, and 25 on the Embarcadero.

The 1906 fire devastated this area but one former Daniel Gibb warehouse at Front and Vallejo Streets was restored. Pictured here in 1971, the building was occupied by the Trinidad Bean and Elevator Company. However, the building did not survive the developers' wrecking ball.

Italian Village Food, conveniently located at the bus stop (numbers 30 and 41 buses), was one of the North Beach Italian Markets noted for its fresh vegetables and fruits. The spires of St. Francis Church are at the right in this 1971 photograph.

Appendix

DONORS OF PIONEER PARK

James R. Bolton
Alexander Boyd
John William Brown
William Burling
William S. Chapman
William T. Coleman
Jacob Z. Davis
Edward E. Eyre
John W. Gashwiler
Matthias Gray
George Hearst
Milton S. Latham
James M. McDonald
Marion Jaspar McDonald
Mark L. McDonald
Darius Ogden Mills
Henry M. Newhall
David Porter
Francis S. Redfield
Christian Reis
Henry E. Robinson
John Skae
Louis Sloss

STREETS OF THE PAST

The following is a list of the different names for Telegraph Hill streets in days gone by, as well as the names and locations of streets which vanished when they were absorbed into adjoining property.

Ada Court: changed to Wells Court; closed 1949.

Agnes Lane: N from Vallejo between Grant and Stockton.

Alleys Court: N from Greenwich between Sansome and Montgomery.

Bannam Place: changed to Bannan Place 1949.

Bellevue Avenue: from Filbert to Greenwich between Grant and Stockton.

Bestole Street: changed to Hodges Alley.

Billings Place: probably same as Napier Lane.

Bond Alley: changed to Brant Alley 1909.

Bone Alley: changed to Green Place.

Bower Place: S from Green between Grant and Stockton.

Card Alley: W from Stockton between Vallejo and Green.

Chambers Alley: changed to Greenwich Alley.

Chestnut Alley: N from Chestnut between Stockton and Powell.

Church Street (Place): changed to Edith Street 1882.

Clairville Place: S from Union between Grant and Stockton.

Clement Place: S from Green between Grant and Stockton.

Dock Street: from Front to Battery between Union and Filbert.

Duncan Court: N from Broadway between Grant and Stockton.

Dupont Street: changed to Grant Avenue 1908.

East Street: changed to Embarcadero.

Edgar Place: changed to Edgardo Place 1909.

Emma Place: S from Chestnut between Stockton and Powell.

Filbert Lane (Place): changed to Genoa Place 1909.

Flint Alley: changed to Cowell Place 1909.

Gaines Street: changed to Icehouse Alley 1969.

Garibaldi Street: changed to Castle Street 1921.

Gavin Place: changed to Grover Place 1909.

Goat Alley: from Vallejo to Green between Battery and Sansome.

Good Children Street: changed to Child Street 1909.

Graham Place: N from Green between Jasper and Stockton.

Grand Place: changed to Harwood Alley (Place).

Green Place: changed to Windsor Place 1909.

Greenwich Alley: from Greenwich to Lombard between Powell and Mason; closed for playground 1908.

Hall Alley: S from Vallejo between Prescott and Bartol.

Hinckley Street: changed to Fresno Street 1936.

Jackson Place: E from Montgomery between Vallejo and Green.

Jasper Alley: E from Jasper Place near Union.

Joseph's Terrace: E from Stockton between Lombard and Chestnut.

Kohler's (Kohler) Place: S from Green opposite Castle Street.

Lafayette Place: from Green to Union between Kearny and Grant; changed to Varennes Street 1909.

Lombard Alley (Place): changed to Tuscany Alley 1909.

Margarette Place: changed to Margrave Place 1909.

Maria Street: N from Vallejo between Kearny and Grant.

Michale Street: from Lombard to Chestnut between Grant and Stockton.

Montgomery Avenue: changed to Columbus Avenue 1909.

Montgomery Place: changed to School Alley.

Moulton Place: changed to Montague Place 1909.

Newell Street: changed to Fielding Street 1882.

Nobili Alley: changed to Noble's Alley.

Norton Place: changed to Darrell Place 1909.

Ohio Street: changed to Prospect Street 1882, back to Ohio Street 1895 and Osgood Place 1909.

Pearl Street: from Front to Sansome between Filbert and Greenwich.

Pierce Row: changed to Price Row.

Pinkney Place: changed to Romolo Place 1913.

Pringle Court: N from Greenwich between Sansome and Montgomery; closed 1943.

Prospect Street: *See* Ohio Street.

Reed Place: changed to Reno Place 1909.

St. Charles Street: W from Kearny between Vallejo and Green; changed to San Antonio Street 1882.

Sloat Street: changed to Sansome 1849.

Sonoma Place: N from Vallejo between Kearny and Grant; changed to San Antonio Street 1882.

Sonora Street: changed to Sonoma Street.

Union Alley: from Union Place.

Union Place: from Green to Union between Grant and Stockton; became part of Jasper Place 1909.

Vincent Street (also St. Vincent): changed to Garibaldi 1909.

Webster Street: changed to Winthrop Street 1882.

Wells Court: S from Lombard between Grant and Stockton; closed 1949.

Notes: Telegraph Hill is included in the 50-Vara Survey of San Francisco, a vara in this instance being 33 inches. City blocks east of Sansome Street are 100 varas or 275 feet square and contain four 50-vara lots. West of Sansome Street the blocks measure 275 by 412½ feet with six 50-vara lots.

Prior to 1860, such streets on Telegraph Hill that were numbered were assigned 24 numbers to each block. After that date the present system of 100 numbers to the block was adopted.

From Chestnut Street, apartment views include Angel Island, Red Rock and Richmond. The building in the foreground occupies the site of the Joshua Hendy Machine Works.

Bibliography

Books

Bancroft's Works, vol. 21. *History of California*, vol. 4. San Francisco, 1886.

Bolton, H. E. *Anza's California Expeditions*, vol. 4. Berkeley: Univ. of California Press, 1930.

Burnham, Daniel H. *Report on a Plan for San Francisco*. San Francisco, 1905.

Harris, Henry, M.D. *California's Medical Story*. San Francisco: Grabhorn Press for J. W. Stacey, 1932.

Hart, Ann Clark. *Clark's Point*. San Francisco: The Pioneer Press, 1937.

Rogers, Fred Blackburn. *Montgomery and The Portsmouth*. San Francisco: John Howell, 1958.

San Francisco City Directory. Various years.

Soulé, Frank; Gihon, John H., M.D.; and Nisbet, James. *The Annals of San Francisco*. New York, 1855.

Williams, Mary Floyd, ed. *Papers of the San Francisco Committee of Vigilance of 1851*. Berkeley: Univ. of California Press, 1919.

Articles and Manuscript Material

Annual Reports of the Telegraph Hill Neighborhood Association, 1904-1917, 1920, 1922.

Ashe, Elizabeth. *Autobiographical Notes—Vol. I*. MS.

Bemistory, Apr. 1944 and Feb. 1961. The Bemis Co.

Carlisle, Henry C. *San Francisco Street Names*. MS.

Conmy, Peter. *Queen of the Avenue*. Unpub. MS.

Howard, Henry T. "The Coit Tower Memorial." *The Architect and Engineer*, vol. 115, no. 3 (Dec. 1933).

Kelley, Rev. D. O. *History of the Diocese of California 1849-1915*. Unpub. MS.

Morphy, Edward A. "Telegraph Hill." In "San Francisco's Thoroughfares," *San Francisco Chronicle*, Aug. 1919.

New York. Int. Tel. & Tel. Corp. *Philo T. Farnsworth, Father of Electronic Television*. Anon. MS., 1967.

One Hundred Years of the First Orthodox Parish in San Francisco. Anon. pamphlet. San Francisco, 1968.

Salesian Boys' Club—Report of Activities. For years ending Sept. 1, 1949, and June 30, 1955.

San Francisco. California Historical Society Library. Amelia Neville and Frederick O. Layman scrapbooks.

Shumate, Albert. "Rincon or Telegraph Hill: Robert Louis Stevenson's Introduction to the South Seas." *California Historical Society Quarterly*, vol. 46, no. 3 (Sept. 1967).

Stephens, W. Barclay, M.D. *Time Balls*. Unpub. MS.

Telegraaf-Seinen van Curaçao. Diagram, 1880.

Weber, Mrs. Fannie McGregor. *Biography of Joseph McGregor*. Unpub. MS.

Government Records and Related Publications

Coit, Elizabeth Wyche. Last Will and Testament, dated Oct. 1, 1924.

Enos, John S., Comm. of Labor Stat. "The Condition of the Laborers Employed by Contractors on the Seawall at San Francisco, Etc." Sacramento, 1886.

Incorporation papers filed with the Secretary of State.

Jackson Novak to Board of Permit Appeals. Ltr. 2/8/51.

Minutes of the Art Commission, Board of Park Commissioners, Meetings of State Harbor Commissioners, and Recreation and Park Commission.

Records in the offices of the assessor, recorder, clerk, Health Department and Recreation and Park Department of San Francisco.

San Francisco Municipal Reports. Various years.

San Francisco Relief Survey. New York: Survey Associates, 1913.

San Francisco Voters' Register, 1873, 1876-77.

Twelfth, Thirteenth and Fourteenth Reports of the State Mineralogist.

U. S. Census for 1880, and Special 1852 Census.

Washington, D. C. National Archives. File of the Federal Communications Commission (Record Group 173). John D. McKee. Mercantile Trust Co. San Francisco.

———. Record Group 24, Microcopy 330. Records of Officers Re: Naval Service of John K. Duer.

Newspapers and Other Publications for Various Years

Alta California°, *The Argonaut*, *California Star*°, *Californian* (Monterey), *Call*°, *Call-Bulletin*°, *Chronicle*°, *Daily Herald*°, *Evening Bulletin*°, *Examiner*°, *Little City News*, *Marin Journal*, *Mining & Scientific Press*, *News*°, *Overland Monthly*, *Pacific News*°, *S. F. Newsletter*, *S. F. Real Estate Circular*, *Sunset Magazine*, *Tel. Hill Alarm*, *Tel. Hill Bulletin*.

°San Francisco newspapers with general circulation.

Litigation

Buchel v. Gray Bros., 115 Cal. 421.

City and County of San Francisco v. Gray Bros., John Kelso et al. No. 38880, Dept 2. Frank J. Murasky, Judge. Dated June 13, 1913. Judgment Record, vol. 66, p. 319.

Cooney v. Furlong, 66 Cal. 520.

Cushing-Wetmore v. Gray, 152 Cal. 118.

Furlong v. Cooney, 72 Cal. 322.

In Re John Kelso, on Habeas Corpus, 147 Cal. 609.

Leese v. Clark, 18 Cal. 535, 20 Cal. 387.

Pacific Rolling Mill v. Tel. Hill R.R., 79 Cal. 340.

Maps

Bache, A. D., Supt., U. S. Coast Survey. City of San Francisco and Its Vicinity, 1853.

Eddy, William M., C.E. Official Map of San Francisco, 1849.

Hicks-Judd Co. *Handy Block Book of San Francisco, 1894*. Ibid., *October 1906*.

Sanborn Map Co. Fire Maps of San Francisco, 1899.

State Harbor Commissioners. Various maps.

Index

°denotes picture reference
†denotes map reference

— A —
Acme Brewery, 209
Agard, William B., 37
Ainsa, Manuel, 201†, 203
Airoldi, Elvetzia, 129
Albro, Maxine, 80
Alemany, Archbishop, 141
American Biscuit Co., 95†, 171
American Sugar Refining Co., 95, 193
Ames, Fisher, 62, 64
Anderlini, Elios, 190
Anderson, David, 33
Arnautoff, Victor, 80, 81°
Ashe, Elizabeth H., 131, 133, 134
Atashkarian, George, 173
Atherton, Gertrude, 76
Autos, 25, 72, 112
Avy, Eugene, 201†, 203

— B —
Bacchus Wine, 207, 208
Bacigalupi, Frank, 127
Bacigalupi, Louis, 51, 99
Bagel Shop, 125, 126
Baptist Church, 127
Barbary Coast, 136, 149
Barnes, Mathew, 80
Barrett, Samuel, 31
Barrows, Albert W., 76
Basque Hotel, 118
Baugh, Theo., 28, 31
Bavaria Brewery, 206
Bay City Wood Co., 95†, 171
Bay Sugar Refinery, 95†
Baylis, Douglas, 127, 140
Beachcomber, The, 211
Beatniks, 125-126
Belfast, 16
Bella Union, 116°, 151
Belli, Melvin (apts.), 106†, 113, 151
Bemis Bag, 95, 199
Bentzen, John, 153
Berg, E. O., 99
Bergantino, Antonio, 35
Berlin, F. A., 207†
Biagini, Pacifico, 128
Big Al's, 126, 146†, 151
Big Daddy, 126
Bigin's, Alex, 113, 179
Bingham & Reynolds, 8°
Bishop, Roy N., 159
Bistro, The, 211
Blakewell, John, Jr., 76
Blasting, 53-55, 60-64
Blossom Rock, 20, 28
Bocce Ball, 140, 149
Bodfish, William, 44
Boehme, Ned, 27, 28
Bohemians, 24, 100, 123, 125, 184
Bond issues, 71, 214°
Booth, Edwin, 36, 37°
Booth, J. B., Jr., 36
Bothin, Henry E., 133
Bowlby, Lady, 167
Boynton, Ray, 80
Brady, William J., 83
Brasch, Caroline, 62, 64
Briones, Juana, 15
Broadsword, 48-50

Broadway Grammar School, 149
Broadway Jail, 139, 146†°, 147
Browell, J., 201†, 203
Brown, Arthur, Jr., 76, 78
Brown, David, 178
Brown, Ida Mae, 187
Brown, Pat (Gov.), 141
Brown, Phillip, 187, 193
Bruce, Edward, 80
Buchel, Ernest, 59
Buckelew, B. R., 167
Buckelew Wharf, 16
Bufano, Beniamino, 157
Bulkhead line, 55
Bullring, 19
Bundschu, Charles, 207
Burgess, Gelett, 70
Burnham Plan, 71
Burton, Stanley, 112
Bus (No. 39), 24, 174°
Byington, L. F., 73, 76

— C —
Caberillo, A., 112
Caen, Herb, 201
California Bible Society, 131
California Historical Society, 33
California Outdoor Art League, 71, 72, 206
California Sugar Refining Co., 95
Callender, M. L., 27
Camels, The, 124°
Campbell, John, 213
Canberra, 33, 74°
Cantella, Sil, 162, 181
Captain's House, 187
Capurro, Nicola, 123
Caraher, Father Terence, 72
Caranzi, 178
Casanova, Henry, 62
Castle St., 160, 164†, 173°
Cats, 115, 193
Cazneau, Mrs. E., 128
Cellar, The, 126
Cemeteries, 19
Center, William, 61
Central Park, 48
Century Furniture Co., 84°
Cereghino, Maria, 160†, 162, 163°
Cervelli, August, 162
Child Street, 125†, 129
Chileans, 17
Chinese, 19, 35, 37, 112, 123
Chiodo, Ernest, 172
Cholera epidemic, 149
Christian, Chester, 211
Christian Hospital Assn., 136
Christopher, George, 24, 197
Chronicle, 73, 106, 196
Chronometers, 31
Chung, Margaret, 112
Churubusco, 27
Cigar manufacture, 36
Cisterns, 20
City Front Assn., 131
City Front Boys Club, 131
City Observatory, 31
City Warehouse, 199
Clark, Maud M. W., 133
Clark, Wm. S., 15-17
Clark's Point, 11, 17, 26°, 27, 28, 29°, 95†, 149, 190
Coe, Edward H., 99
Coffee Gallery, 122°, 124°, 126
Cogswell, H. D., 139
Coit, Lillie H., 75-76, 139, 142

Coit Tower artists, 83
Collapsed bldgs., 129
Collett, Thomas, 199
Columbus Ave., 134°, 139, 141, 214°
Columbus Square, 139
Columbus statue, 79°, 83
Column of Progress, 73
Compound (Greenwich), 193
Compound (Hoeffler), 99-101
Compound (Lafler), 112
Compound (Wilhite), 153
Condor, The, 149-151
Congress, 19
Conrad, B., 149, 188
Cookbook, 132
Cooney family, 167-169
Coral Sea, U.S.S., 83
Cosenza, Milanelli, 120
Costa Bros., 123
Costa, Giacomo, 201†, 203
County Hospital, 137
Cousins Dry Dock, 54°
Cravath, D. P., 83, 181
Creation, 190
Crescent, 28
Cresta Blanca winery, 67
Crocker Research Laboratory, 159, 160†
Crowley, M., 107°, 113
Cruz, Domingo, 17
Cugia, Mario, 85
Cummings, Melvin E., 140†, 141°
Cuneo, Joseph, 203
Cuneo, Rinaldo, 82°
Cunningham, James E., 62, 64
Cunningham Wharf, 16
Curaçao, 31
Cushing, Sidney B., 67
Cushing-Wetmore Co., 67

— D —
Dailey, Gardner, 113, 181, 185°, 200
D'Angers, Yvonne, 151
Daniel Grant, 28
Dark Victory, 87
Darling, Dr. Herb, 107°
Darrell Pl., 109°, 184†, 187-190°
Davalle, Vincenzo, 106
Davis, Sgt. Owen, 48
de Colbertaldo, V., 83
De Martini, Armond, 85
De Martini, Louis, 209°
de Matti, Louis, 142
De Vries, Thomas, 55
de Young Museum, 78, 80
Dead Fish Cafe, 167
Dean, Mallette, 80
Decker, Elwood, 179, 181
Deutscher Verein, 207
Dewitt & Harrison, 19
Di Grazia Bros., 123
Di Maggio, Joe, 142
Diaz, Frank, 111
Dirty Harry, 84°
Dixon, Maynard, 80
Doda, Carol, 151
Doneri, Giovanni, 22, 23
Dong, Dr. Collin H., 121
Dry Dock Exchange, 54
"Duck House," 178, 180°, 181, 185°
Duer, Lt. John K., 27, 28
Duncan, C. S., 78, 83
Dunn, Baby Jane, 126

— E —
Earthquake, 20, 22
Eastwood, Clint, 84°
Eccles, Marriner, 200
Edgardo Pl., 125†, 127, 144°, 145°
Edith St., 125†, 127°, 128, 197
Eggert, Henry, 171
Ehlers' Corners, 120, 157°
Ehlers, W., 117, 120
El Matador, 149
Ellis, John S., 147
Empire and Lyon breweries, 209
English, 165, 177, 187, 203, 206
English, W. D. & Co., 55
Enrico's Coffee House, 121°, 151°
Episcopal Church, 131, 143
Erckenbrack, Mary, 111
Erskine, Mrs. (Dorothy) Morse, 25, 141, 200-201
Eureka Flour Mills, 213
Eureka Grain Whse., 207†, 211
Evers, Kenneth, 86
Everson, George, 159

— F —
Farnsworth, Philo T., 92°, 159
Fazackerley, J., 44, 47
Fibreboard Corp., 211
Figoni, Louis, 123
Finocchio's, 149
Fior D'Italia, 105, 148°
Fire (1906), 20-23, 25°, 138°, 139, 143, 149, 159, 197, 208
Fire Department Repair Shop, 137
Fires (other), 18°†, 19, 20, 27, 50, 51, 56, 107°, 113, 128, 143, 153, 162, 182°, 183, 199
Fireworks, 19, 20
Fisherman's Wharf (Union St.), 172°
Fitch, William S., 37
Fleishhacker, H., 76
Fletcher, R. H., 70
Flood, James, 188
Flynn, Dennis, 120
Forbes, H., 39, 112, 181, 185°
Fort Montgomery, 15, 29°, 92°, 93, 95†, 158°
Francisco Junior High School, 209
Franklin, Benjamin (statue), 139, 140†, 143°
Franklin, Dr. Walter Scott, 133
Frauenhalz, Philip, 207, 209
Freddie's, 212†, 213
Fredericksburg Brewing Co., 44
Freeman, Ray, 173
Fremont Hotel, 17, 29°, 93°, 95†, 152°
Frescoes, 80, 181
Fresno (Hinckley) St., 116†, 117, 119°
Friml, Rudolph, 100
Fugazi Hall, 141
Furlong, T., 168

— G —
Garfield Market, 175
Garfield School, 22, 142°, 191°
Gazebo, 188
Genoa Place, 164†, 169, 184†, 191
Gentry, Curt, 209
Gerke Alley, 89°, 125†, 127
Gerke, Henry, 127
German General Benevolent Society, 207
German Savings & Loan Society, 207

254

Germans, 35, 120, 165, 177, 178, 187
Ghiradelli, Mrs. Louis, 200
Gibb, Daniel, 152°
Gibbons, H. & W. P., 93
Gifford, Mabel F., 196
Gilbert, Ed, 19
Gilliam, Harold, 197
Gimbel, W. B., 208
Ginsberg, Allen, 125
Giusti, S. A., 159
Gledhill, Honore, 167
Globe Brewery, 209
Globe Grain & Milling Co., 67
Goat Hill, 11
Goats, 39, 120, 203, 208°
Godfather, The, 173
Gogna, Pasquale, 117
Gold, disc., 190
Gold Rush, 17, 53
Golden Gate Kindergarten Assn., 164†, 173, 175
Golden Gate Tile, 62
Goldtree, Sidney, 163
Gorrell, Leslie, 159
Graham, Billy, 126
Grannis, G. W., 37
Grannucci Groc., 123
Grant Avenue Street Fair, 122°, 123
Graves, H. T., 198°, 201
Graves, Roy D., 201
Gray Bros., 50, 51, 56, 58°, 59-66, 69, 92°, 95†, 97, 165
Gray, Matthias, 42, 201
Graziotti, Ugo, 83
"Great Blow Out," 53
Green St. Italian Church, 162
Green St. Theater, 163
Greene, Lucius E., 75
Gremminger, Joseph, 142
Griffith, Alice S., 131, 133, 134
Griffith, Capt. Millen, 54°, 131
Grossman, John, 187
Grosso, A. G., 96°, 207†, 208
Grunsky, C. Ewald, 69-71
Gulf Bag Co., 95†, 199
Gundlach, Jacob, 206

– H –
Hale, Randolph, 115
Halleck, Peachy & Billings, 37
Hallidie, A. S., 41, 43, 201
Halprin, Lawrence, 140
Harmon, John, 173
Harrington, J., 106°, 110
Harrold, James, 209
Harwood Alley, 184†, 191
Hawaii, 35, 39, 110, 167, 188
Hearst Free Kindergarten, 175
Hearst, Mrs. Phoebe, 175
Heatley, E. D., 206
Hebrew Home, 203
Height limits, 25
Heil, Dr. Walter, 78, 80, 83
Heintz, Ralph M., 201
Helping Hand Kindergarten, 175
Henning, J. S., 29
Herrero, R. & A., 112
Heynemann, H., 207†, 208
Higgins, M., 201
High Living – Receipts, 132
Hildebrandt, Carsten, 117
Hill Farm, 133
Hippies, 126
Hitchcock, C. M., 75

Hoeffler, Ian, 100, 102°, 103
Hoelscher, Eda, 115
Holmes, Ahira, 149
Home (Inebriate), 136
Hoppe, Jay, 125
Horre, Mrs. A., 184†
Horstmeyer, A. L., 78
Hounds, 17
House on Telegraph Hill, The, 84°, 87
Houston, A. H., 53, 55
Houston, Mrs. B., 55
Howard, Henry T., 78
Hudson, H. C., 33°, 106
Hughson, William L., 201
Hunchback, The, 28
Hungry i, 126, 150°

– I –
Iacopi, Frank, 96°
Iacopi Meats, 175
Ice House, 92°, 95†, 97
Internat. Settlement, 118°, 146†, 149
International Workers' Defense League, 66
Iran, Shah of, 39
Irish, 35, 177, 178, 184
Irwin, Mrs. William, 134
Irwin, Wallace, 86
Italian-American Paste Co., 162
Italian Bersaglieri Mutual Benefit Society, 131
Italian Church, 141
Italian French Bakery, 123
Italian Vil. Mkt., 162
Italians, 20, 23, 35, 139, 159, 171, 178, 200

– J –
Jean Parker School, 146†, 149
Joe's Wine Cellar, 160
Johnson, Daisy, 132
Johnson, Edmund, 86
Johnson, Hiram, 115
Joost, John, 213
Joshua Hendy Machine Works, 211, 212†
Julia, 176°
Julius' Castle, 23, 87, 107°, 109°, 113, 195°

– K –
Kahn, Sidney, 101°, 103
Keane, Laura, 37
Keane, Walter, 149
Kearney, Tom, 39
Kelham, George W., 76
Kelleher, Eliza, 56
Kelso, John, 56, 61, 64
Kern, Mr., 187, 188
Kerouac, Jack, 125
KFDB (radio), 72°, 201
King, Thomas Starr, 136
Kitterman, James, 203
Klussman, Frieda, 159
Knickerbocker Engine Co. No. 5, 75
Knop, Henry, 117
Knorp, Alfred F., 47
Kohler, Henry, 120
Kohler Place, 116†, 120, 160†
Kramer, Jacob, 127
Kramer Place, 125†, 127, 192°
Krikorian, Leo, 126
Kuh, Fred, 162

– L –
La Ferrera Ter., 116†, 121
La Vero Players, 86
Lady Godiva, 111
Lafler, Harry, 112, 113
Lafler, Mary, 112, 113, 120
Lammers, Martin, 171
Landreth, J. B., 178
Lane, Franklin K., 208
Langdon, Gordon, 80
Lange, F. W., 198°, 199
Lansburgh, G. A., 73
Lathrop, Allen, 169
Laughter on the Hill, 85
Law's Wharf, 16
Lawson, Mrs. J. F., 61
Layman, F. O., 41-44, 47-48
Layman's Folly, 50, 51
Leahy, Pat, 112
L'Eco d'Italia, 85
Leese, Jacob P., 17
Legers, Ben, 86
Leidesdorff, Wm. A., 17
Levin, Marvin, 187
Liebman, Otto, 50
Lighters, 16, 131
Lignite, discovery, 190
L'Italia, 162
Little Chile, 17
Little City News, 85
Lococo, Joseph, 64, 65, 66
Loma Alta, 11, 15
Lombardi, Lorenzo, 172
Long, Percy V., 62
Long Wharf, 8°, 16

– M –
Maas, Johan H., 179
McCandless, J. C., 200
Macchiarini, Peter, 100, 123
McDonald, J. M., 69
McDougal, Gov. John, 190
Mace, Harriet, 36
McEvoy, James, 165
McGlynn, Frank, 208
McGreggor, J., 33, 55
McHenry, John, 55
McKew, John, 41
McLaren, John, 72, 73, 206
McLaren, Mrs. Norman, 132
McNear, Fred, 177, 178†
McNear, Jake & Bob, 39
McSheehy, James B., 76, 78
Maffei, Michael, 162
Magee, Thomas, 207
Maguire's Opera, 36
Malloch, Jack, 115
Malony, 28
Manning, J. E., 64
Marchant, Grace, 90°, 184
Marchi Club, 173
Margaret, Princess, 39
Margrave Place, 145°
Marine Exchange, 31
Marine Tel., 27-33, 68†
Marini, Frank, 141, 157
Marsh, Mrs. George T., 72
Marsky, Emile, 50
Marsten, A. L., 107°
Martedi Grasso, 140
Martin, Mayris C., 39
Martinez, Roque, 35
Massucco, Lena, 169
Mastick, E. B., 37, 168
Maybeck, Bernard, 133, 134

Maybeck bldg., 130°, 131, 132†
Meiggs, Henry, 36, 147
Meiggs' Wharf, 36, 53, 56°, 198°
Meisel, Herman A., 165
Menken, Adah Isaacs, 37
Mercantile Trust Co., 201
Merchants Dry Dock, 54°
Merchants' Exch., 25°, 27, 28
Mercier, William, 27
Merrill, Al, 193
Merrill, Victor, 113
Methodist Church, 149
Metropolitan Theater, 37
Mexicans, 20
Meyer, Fred, 24
Mike's Grocery, 197
Miller, John S., 177, 178
Milliken, W. H., 43, 44, 47
Mini, John B., 113
Miniature golf, 127
Miss Smith's, 126
Missroon, Lt. John S., 15
Mitchell, Charlie, 50
Monarch, 54°, 60°
Montague, Marion, 111
Montclair Rest., 173
Montez, Lola, 37
Montgomery Ave., 214°
Montgomery Hill, 37
Montgomery, J. B., 9, 15
Montgomery Lake, 53
Montparnasse of the West, 187
Mooney's Irish Pub, 123, 125†
Mooshake, Rev. F., 197
Moran family, 177
Morgan, Helen, 115
Morton, George, 177, 178†
Mounted sword contests, 40°, 48-50
Murasky, Judge, 61, 62, 64
Myrtokleia, 179

– N –
Napier Lane, 184†, 186°, 187
National Paper Products Co., 211
Neutra, R., 103, 112
New Joe's, 149, 181
New Pisa, 123, 125†
New Union Grocery, 169-173
New York Vols., 17
Night clubs, 118°, 149-151, 179
Nightengale, George, 99, 165
Noonan, W. R., 178
Nord, Eric, 126
North Beach, 11, 36, 85, 93, 123, 140-142, 149
  Improvement Club, 69
  Library, 197
  Merchants Assn., 73
  Playground, 194†, 197
  Promotion Assn., 72
  Record, 85
North Central Improvement Assn., 69
North End Protective League, 71
North End Review, 71, 85
North Point, 54°, 211, 212†
North Point Dock Whse., 94°, 95†, 96°, 210°
Northpoint (apt.), 213
Norton Place, 188
Norway, 35, 99
Novak, Jackson, 112
Novak, Kim, 87
Nuevo Teatro, 162

255

— O —

O'Brien, Robert, 106
O'Connor, Dan, 128
Off Broadway, 121°, 149
Old People's Home, 132†, 137
Old Spaghetti Factory, 160†, 162, 163°
Oldfield, Otis, 80, 112
Omnibus R.R. and Cable Co., 47, 48
On the Road, 125
Onderdonk, Andrew, 55
Organization, The, 84°
O'Rourke, Austin, 175
Ortega, Juan, 111, 167, 188-190
O'Toole, Coleman, 193
Overend, Eliz., 56
Overend, John A. T., 37
Oxnard, Robert, 95

— P —

P.&O.-Orient Lines, 33
Pacific Coast Steamship Co., 177
Pacific Hospital, 136
Pacific Rolling Mills, 47
Pacifica, 190
Padrinas, Alfonso, 115
Pal Joey, 87
Panama-Pacific Exp., 35, 72, 73
Panattoni, Mary, 170°, 171
Paper Doll, 173
Pardee Alley, 89°
Pargeting, 168
Parsons, Mike, 85
Parthenon, 72
Parton, Margaret, 85
Party Pad, 126
Pasquale's Tower, 117
Patigian, Haig, 75, 83, 139, 142°, 190
Paul Smith House, 74°, 196
Peach Blossom Fest., 181
People's Place, 134
Pera, Guillo, 123
Pfeiffer, W. A., 197, 213
Pfeiffer's Castle, 132†, 135°, 136, 212†, 213
Pioneer Park, donors, 215
Place, The, 126
Point Lobos, 28, 29, 30°, 31, 32†
Poitier, Sidney, 84°
Pond, Rev. W. C., 197
Poniatowski, Marie Anne, 115
Pony Express, 20
Porter, Bruce, 70
Porter, Langley, 133
Portolá, 15
Portuguese, 35, 178
Pos, Bernard, 59
Prendergast, J. G., 85
Prescott Court, 153, 155†
Pringle Court, 193, 194†
Prospect Hill, 11, 16°
Prostitution, 100, 105, 118, 193
Puccinelli, Dorothy, 83, 181
Puck, Johann H., 205
Puvogel, John, 134

— R —

Railroads, 97°, 197°, 199, 201†
Rea, L. Achille, 85
Rebmann, Carl, 112
Redmond, Mrs. Anna, 61
Regulators, The, 17
Reno Place, 160†, 162, 163°
Robinett, Clyde, 112, 167
Robinson, David G., 99, 100°
Rock Rollers, 35
Rockrise, George T., 153
Rodriguez, Juan, 167
Rogers, Henry D., 128
Rolando's, 173
Roma Macaroni Factory, 171, 211, 212†°
Romolo (Pinkney) Place, 89°, 116†, 117, 118, 147
Roncovieri, Alfred, 118
Roosevelt, Mrs. F. D., 39, 83
Ross, Duncan C., 48-50
Ross, James, 37, 159
Rossi, Angelo, 78
Rossi Drug, 175
Ruef, Abe, 60, 116°, 201†, 203, 209
Runge, John, 193, 194†
Russell, Mrs. H. P., 113
Russian Church, 51°, 140†, 143
Russian Hill, 9, 11, 86, 117, 138, 141°, 174°, 192°, 196, 197

— S —

St. Francis Church, 154°, 157
St. Mary's Hospital, 131
St. Peter's (Episcopal) Church, 51°, 140†, 143
SS. Peter and Paul's Church, 51°, 125†, 127, 140-142
Salesian Boys' Club, 100, 140°, 143
San Antonio St., 116†, 120°
San Francisco: Art Comm., 33, 76, 78, 83; Bible Society, 131; Brick Co., 59; Neighbor. Assn., 134; Observatory, 33; Park Comm., 73, 76, 206; Private Hospital, 93
Sanchez, Ignacio, 118
Sangiacomo, Angelo, 173
Sarmiento, 15
Satchell, Rev. C., 127
Savannah, 19, 27
Savoy-Tivoli, 123, 125†
Sawvelle, C. F., 179
Schaeffer School of Design, 24, 140, 173
Scheuer, Suzanne, 81°
School Alley, 106†, 111, 162°
Schools, 22, 51°, 142°, 149, 173, 191
Sea Wall Whse., 94-95, 199
Sea walls, 52-53, 55-56
Selby, T. H., 29
Semaphore, 27-33
Semaphore, The, 24
Sempione Hotel, 123
Seone, Francisca, 35
Sgraffito, 114°, 115
Shadows, The, 109-112
Shaefle, Frederick, 33
Shanghaiing, 110, 187
Sharon, Mrs. A. D., 71
Shellard, Benj., 106
Shelley, John F., 141
Sherwood, Robert, 31
Shootings, 62, 65
Signal Hill, 11, 28, 32†
Signals (chart), 28, 30°
Silver Star Hall, 131-132
Sims, Richard M., 207
Slate, Marjorie, 169
Smith, La Veta M., 126
Smith, "Tubby," 165
Society of California Pioneers, 28
Sonorans, 17
Sour dough bread, 123
Southampton, 27
Spanish, 23, 35, 110, 167, 171, 172, 178, 183, 188, 203
Spanish Coop., 171
Spanish Lot, 15
Spediacci family, 169-173, 178
Speedy's, 87, 115, 169-173, 184
Spreckels, Claus, 95
Spreckels, J. B., 60, 64
Stackhouse, John L., 37
Stackpole, Ralph, 80, 190, 191
Standard Biscuit Co., 171
Stanton, W. P., 76
State Marine Hospital, 131
Stearns, H., 103°, 115
Steinhart, J. H., 62
Stella Pharm., 148°
Stergois, Alex, 211
Sterling, G., 85, 112
Stevenson, Adlai, 141
Stevenson, Robert L., 39
Stoddard, C. W., 38°, 39
Street dances, 103°
Street names (changes), 215-216
Street numbering, 199
Streetcars, 24, 96°, 97, 118°, 174°
Sugar beets, 95
Sugar factory, 66°, 95
Sullivan, John L., 50
Sullivan, John T., 56
Summit(s) of Tel. Hill, 9, 169
Sunny Side, 35
Sutch, John, 17
Sutro & Co., 42, 44
Sutro, Charles, 50
Sutro, Gustav, 42, 44, 47, 48, 50
Swat, Mr., 28
Sweeny, George F., 28, 31
Sweeny, Myles D., 28
Sweet, Harry, 127
Sydney Ducks, 17, 99
Sydney Town, 17

— T —

Tahiti Club, 211
Tantau, Clarence, 107°
Taylor, Samuel P., 37
Telegraph (elec.), 28
Telegraph Hill: Alarm, 85; Apartment, 173; *Bulletin*, 86; Cafe, 123; Country Club, 125†, 127; Dwellers, 24, 86, 120; Hotel, 197; Neighbor. Assn., 130°, 131; Neighbor. Assn. Auxiliary, 134; Neighbor. House, 131, 132; name, 28, 29; Players, 86; R.R. Co., 41-44, 47-48; Sage of, 205; *Semaphore*, 86; Sherry, 172; Sorosis Club, 132; Tavern, 85, 178†, 179, 181
Tel., Marine, 27-33
Telescope, 29, 104°
Television, 159
Telhi, City of, 133
"Telygraft Hill," 86
Tempany, Maria T., 209
Thayer, Mrs. Sarah, 36, 37
Theater, 36-37
Theill, Mrs. Raymond, 24
Thompson, Ernie, 173
Thornton, M., 184
Thousand Steps, 183
Time ball, 31, 33
Tin Can Hill, 11
Toetge, Henry, 165
Toland, Dr. Hugh H., 136
Toland Medical College, 132†, 135°, 136-137°
Tonquin Point, 211
Trees, 13, 25
Trinchieri, Father Oreste, 142
Tully, John, 95
Tunnel, 69, 70, 147, 190
Turntable, 109°, 113
Turtle races, 191
Twentieth Century-Fox, 84°, 87
Twilight Side, 35

— U —

Under the Yum Yum Tree, 86
Union Grammar School, 23, 39, 168, 173, 213
Union Primary School, 191
U.S. Bonded Warehouse, 93
U.S. Coast & Geodetic Survey, 139

— V —

Van Sicklin, F. W., 72
Vanessi's, 146†, 149
Varacchi's Groc., 105, 155†
Ver Mehr, Dr., 131
Vice, Martin, 54°
Vienna Garden, 47, 48
Vigilance Comm., 17
Vincent, Emile, 50, 51
Vision, Street of, 183
Vol. Fire Dept., 75, 139
Vorpal Galleries, 95†, 97
Vulcan Iron Wks., 67, 211
Vulcan Quarry, 67

— W —

Waller, George C., 37
Walsh, Sgt. Charles, 50
Walter, Edgar, 76, 78, 83
Walter, Gustav F., 47
Walters whse., H. G., 183, 184†, 189°, 190
Wands, A. H., 48
Ward, Frank, 131
Warren, Whitney, 39
Washington Irving School, 149
Wasp, The, 43
Waterfalls, 72, 73
Weise, Harold, 106
Weissel, Mrs. Adam, 61
WELCOME (sign), 71, 112, 195°, 196
Wells Fargo Bank, 75, 93, 201
Western Development Syn., 62
Wetmore Bros., 56, 63, 64, 67
White, Mrs. Lovell, 71
Wiatrak, Leon, 173
Wilhite, James O., 153
Wilson, Mrs. Persis, 60
Windmill, 33°, 213
Windmill Hill, 11
Windsor Place, 160†, 162°
Wine making, 160, 172, 178
Winkler, Otto, 112, 113
Winthrop St., 63, 119°, 205, 207†

— Y —

Yeomans, George, 205
Yone, Inc., 164†, 175
Yureska, 111

— Z —

Zakheim, Bernard, 80, 83